# The Actuality of Communism

# The Actuality of Communism

## BRUNO BOSTEELS

VERSO

London • New York

First published by Verso 2011
© Bruno Bosteels 2011

1 3 5 7 9 10 8 6 4 2

**Verso**
UK: 6 Meard Street, London W1F 0EG
US: 20 Jay Street, Suite 1010, Brooklyn, NY 11201
www.versobooks.com

Verso is the imprint of New Left Books

ISBN-13: 978-1-84467-695-8

**British Library Cataloguing in Publication Data**
A catalogue record for this book is available
from the British Library

**Library of Congress Cataloging-in-Publication Data**
A catalog record for this book is available
from the Library of Congress

Typeset in Bodoni Book by Hewer Text UK Ltd, Edinburgh
Printed in the US by Maple Vail

# *Contents*

# *Introduction*

Communism is the solution of the riddle of history, and knows itself to be the solution.

— Karl Marx, *Economic and Philosophic Manuscripts of 1844*

More than a solution to the problems we are facing today, communism is itself the name of a problem: a name for the difficult task of breaking out of the confines of the market-and-state framework, a task for which no quick formula is at hand.

— Slavoj Žižek, *First as Tragedy, Then as Farce*

## In the Name of Communism

"Of What Is Communism the Name?" Such was the guiding question behind a recent special dossier of *ContreTemps*, the French journal of communist critique co-founded by the late Daniel Bensaïd. Partly in response to the March 2009 London conference "On the Idea of Communism," organized by Costas Douzinas and Slavoj Žižek, partly as a tongue-in-cheek allusion to Alain Badiou's bestseller *The Meaning of*

*Sarkozy*, the original French title of which would translate literally as *Of What Is Sarkozy the Name?*, partly to defy the half-hearted celebrations of November 2009 in honor of the twentieth anniversary of the collapse of the Berlin Wall, and partly in preparation for another international conference, "Potentialities of Communism: Of What Is Communism the Name Today?," held in Paris in January 2010 just days after Bensaïd succumbed to a long-term illness, a number of authors from a variety of backgrounds were asked to define the possible stakes involved in the current revival of interest in the idea and practice of communism: "Have the communist idea and the communist name been historically compromised in the last century by their statist and bureaucratic uses, to the point of having become unpronounceable? Or else, of what—idea of another world, critical utopia, emancipatory movement, strategic hypothesis—can communism be the name today? And wherein lies its still active actuality?"[1]

---

1   Daniel Bensaïd, Stathis Kouvélakis, and Francis Sitel, "De quoi le communisme est-il le nom?" *ContreTemps: Revue de critique communiste* 4 (Winter 2009): 12. In the first section of the introduction here, I rework and expand my original answer to the editors' opening question. Other contributors to the *ContreTemps* dossier include Véronique Bergen, Olivier Besancenot, Alex Callinicos, Pierre Dardot, Isabelle Garo, Michel Kozlowski, Christian Laval, Michel Surya, and Ellen Meiksins Wood. The proceedings from the March 2009 London conference have been published in English as *The Idea of Communism*, ed. Costas Douzinas and Slavoj Žižek (London: Verso, 2010). Alain Badiou's *De quoi Sarkozy est-il le nom?* (Paris: Lignes, 2007) has been translated into English as

In homage to Bensaïd—whom I met in person only once, in Lisbon, but whose unparalleled internationalist vision and generosity serve as a constant reminder of what an intellectual can and should do—I would want the following chapters to be read as ongoing attempts to answer his request and its guiding question.

My original response, like that of many other contributors not only to the special dossier of *ContreTemps* but also to the proceedings from the Paris conference partially published in a special issue of the journal *Actuel Marx*, consisted rather coyly in raising a new set of subsidiary questions.

Firstly, indeed, what is to be done with the past and with the burden of history? Can we formulate a form of communism—as idea, as movement, as hypothesis, or as program; for the time being this dispute would not matter

---

*The Meaning of Sarkozy*, trans. David Fernbach (London: Verso, 2008). This book's last part was also published separately as "The Communist Hypothesis," *New Left Review* 49 (2008): 29–42. The program for the January 2010 Paris conference "Puissances du communisme (De quoi communisme est-il aujourd'hui le nom?)," organized by Daniel Bensaïd, can be found on-line at www.contre-temps.eu together with several videos; its participants partially overlapped with those from the London conference, most notably in the persons of Toni Negri, Jacques Rancière, Alberto Toscano, and Slavoj Žižek, while other speakers, including Etienne Balibar, Alex Callinicos, and Isabelle Garo, despite an underlying sympathy, were openly or covertly critical of Badiou's initiative. Some of the contributions to this conference can also be found in the special dossier titled *Communisme?*, edited by Jacques Bidet for the journal *Actuel Marx* 48 (2010).

much—without automatically having to face up to the disastrous evidence stored in the official and unofficial archives? Or is the choice of one of these options, say in favor of communism as an ideological hypothesis rather than as a real movement, already bound to impact our capacity to confront this history critically? This is a generational question, no doubt, even though the notion of generation, steeped as it is in the ideology of consumerism based on the model of the parallel development of individuals and eras, seems to me to provide a false window. But it is also a question of transmission and contestation between and across generations, a problem of which Bensaïd toward the end of his life became acutely aware. "So something has come to an end together with the twentieth century, between the fall (or the toppling) of the Berlin Wall and the 9/11 attacks. Something, but what? From this question in suspense is borne an undeniable malaise in transmission," Bensaïd wrote in an homage of his own, to the Trotskyist intellectual, militant, and editor Jacques Hassoun, before addressing this malaise or discontent under the rubric of the following questions: What is to be transmitted? How to transmit? And why transmit? But also, I would add so as to make explicit an understated self-criticism: to what extent should we trust the old masters in terms of what they decide to transmit or not in the first place?[2]

---

2    Daniel Bensaïd, "Malaise dans la transmission. Jacques Hassoun ou le Sage engagé" (author's typescript). Bensaïd's homage, with the

If it is communism that is a new idea in Europe today, as Badiou claims, why are the *soixante-huitards*, whether Trotskyist, Maoist, anarchist or other, the ones to proclaim this novelty, all the while repeating their old quibbles in the process? Should communism not abandon this "most intolerable burden" that is also the "once upon a time" or the "it was" of the past, of *Es war*, as Nietzsche used to say in *Thus Spoke Zarathustra*, to which Freud seemed to reply with his own maxim of *Wo es war soll ich werden*, "Where it was, I shall come to be," as if to echo Zarathustra's *So wollte ich es!* as the decisive act of the will that solves the riddle of every *Es war* ("All 'it was' is a fragment, a riddle, a dreadful chance—until the creative will says to it: 'But I willed it thus!'")[3]? From

---

pun in its title on Sigmund Freud's *Civilization and Its Discontents* (usually translated into French as *Malaise dans la civilisation*), specifically takes the form of a review of two books by Jacques Hassoun, *Les Contrebandiers de la mémoire* (Paris: Syros, 1994) and *Actualités d'un malaise* (Paris: Erès, 1997). For a portrait of Bensaïd's life, character, and work that should help the cross-generational transmission, see Sebastian Budgen, "The Red Hussar: Daniel Bensaïd, 1946–2010," *International Socialism: A Quarterly Journal of Socialist Theory* 127 (June 2010), available on-line at www.isj.org.uk. See also the special issue of *Lignes* 32 (May 2010), with contributions from Alain Badiou, Etienne Balibar, Stathis Kouvélakis, Michael Löwy, Enzo Traverso and others.

3  Friedrich Nietzsche, "Von der Erlösung," *Also sprach Zarathustra* in *Werke: Kritische Gesamtausgabe*, ed. Giorgio Colli and Mazzino Montinari, vol. 6: 1 (Berlin: Walter de Gruyter, 1968), 177; *Thus Spoke Zarathustra*, trans. R. J. Hollingdale (London: Penguin, 1969), 163. Sigmund Freud's maxim *Wo es war soll ich werden* ("Where it was, I shall come to be" or "Where id was, there

all sides, we are bombarded with calls to live up to our duty to remember the past disasters of humanity, lest history repeat itself, but more often than not this inflation of memory comes at the cost of postponing a genuinely critical history of ourselves from the point of view of the present. "As history becomes opaque, a mania for commemoration has developed. A tyrannical one-way 'duty of memory' has gradually silenced the necessary dialogue between history and memory. Memory is then no longer the critical obverse of history but its censor," Bensaïd also writes. "And when history is on a downward trend, politics—let us be clear, not parliamentary and administrative politics but politics as strategic anticipation of the day after—perishes."[4] Confronted with so many lessons patiently taught and instantly forgotten, so many languishing memories and lukewarm commemorations, so many unabashed apostasies and shameful repentances, so many lost illusions and so much undigested nostalgia for the happy days of yesteryear, do we not need a strong dosage of active forgetfulness to combat the culture of memory?

Then again, do we not also cause actual emancipatory politics to perish when we simply ignore the long history of communism, or of communisms in the plural—of that

---

shall ego be," frequently commented upon by Jacques Lacan and his followers, including Slavoj Žižek who made it into the title of his book series for Verso), appears in his *New Introductory Lectures on Psycho-Analysis*, trans. James Strachey (New York: W. W. Norton, 1990), 100.

4    Bensaïd, "Malaise dans la transmission."

communism which is not one, but multiple? As Véronique Bergen argues:

> Furthermore, to try by some discretionary decree to amputate the name and idea of communism from the connotations that are attached to it—collective homogenization of differences (on the conceptual level), Stalinist dictatorship, bureaucratic regime muzzling individual liberties, statist control (on the level of its incarnation)—does not suffice to enact the renewal of the term: ideologically, in the collective unconscious, it remains burdened by its conceptual recodings and historical slippages.[5]

A question, this last one, concerning the risk of succumbing to the other, antihistoricist extreme of a purely moralizing self-referentiality—that of communism as a beautiful soul refusing to bother with the inscription, here and now, of its noble idea in a concrete historical program. "The word and the thing cannot remain outside of the time frame and the historical trials to which they have been subjected," as Bensaïd warns. "The temptation to subtract oneself from a critical historical inventory would reduce the communist idea to its atemporal 'invariants,' making it synonymous with indeterminate ideas of justice or emancipation, and not with

---

5  Véronique Bergen, "Un communisme des singularités," *ContreTemps: Revue de critique communiste* 4 (2009): 18.

the specific form of emancipation in the age of capitalist domination. The word then loses in political precision what it gains in ethical or philosophical extension."[6]

As Isabelle Garo suggests in her answer to Bensaïd's guiding question, it is very well possible that the recent revival of interest in communism is the result of, if not also an overcompensation for, the absence of its historical referentiality:

> One might consider first that communism is a signifier that resurfaces at the very moment when its referent seems to have disappeared, less undone by its adversary than collapsed on its own. On this ground, it is logical but also very problematic that this return takes place above all on the terrain of theory and more specifically of philosophy, while its political pertinence remains very uncertain, contrary to what was for a long time its strong political presence and its lesser theorization.[7]

On the other hand, we could also argue that the positive anticipation of a future, beyond the current status quo, is precisely what gives communism its force: "Reappearing at the same time that capitalism becomes once more nameable, fusing anti- and post-capitalism into a unique positive

---

6   Daniel Bensaïd, "Puissances du communisme," *ContreTemps: Revue de critique communiste* 4 (2009): 14.

7   Isabelle Garo, "Le communisme vu d'ici ou la politique au sens plein," *ContreTemps: Revue de critique communiste* 4 (2009): 40.

name that is not a simple negation of its other, communism remains the name of an emancipated future."[8] What this implies is that the reappearance of the name communism today, far from merely signaling a philosophical flight of fancy, opposed to its actuality in the ordinary sense of the term, could be the leverage that opens up the present to the historicity of its possible alteration. "Thus, if in a first approach, communism presents itself as that contradiction that would be merely internal to it and that puts at logger-heads the possible actualization of the term and the perma-nent threat of its obsolescence and its ineffectiveness, this contradiction more fundamentally reveals itself to be that which splits the real itself and reopens history as the space of collective political decision," adds Garo. This is where what I will call the actuality of communism comes to light in a way that is neither a dogmatic continuation of party politics as we know them nor a philosophical speculative dream: "This actuality, if it must last, stems neither from the reduction of its usage to the labeling of organizations, nor from the poeticization of the political into a finality that

---

8  Ibid. Alberto Toscano, in his contribution to the London conference, convincingly shows the extent to which philosophy (or theory) is an intrinsic part of communism as a non-dogmatic anticipation beyond the current state of affairs, not only for the young Marx but even later on in Marx's politico-economical writings. See Alberto Toscano, "The Politics of Abstraction: Communism and Philosophy," in Douzinas and Žižek, eds., The Idea of Communism, 195–204.

is as sublime as it is vague. Its possible actualization plays itself out very exactly in the in-between of the question of organization and that of political finalities, by interrogating one and the other, and one by the other."[9]

Second, there is the set of never-ending questions concerning the relation of communism to Marxism. As Toni Negri also asks: "Can one be communist without Marx?"[10] Is there necessarily a link between the two, whether in terms of doctrinal body, the history of the workers' movement and its so-called fusion with Marxist ideas, the state-sponsored efforts to promote Marx's thought, or purely and simply the scholastic authority of sacred texts? In the absence of a quick formula to break out of the confines of our present state of affairs, the

9   Garo, "Le communisme vu d'ici ou la politique au sens plein," 40–1.

10   Toni Negri, "Est-il possible d'être communiste sans Marx?" *Actuel Marx* 48 (2010): 46–54. The Italian version can be found on-line at http://uninomade.org. Other investigations in the recent special dossiers that return to the question of Marx's communism(s) include Pierre Dardot, "Le 'communisme scientifique' pouvait-il être politique?" *ContreTemps: Revue de critique communiste* 4 (2009): 33–9; Franck Fischbach, "Marx et le communisme," *Actuel Marx* 48 (2010): 12–21; Etienne Balibar, "Remarques de circonstance sur le communisme," ibid., 33–45; and Jacques Bidet, "Le communisme entre philosophie, prophétie et théorie," ibid., 89–104. Christian Laval, in a defense of communism as the institution of the commons, holds the exact opposite thesis: "If communism is meant to have a future, it can only be by breaking with its Marxist interpretation," in "Réinventer le communisme, instituer les communs," *ContreTemps: Revue de critique communiste* 4 (2009): 53.

temptation is obviously great to resort to the authority of Marx's
changing views on the subject of communism, in particular
his shift from the purely philosophical register to the material
conditions of communism laid bare in the critique of political
economy and the political form finally discovered in the Paris
Commune: "From the foundational experience of 1848 to
that of the Commune, the 'real movement' that tends to abolish the existing state of things took form and force, dissipat-
ing the 'sectarian crotchets' and ridiculing 'the oracular tone
of scientific infallibility.' In other words, communism, which
was first of all a state of mind or a 'philosophical communism,'
found its political form."[11] There are certainly worse things
to do with our time than revisiting this trajectory behind
Marx's communism. In a familiar compensatory move, textual
exegesis in that case comes to serve as an academic stand-in
for a missing political strategy, which in any case is already
better than having no placeholder for the lack whatsoever. But
then what is to be done with non-Marxist, pre-Marxist or even
anti-Marxist, utopian or libertarian, primitive or communitarian, precolonial or postcolonial, literary-artistic or artisanal
communes and communisms?

---

11    Bensaïd, "Puissances du communisme," 13. Bensaïd is summa-
rizing the shift from Marx's correspondence with Arnold Ruge,
through the well-known statements from *The German Ideology* and
*The Communist Manifesto*, all the way to the discussion of the Paris
Commune in "The Civil War in France," here quoted from Karl
Marx, *Political Writings*, vol. 3: *The First International and After*, ed.
David Fernbach (London: Penguin, 1974), 213.

Even assuming that we accept the blackmail of scholastic exegesis, what to do, above all, with the orthodox Marxist tradition on the questions of communism and the withering away of the State? The old masters recall for us that today this traditional debate puts us inexorably on the wrong track, with Eurocommunism and its failure, to say nothing of the infamous common programs and historical compromises with socialism, having done for Western Europe what the debacle of the Stalinist or Maoist State did for the East, namely, to show that communism as an idea must be completely severed from the question of the takeover of power. The invocation of history, in that case, serves as a strange defense mechanism—preventing us from taking into account not only the complexity of the past but also the actuality of other experiments, some of which are currently still ongoing, as in the cases of Chiapas or Bolivia. "Sheer prehistory," some will whisper, while others wave the banner of "primitive communism" before our eyes only to predict that Latin America will still have to experience the same mistakes that Europe had the dubious privilege of making a century or more in advance of the Third World.

And yet, as Etienne Balibar also argues in his contribution to the "Potentialities of Communism" conference, the aporia contained in the formula of the withering away of the State—that is, the idea of a State capable of functioning as a non-State—may well be one of the most productive problems in the entire Marxist political legacy. "Rather than reflecting upon communism as 'overcoming of socialism,' think of the modalities of a bifurcation at the heart of revolutionary discourses that have in common the reference to 'the people' vis-à-vis the State, and hence as an *alternative to populism*," proposes Balibar, before alluding to Bolivia, and to the theoretical work of Álvaro García Linera in particular, as a case in point:

I propose to invert, in some way, the aporia of communist politics as the dialectic of a "State-non-State," by seeing in it not so much a supplement of radicalism in socialism but rather a paradoxical supplement of democracy (and of democratic practices) capable of altering the representation that the people make for themselves of their own historical "sovereignty": another interior (or rather, an *interior alteration*) of populism, or the critical alternative to the becoming-people of anti-capitalism as well as, in certain historico-geographic conditions, of anti-imperialism.[12]

---

12   Balibar, "Remarques de circonstance sur le communisme," 44–5. In a footnote Balibar refers to Álvaro García Linera's collection *La potencia plebeya. Acción colectiva e identidades indígenas, obreras y populares en Bolivia*, ed. Pablo Stefanoni (Buenos Aires: Prometeo/CLACSO, 2008), to which I return below in Chapter 5. Bensaïd, as always, had the internationalist foresight to include a translation of García Linera's text on the missed encounter between indigenist (or indianist) and Marxist logics as part of the same special issue of *ContreTemps*, "De quoi le communisme est-il le nom?" See García Linera, "Indianisme et marxisme: La non-rencontre de deux raisons révolutionnaires," *ContreTemps: Revue de critique communiste* 4 (2009): 67–75.

What this proposal suggests, above all, is that the question of the relation between communism and the State cannot be addressed without adopting a truly internationalist perspective from where even the broad typology of pre-Marxist and non-Marxist communisms—Balibar himself mentions the examples of *Christian* communism, from the Anabaptists to Negri, as well as *egalitarian* or *bourgeois* communism, from the Levellers to Babeuf to Rancière—will turn out to have been exceedingly Eurocentric.

Third, and finally, what is to be done with communism in relation to the multiple forms of political organization that seek to give body to the idea, from the party to social movements both old and new, all the way to the so-called revolution of everyday life inspired by council communism? "Thus, against all expectations and in spite of the final resonances of the term, communism also has the merit of relaunching the question of mediations and transitions, of forms of organization and struggle, of strategic and programmatic elaborations."[13] Conversely, what is left if communism as an egalitarian discipline of anti-property, anti-hierarchy, and anti-authority principles is subtracted from the State, from the party, perhaps even from all clubs, leagues, unions, councils, and social movements? As Badiou writes in "The Communist Hypothesis": "Marxism, the workers' movement, mass democracy, Leninism, the party of the proletariat, the socialist

---

13    Garo, "Le communisme vu d'ici ou la politique au sens plein," 41.

state—all the inventions of the 20th century—are not really useful to us any more. At the theoretical level they certainly deserve further study and consideration; but at the level of practical politics they have become unworkable," so that today, in any case, "the solution will be neither the formless, or multiform, popular movement inspired by the intelligence of the multitude—as Negri and the alter-globalists believe—nor the renewed and democratized mass communist party, as some of the Trotskyists and Maoists hope. The (19th-century) movement and the (20th-century) party were specific modes of the communist hypothesis; it is no longer possible to return to them."[14] Is what remains then purely and simply a kind of generic communism that is everywhere and nowhere—like God, that "impossible possibility" as Karl Barth said as early as 1919 in his commentary on Paul's *Epistle to the Romans*—which is never far removed from the idea of communist politics not just as the "art of insurrection" (as Lenin said) but also as the "art of the impossible" (as both Badiou and Žižek say today)? Could something of the kind be what Marx already had in mind when he waxed sarcastic about the public's perceptions of the Paris Commune: "But this is communism, 'impossible' communism," something which the cooperative production of the workers nonetheless turned into an actuality overnight, thus rendering the impossible possible as if by miracle: "What else, gentlemen, would it be but communism,

---

14   Badiou, "The Communist Hypothesis," 37.

'possible' communism?"[15] Does this mean that we should come
to embrace the impossible possibility of generic communism
as a new religion, or as a renewal of political theology—not
even excluding the whole theatrical procession of grace, miracles, apostles, and saints? In other words: *Deus sive Revolutio*?[16]
Or else, subsequent to a robust secularization, is what remains
of communism subtracted from all hitherto existing forms
of political organization perhaps nothing more than a pure
ethics of courage and commitment—the ethics of not giving
up on one's desire for, or one's fidelity to, communism as an
Idea? This is Bensaïd's principal objection against Badiou's
formulation of the communist hypothesis, which in this sense

---

15    Marx, "The Civil War in France," 213. Karl Barth discusses
the notion of "impossible possibility" throughout his commentary
on Paul, in *The Epistle to the Romans*, trans. Edwyn C. Hoskins
(London: Oxford University Press, 1968). I owe this reference
to my friend Geoff Waite, who also draws the comparison with
Badiou's communism in his "Bataille, or, Communism: *Supplice* &
Euphemism, Tautology & Suicide Bombs (*Summa theologica-poli-
tica*)," originally intended for inclusion in the volume *The Obsessions
of Georges Bataille: Community and Communication*, ed. Andrew J.
Mitchell and Jason Kemp Winfree (Albany: State University of New
York Press, 2009), for which in the end it must have been deemed
too radical or not euphemistic enough. For a discussion of the category of the impossible in Badiou's work, and a comparison with both
Žižek and Derrida, see Chapter 7, "From Potentiality to Inexistence,"
in my *Badiou and Politics* (Durham: Duke University Press, 2011).
Finally, Roberto Esposito offers an "impolitical" reading of Barth's
commentary on Paul's *Epistle to the Romans*, in "Opera," in his *Nove
pensieri sulla politica* (Bologna: Il Mulino, 1993), 137–57.
16    Balibar, "Remarques de circonstance sur le communisme," 37.

would remain a purely hypothetical communism, one that would be unable to mediate between the ideal and the real, between politics and history, or between perennial philosophy and the discordant realities of the present. "The philosophical hypothesis of the escape from the cavern by way of the event, or of the Paulinian revelation, does not allow the articulation of the event with history, of contingency with necessity, of the goal with the movement," Bensaïd concludes in a book review of *The Communist Hypothesis*, reiterating a common criticism, shared by many others, of Badiou's doctrine of the event in general. "Now, for us there is no exteriority, no absolute outside of politics with regard to institutions, of the event with regard to history, of truth with regard to opinion. The outside is always within. Contradictions explode from inside. And politics does not consist in eluding them but in installing oneself in them so as to bring them to the point of rupture and explosion."[17]

---

17   Daniel Bensaïd, "Un communisme hypothétique. À propos de *L'Hypothèse communiste* d'Alain Badiou," *ContreTemps: Revue de critique communiste* 2 (2009): 107. See also Peter Hallward's review of Badiou's book *The Meaning of Sarkozy*, which ends with a comparable critical note on the political insufficiency of the communist Idea, in *Radical Philosophy* 149 (2008): 50–2. Other criticisms along similar lines, referring to Badiou's more recent book *The Communist Hypothesis* (London: Verso, 2010) in particular, include Emmanuel Barot, "Le communisme n'est pas une Idée (Court état du marxisme en France)," *ContreTemps: Revue de critique communiste* 7 (2010), available on-line at www.contre-temps.eu; and Pierre Khalfa, "Vérité et émancipation. À propos du livre d'Alain Badiou, *L'Hypothèse communiste*," *Mouvements* 60 (2009): 152–7.

Why should we have to choose, though, among the
different communisms, whether as movement, as process, or as goal; among utopian, scientific, or really existing
communisms and socialisms; or among crude, political, or
fully developed and thus presumably anti- or suprapolitical
communisms? Beyond the endless polemics, the bitter self-
criticisms, and the vicious internecine strife that continues
to divide the Left more efficiently than the Right could ever
hope to accomplish, could we not propose a kind of communism of communisms? Or—and here the admonishing voice
of the old masters makes itself heard one last time—does all
this not reek of the politics of popular fronts whose historical outcome, especially in Latin America, more often than
not led to violent anti-communist military coups? In brief,
regardless of the question of age in a vulgar biological or a
naïve generational sense, is it possible to be a young communist today without being either an ignoramus (of history) or
an ingénue (of morality)?

Extending this set of questions, then, the present book
seeks to intervene in the contemporary debate on politics
and philosophy by addressing the legacy of leftism and
communism in the wake of both the crisis of Marxism and
the critique of metaphysics. In particular, on the basis of
the assumption that the reaffirmation of communism as
an idea or hypothesis untainted by its actual history is as
naïve and ultimately as ineffective as its wholesale refutation in the name of so-called hard empirical evidence, the
chapters in this book seek to work out a dialectic between

leftism and communism, itself transversal to the dialectic between philosophy and actuality, or rather, as I prefer to think of it, between theory and actuality. The point is to verify whether communism, aside from being a relic of the past and the object of incriminating or nostalgic reminiscences, can be something more than a utopia for beautiful souls—something more than what Lenin described as the "infantile disease" of "left-wing communism," which today seems to be making a comeback in the guise of "speculative leftism" as diagnosed by, among others, Rancière and Badiou.

"Communism is for us not a *state of affairs* which is to be established, an *ideal* to which reality [will] have to adjust itself," Marx and Engels famously wrote in the still heavily Hegelianized language of *The German Ideology*. "We call communism the *real* movement which abolishes the present state of things [*die* wirkliche *Bewegung, welche den jetzigen Zustand aufhebt*]."[18] Can this abolition, this destruction, or this suppression and supersession of the present state of things also bring about an equally *real* movement of recomposition? In the end, wherein lies the reality or, rather, the actuality of communism? Is this actuality under the present circumstances necessarily limited

---

18   Karl Marx and Friedrich Engels, *Die deutsche Ideologie*, in *Werke*, vol. 3 (Berlin: Dietz Verlag, 1962), 34; *The German Ideology*, *Collected Works*, vol. 5 (New York: International Publishers, 1976), 49. In the recent flurry of publications and special dossiers, there is almost no contribution that does not quote or allude to this passage.

to being a pure movement of critique and destruction? Or is there place for a unified front of common affirmation and overcoming?

## The Speculative Left

Now if there is one thing on which all authors involved in the current return of communism seem to be in complete agreement, it is the need to draw a sharp line of demarcation between communism and socialism. "Negri's anti-socialist title, *Goodbye Mr. Socialism*, was correct: communism is to be opposed to socialism, which, in place of the egalitarian collective, offers an organic community," writes Žižek in his own version of "The Communist Hypothesis," in *First as Tragedy, Then as Farce*; just as, much earlier, Badiou already had made the same claim in his *Theory of the Subject*: "If there is a major point in Marxism, which this century confirms almost to the level of disgust, it is that we should certainly not inflate the question of 'socialism,' of the 'construction of socialism.' The serious affair, the *precise* affair, is communism. This is why, all along, politics stands in a position of domination over the State, and cannot be reduced to it."[19] In

---

19   Slavoj Žižek, *First as Tragedy, Then as Farce* (London: Verso, 2009), 95; and Alain Badiou, *Theory of the Subject*, trans. Bruno Bosteels (London and New York: Continuum, 2009), 7–8. For a good combined criticism of Badiou and Žižek's positions, see also Alex Callinicos, "Sur l'hypothèse communiste," *ContreTemps: Revue de critique communiste* 4 (2009): 28–32. The only exceptions to this chorus in praise

what follows, however, I would like to displace the focus of attention away from the debate over communism and socialism toward a slightly different dialectic: that between the actuality of communism and the attraction of so-called speculative leftism that often lurks behind wholesale rejections of the problematic of the construction of socialism and the related thematic of the withering away of the State. If today communism is indeed the name of a problem rather than the solution, I would argue that this last dialectic can still teach us a great deal about the nature of the problem in question as part of an ongoing critical history of the Left.

For the purposes of our argument, we can adopt the following definition of the Left that Badiou provides in the context of his analysis of the Paris Commune: "Let's call 'the Left' the set of parliamentary political personnel that proclaim that they are the only ones equipped to bear the general consequences of a singular political movement. Or, in more contemporary terms, that they are the only ones able to provide 'social movements' with a 'political perspective.'"[20] Needless to say, this is a heavily historically

---

of communism and against socialism are Ellen Meiksins Woods, "Redéfinir la démocratie," *ContreTemps: Revue de critique communiste* 4 (2009): 59–62; and Chantal Mouffe, "Communisme ou démocratie radicale?," *Actuel Marx* 48 (2010): 83–8. Both these authors not only argue in favor of a radical socialist democracy, they also believe that communism is not worth returning to.

20    Alain Badiou, "The Paris Commune: A Political Declaration on Politics," in *Polemics*, trans. Steve Corcoran (London: Verso, 2006), 272.

charged definition or stipulation that purports to take into account the burden of the parliamentary and State-oriented destiny of politics, which for the past two centuries has weighed down on the idea of communism, to the point of conflation with the question of the construction of socialism. And, insofar as for Badiou "the Commune is what, for the first and to this day only time, broke with the parliamentary destiny of popular and workers' political movements," we can also understand why on his account the task of communist politics today somehow must entail a resurrection of the politics of the Paris Commune. Or, rather, the new sequence of the communist hypothesis, while entailing no mere return to the saturated forms of movement and party-State, will have to learn its lesson from the problems left unresolved in the wake of the events of 1871: "Today, the Commune's political visibility must be restored by a process of disincorporation: born of rupture with the Left, it must be extracted from the leftist hermeneutics that have overwhelmed it for so long."[21]

In view of the cycles of hope and disappointment that like a curse seem to bewitch the parliamentary-electoral Left, from François Mitterrand to Barack Obama, nothing indeed makes more sense than the desire to extract oneself from this leftist hermeneutics and to define an emancipatory politics outside of, or at a distance from,

---

21   Ibid., 272–3.

the entire framework of classes, social movements, political parties, and socialist States inherited from a certain interpretation of Marxism. In this sense, we could even call "communism" the ensemble of struggles, desires, and impulses that aim to exceed the parliamentary Left with its predictable oscillation between enthusiasm and betrayal. This excess is not just an ideological deviation, it is also the repeated beginning of a necessary drive toward continued emancipation. In fact, communism acquires much of its strength precisely from immersion in this excess, which in many regards may well be the very source of its political actuality. However, insofar as the ensemble of struggles, desires, and impulses to exceed the parliamentary destiny of the Left may also appear to sidestep all questions of mediation except to posit that everything must be invented from the ground up, the ensuing definition of "communism" often becomes indistinguishable from another kind of "leftism," namely, "speculative leftism."

To my knowledge, Rancière is the first to define "speculative leftism" as one of the two historical outcomes of Althusserianism—the other being Zhdanovism, or what we might also call the "speculative rightism" of the class struggle. As early as in *Althusser's Lesson*, Rancière writes: "The double Althusserian truth after May '68 is shattered into two poles: the speculative leftism of the all-powerful ideological apparatuses and the speculative Zhdanovism of the class struggle in theory that interrogates each word to make it confess its class."[22] As a matter of fact, what defines the first of these poles of the Althusserian legacy is not the all-powerful role of the ideological state apparatuses but the desire—in the name of science, theory, or philosophy as the class struggle in theory—radically to break with their power of subjection. Speculative leftism thus comes to represent an uncompromising purification of the notion of communism, not so much as the abolition but rather as the complete tabula rasa of the present state of things, including all classes, parties, and ideological apparatuses of the State.

The influence of French Maoism is key in this portrayal of the destiny of Althusser's legacy after May '68. "In a first phase, some enthusiastically adopted a reading of Marx

22    Jacques Rancière, *La Leçon d'Althusser* (Paris: Gallimard, 1974), 146. Interestingly enough, Žižek also uses the expression "speculative positivism" in his reading of Schelling: "Today, it is clearly established that Schelling prefigures a series of key Marxian motifs, up to Marx's 'revolutionary' reproach to Hegel's dialectics according to which the speculative-dialectical resolution of the contradiction leaves the actual social antagonism intact (Hegel's 'speculative positivism')." Slavoj Žižek, *The Indivisible Remainder: An Essay on Schelling and Related Matters* (London: Verso, 1996), 4. Žižek would have no trouble pointing out the pseudo-Hegelian nature of this understanding of the "speculative" dialectic. For alternate readings, see also Jean-Luc Nancy, *The Speculative Remark (One of Hegel's Bons Mots)*, trans. Céline Surprenant (Stanford: Stanford University Press, 2001); and Jean-François Lyotard, "Analyzing Speculative Discourse as Language-Game," in *The Lyotard Reader*, ed. Andrew Benjamin (Cambridge: Basil Blackwell, 1989), 265–74.

privileging the moment of rupture with previous ideology," Rancière also writes, quoting an early account of the rise of Maoism among young Althusserians in France: "Yet they visibly gave this approach a leftist slant and pushed it to absurdity, making Marxism into a kind of absolute commencement, the negation of all past culture, disregarding hundreds of texts by Marx and Lenin. They thus needed to accomplish a new 'leap forward': then 'Mao Zedong thought,' or at the very least what was actually put in the spotlight under this name, offered its linearity and its schematism."[23] What is speculative about this leftism is not the simple fact of being out of touch with reality in the style of plain old idealism but the way in which actual political events and historical filiations, while purportedly taken into account, in reality vanish and are replaced by theoretical operators that continue to be the sole purview of the Marxist philosopher as the master and proprietor of truth. "These operators, in the Hegelian fashion, transform the empirical into speculation and speculation into the empirical, reducing historical phenomena such as Stalinism to flimsy abstractions such as economism and incarnating concepts such as humanism into the empirical existence of individuals," maintains Rancière, still referring to Althusser's operation and its fateful effect on the history of the Left: "Such is the necessity of the 'class struggle in theory':

---

23  Claude Prévost, "Portrait robot du maoïsme en France," *La Nouvelle Critique* (June 1967), quoted by Rancière in *La Leçon d'Althusser*, 110 n.1.

it functions only by reducing the actual to the eternal and the other to the same."[24]

At this point, anyone familiar with Bensaïd's criticisms of the way Badiou defines the eternal invariance of the communist Idea cannot but be struck by the remarkable coincidences with Rancière's early criticisms of Althusser. Just as Bensaïd in his review of Badiou's *The Communist Hypothesis* speaks of a "libertarian, or, rather, authoritarian anti-statist Platonism" of the eternal "philosopher-king against the sophist," so too, Rancière explains sarcastically, "the philosophers did not become kings" upon reading *For Marx* in spite of, or due to, Althusser's "ultraleft Platonism."[25] And yet, surprisingly, one of the most succinct diagnostics of speculative leftism as a twin deviation next to statism comes to us from the hand of Badiou himself, in *Being and Event*. Even more surprisingly, this diagnostic still relies on some of the very same terminology found twenty or so years earlier in *Althusser's Lesson*.

In his pivotal meditation "The Intervention," in *Being and Event*, Badiou declares:

We can term *speculative leftism* any thought of being which bases itself upon the theme of an absolute

---

24   Rancière, *La Leçon d'Althusser*, 193–4.
25   Daniel Bensaïd, "Un communisme hypothétique. À propos de *L'Hypothèse communiste* d'Alain Badiou," 107, 113; and Rancière, *La Leçon d'Althusser*, 54, 146.

commencement. Speculative leftism imagines that intervention authorizes itself on the basis of itself alone; that it breaks with the situation without any other support than its own negative will. This imaginary wager upon an absolute novelty—"to break in two the history of the world"—fails to recognize that the real of the conditions of possibility of intervention is always the circulation of an already decided event. In other words, it is the presupposition, implicit or not, that there has already been an intervention. Speculative leftism is fascinated by the evental ultra-one and it believes that in the latter's name it can reject any immanence to the structured regime of the count-as-one.[26]

Badiou's philosophy, as I argue elsewhere, does not pretend to save the purity of the event by haughtily withdrawing from all immanence and situatedness. Rather, for him, the point is to study the consequences of an event within the current situation or world, not to elevate the event into a dimension that is wholly or even mystically otherwise than being: "What the doctrine of the event teaches us is rather that the entire effort lies in following the event's consequences, not in

---

26    Alain Badiou, *Being and Event*, trans. Oliver Feltham (London: Continuum, 2005), 210. For a more detailed commentary, see Bruno Bosteels, "The Speculative Left," *South Atlantic Quarterly* 104 (2005): 751–67; now reworked as the conclusion to my *Badiou and Politics*.

glorifying its occurrence. There is no more an angelic herald of the event than there is a hero. Being does not commence."[27] In this sense, the repudiation of leftism is even a constant in all of Badiou's work, from his early attacks on the revisionism of the New Philosophers, but also against the Deleuzian and Lacanian philosophers of desire who throw the dissidence of the formless masses or plebes directly against the oppressive machinery of the State, all the way to his recent attempt at an ideological mediation between politics and history that precisely would be the task of the communist Idea.

Thus, for example, in Badiou's *Ethics* both the temptation of "total reeducation" dreamed of by some of Mao's Red Guards and Nietzsche's mad dream of a "grand politics" are diagnosed as disastrous forms of extremism. These are attempts to draw a rigid and dogmatic line of demarcation between truth and opinion, in the name of which all immanence to the existing state of things is denied as sheer decadence or bourgeois revisionism. To be more precise, these are attempts to perform a complete tabula rasa of the past for the sake of truth's absolute present. "When Nietzsche proposes to 'break the history of the world in two' by exploding Christian nihilism and generalizing the great Dionysian 'yes' to Life; or when certain Red Guards of the Chinese Cultural Revolution proclaim, in 1967, the complete suppression of self-interest, they are indeed inspired by a vision of a situation in which all opinions have been replaced by the truth to which Nietzsche and the Red

---

27    Badiou, *Being and Event*, 210–11.

Guards are committed," claims Badiou. But these are forms of absolutization of the power of truth that amount to a disastrous Evil: "Not only does this Evil destroy the situation (for the will to eliminate opinion is, fundamentally, the same as the will to eliminate, in the human animal, its very animality, i.e. its being), but it also interrupts the truth-process in whose name it proceeds, since it fails to preserve, within the composition of the subject, the duality [*duplicité*] of interests (disinterested-interest and interest pure and simple)."[28] To avoid the trap of speculative leftism, therefore, a certain degree of duplicity and impurity must be preserved in the articulation between the old state of things and the new emancipatory truth.

Badiou's proposal of the communist Idea is in part meant to ensure a similarly impure mediation, this time between history, politics, and subjectivity. "A formal definition of the Idea can immediately be given: an Idea is the subjectivation of an interplay between the singularity of a truth procedure and a representation of History," which is how Badiou sees the function of the communist Idea: "For about two centuries (from Babeuf's 'community of equals' to the 1980s), the word 'communism' was the most important name of an Idea located in the field of emancipatory, or revolutionary politics."[29] Far from remaining a utopian principle,

---

28    Alain Badiou, *Ethics: An Essay on the Understanding of Evil*, trans. Peter Hallward (London: Verso, 2001), 84–5.
29    Badiou, "The Idea of Communism," in Douzinas and Žižek, eds., *The Idea of Communism*, 3.

communism would thus be what allows for the historical inscription of politics in a concrete situation. It is what operates in the space in-between the local and the universal, the singular and the eternal, the interested individual and the disinterested subject of a cause greater than him or herself. In this sense, communism actually would be able to avoid the pitfalls of speculative leftism thanks to the triangulation of history, politics, and subjectivity enabled by the Idea.

And yet, a profound ambiguity surrounds this recasting of communism as Idea. Not only does Badiou warn against the "short-circuiting between the real and the Idea," in which he perceives the "long-term effects of the Hegelian origins of Marxism," but what is more, both the nomination of the communist Idea or hypothesis and the maintenance of the distance separating it from the real seem to be tasks reserved if not exclusively then at least primarily for philosophy. "In fact, what we are ascribed as a philosophical task, we could say even a duty, is to help a new modality of existence of the hypothesis to come into being," absent which the people appear once again disoriented and confused, if not waiting for the intervention of the philosopher: "Lacking the Idea, the popular masses' confusion is inescapable."[30] By way of

---

30   Badiou, *The Meaning of Sarkozy*, 115 (the version in "The Communist Hypothesis" is less specifically tied to the work of the philosopher: "This is our task, during the reactionary interlude that now prevails: through the combination of thought processes— always global, or universal, in character—and political experience, always local or singular, yet transmissible, to renew the existence

the Idea, supposed to guarantee the historical inscription of a singular political experience, the energy of communism thus ends up being absorbed into the sole purview of the philosopher's act. This is why Judith Balso and Alessandro Russo, two of Badiou's closest allies in terms of a shared Maoist or post-Maoist political orientation, distance themselves from their friend and mentor's main thesis. "I consider this thesis above all a *defence of philosophy*," Russo starts out by saying. "It is the name for a desire of the philosopher, a desire that perhaps the present conditions of de-politicization make even more acute."[31] In fact, contrary to the original premise behind the London conference as stated in the invitation sent out to all participants, both Balso and Russo argue that, if it is a possible hypothesis for philosophy, communism can no longer be the name or hypothesis for militant politics. Instead, they urge participants to find ways of "identifying politics as an absolutely singular thought, one wholly internal to the organized processes of politics itself; abandoning the *dispositif* which consists in asking philosophy questions which only politics can answer; ceasing to think that it is possible to proceed from philosophy (or science) to politics," in the way that Althusser is said to have proceeded. "Above all, ceasing to require of philosophy that it provide

---

of the communist hypothesis, in our consciousness and on the ground" [42]); and Badiou, "The Idea of Communism," 13.
31     Alessandro Russo, "Did the Cultural Revolution End Communism? Eight Remarks on Philosophy and Politics Today," in Douzinas and Žižek, eds., *The Idea of Communism*, 180, 190.

new foundations or a completed form for politics, or that it serve as a palliative for the seeming absence or weakness of politics."[32]

If, in light of these demands, we return to a text such as *Of an Obscure Disaster: On the End of the Truth of the State*, which is Badiou's take on the fall of the Berlin Wall and the so-called death of communism, the ambiguity is by no means lifted. On one hand, there is agreement about the need for a separation between philosophy and politics. "I speak here as a philosopher instructed by the fact that, as I contend, the fusion between philosophy and its political condition ruins both," says Badiou. "In reality, the fact that the identification of the philosophical and the political, their identification as *thoughts*, has only a policing, not to mention a criminal, reality, is established since—at least—let's say book X of Plato's *Laws*."[33] The point is to think history, for example, as an intrinsic periodization of politics and not the other way around, to think politics from within the necessary course of history: "Politics alone, from the point of the prescription that opens it up, *thinks* the lacunary periodicity of political subjectivity."[34] And yet, on the other hand, philosophy also

---

32  Judith Balso, "To Present Oneself to the Present. The Communist Hypothesis: A Possible Hypothesis for Philosophy, an Impossible Name for Politics?," in Douzinas and Žižek, eds., *The Idea of Communism*, 31.
33  Alain Badiou, *D'un désastre obscur: Sur la fin de la vérité d'État* (La Tour d'Aigues: De l'Aube, 1998), 43.
34  Ibid., 13.

steps into the arena as a formidable competitor as soon as the question of political truth arises: "Philosophy and only philosophy, which is conditioned by politics, can say what the rapport of politics to truth is all about, or more precisely what politics as a procedure of truth is all about."[35]

I read in this ambiguity the sign of a still tentative unsuturing of politics and philosophy and the symptom of philosophy's constant hegemonic desire for and above politics. How else should we interpret the need for the limiting clauses in definitions such as the following in which it is said that "politics, *inasmuch as it is a condition of philosophy*, is a subjective procedure of truth. It finds in the State neither its primary stake nor its incarnation"; or again, "the essence of politics, *such that philosophy traces the concept thereof as condition for its own exercise of thought*, i.e. politics as the free activity of the thought of the collective under the effect of always singular events, *this* politics is by no means power or the question of power."[36] Politics, as one condition of philosophy among others, thus appears to be absorbed back into the conditioned. In the end, this is how I would describe the temptation of speculative leftism, namely, as a name for the philosophical appropriation of radical emancipatory politics, as if this radicality depended on philosophy in order to be able to subtract itself from the questions of power and the State. Yet speculative leftism is not just the name for an ideologi-

35  Ibid., 48.
36  Ibid., 54 (emphases added).

cal deviation to be corrected by following the correct line of communism; it also and at the same time serves as a possible passageway through which philosophy communicates with the struggles, desires, and impulses that define its actuality.

## The Idea of Actuality

Actuality and communism, to be sure, are two words that few people in their right mind would want to see used in the same sentence today. At least in this regard, the sophisticated philosopher and the mainstream opinion-pollster are surprisingly well-attuned to one another, insofar as the critique of metaphysics has for the most part served to complement and give theoretical credence to the dominant impression that communism is morally bankrupt and politically obsolete in light of the complete crisis of Marxism and the collapse of the Soviet Union. At best, thanks to half a century of dogged deconstruction, we have grown accustomed to the retrieval of communism as an element of ghostly spectrality, without the threat of its manifesto-like realization, or to the repetition of communism as an ever-present but always untimely potentiality without actuality.

Even Badiou's notion of the communist hypothesis runs the risk of inactuality to the extent to which it would be only an Idea of Reason in the Kantian sense, never a concept of the Understanding for which there might be a corresponding sensible intuition. This is how Badiou defines communism in "The Communist Hypothesis": "It is what Kant called an Idea, with a regulatory function, rather than a programme."[37] A few months later, in his talk "The Idea of Communism" presented at the London conference, Badiou admittedly seems partly to abandon this claim. Or, perhaps in response to some of Žižek's objections, he now softens the Kantian edge of his earlier statement by opting instead for the claim that, philosophically speaking, the exact status of the communist hypothesis is necessarily undecidable:

> The Idea, which is an operative mediation between the real and the symbolic, always presents the individual with something that is located between the event and the fact. That is why the endless debates about the real status of the communist Idea are unresolvable. Is it a question of a regulative Idea, in Kant's sense of the term, having no real efficacy but able to set reasonable goals for our understanding? Or is it an agenda that must be carried out over time through a new post-revolutionary State's action on the world? Is it a utopia, perhaps a plainly dangerous, and even criminal, one? Or is it the name of Reason in History? This type of

---

37  Badiou, "The Communist Hypothesis," 35. Lyotard is, of course, the greatest proponent of this return to the Kantian Idea as part of a rethinking of politics and aesthetics after (and against) Hegel but also after (and against) Marx. See the sadly ignored book that he considered his philosophical masterpiece, Jean-François Lyotard, *The Differend: Phrases in Dispute*, trans. Georges Van Den Abbeele (Minneapolis: University of Minnesota Press, 1988).

debate can never be concluded, for the simple reason that the subjective operation of the Idea is not simple but complex.[38]

Even so, the reader may be forgiven if she has the impression of a lingering Kantianism. As Véronique Bergen wonders:

> By the disjunction between the idea or the hypothesis and its realization, does one not have recourse to an operation that is doubly problematic, on one hand, because of the openly declared presuppositions (establish a difference in nature between a concept and the historical figures of its realization), and, on the other hand, because of the ensuing consequences (return to a Kantian scene based on the split of the transcendental and the empirical, the intelligible and the sensible, the regulative Idea and the fact, or return to the Deleuzian version of the virtual and the actual)?[39]

Viewed in this light, none of the concrete actualizations of the communist idea would discredit its intrinsic philosophical coherence. But then are we not back in a form of speculative leftism? "How not to fall back into the impasse of a split between the valorization of communism as pure movement and the stigmatization of its relapses?" Bergen also

---

38    Badiou, "The Idea of Communism," 8.
39    Bergen, "Un communisme des singularités," 17.

asks: "How not to remain at the level of sterile praise for the insurrectionary movement, well short of its consequences and its basis in being?"[40] Perhaps the alternative to this form of speculative leftism, then, must also break with a certain legacy of Kant?

Over and against the perceived Kantianism behind the proposal of communism as a purely regulative Idea, Marx's reference to the actuality of communism, as in the *real* or *actual* movement that abolishes the present state of things, here reveals its wide-ranging Hegelian orientation. If we manage to think outside the guided adventure of the spirit with which dialectical thought is all too often lazily equated, this orientation has lost nothing of its force. Indeed, as Fredric Jameson recently highlights in *The Hegel Variations*:

> The word actuality—an English translation more pointed and useful than its German equivalent *Wirklichkeit* or reality as such—is a whole Hegelian program here; and we can best approach the Hegelian doctrine of immanence by understanding that for Hegel actuality already includes its own possibilities and potentialities; they are not something separate and distinct from it, lying in some other alternate world or in the future. Qua possibility this promise of the real is already here and not simply "possible."[41]

40   Ibid.
41   Fredric Jameson, *The Hegel Variations* (London: Verso, 2010), 70.

Here, in other words, we should overcome a common misconception surrounding the notion of actuality, which is often equated with dumb reality or, more subtly, with historical effectivity, in contrast to the pristine but ineffective purity of thought or of the Idea.

Hegel explains in an addition to §142 of *The Encyclopaedia Logic*:

> Actuality and thought—more precisely the Idea—are usually opposed to one another in a trivial way, and hence we often hear it said therefore that, although there is certainly nothing to be said against the correctness and truth of a certain thought, still nothing like it is to be found or can actually be put into effect. Those who talk like this, however, only demonstrate that they have not adequately interpreted the nature either of thought or of actuality. For, on the one hand, in all talk of this kind, thought is assumed to be synonymous with subjective representation, planning, intention, and so on; and, on the other hand, actuality is assumed to be synonymous with external, sensible existence.[42]

---

42　G. W. F. Hegel, *The Encyclopaedia Logic*, trans. T. F. Geraets, W. A. Suchting, and H. S. Harris (Indianapolis: Hackett, 1991), 214. Fischbach draws the connection with the passage from *The German Ideology*, in "Marx et le communisme," 20.

Contrary to these common interpretations, the notion of actuality as used in connection with communism presupposes the immanence of thought and existence, going so far as to accept the much maligned identity of the rational and the real, not as a dogmatic given guaranteed by the objective course of history, but as an ongoing and open-ended task for politics: "As distinct from mere appearance, actuality, being initially the unity of inward and outward, is so far from confronting reason as something other than it, that it is, on the contrary, what is rational through and through; and what is not rational must, for that very reason, be considered not to be actual."[43] The point is somehow to perceive communism not as a utopian not-yet for which reality will always fail to offer an adequate match, but as something that is always already here, in every moment of refusal of private appropriation and in every act of collective reappropriation. "The ontological background of this leap from 'not-yet' to 'always already' is a kind of 'trading of places' between possibility and actuality: possibility itself, in its very opposition to actuality, possesses an actuality of its own," writes Žižek, in a slightly different context that should nonetheless prove relevant for the debate concerning the actuality of communism. "Hegel always insists on the absolute primacy of actuality: true, the search for the 'conditions of possibility' abstracts from the actual, calls

---

43  Hegel, *The Encyclopaedia Logic*, 214.

it into question, in order to (re)constitute it on a rational basis; yet in all these ruminations actuality is presupposed as something given."[44]

It is with an eye on this understanding of the relation between the actual and the possible that, in the chapters to follow, I will study a series of thinkers and trends that all somehow claim to contribute to the reinvigoration of a tradition of thought for the Left. Do these proposals open up a perspective for the actualization of communism, or does our current ontological background, always more attuned to Kant's analytic of finitude than to Hegel's dialectic of the infinite, run counter to this orientation? Before we can answer this last question, however, we must come to an understanding of the way in which some of our most radical leftist thinkers posit the need for a return to ontology in the first place. They thus propose that a socialist or communist mode of doing politics must necessarily pass through the detour of a prior ontological investigation into the very being of politics. In her short book *On the Political*, for example, Chantal Mouffe contends "that it is the lack of understanding of 'the political' in its ontological dimension which is at the origin of our current incapacity to think in a political way"; or, as Toni Negri writes: "Here is where communism is in need of Marx: to install itself in the common, in ontology.

---

44   Slavoj Žižek, *Tarrying with the Negative: Kant, Hegel, and the Critique of Ideology* (Durham: Duke University Press, 1993), 157.

And vice versa: without historical ontology, there is no communism."[45] The first trend to be studied, then, is this ontological turn in the contemporary political philosophy of the Left.

45    Chantal Mouffe, *On the Political* (New York: Routledge, 2005), 8; and Negri, "Est-il possible d'être communiste sans Marx?," 49.

# 1

## *The Ontological Turn*

Which imbecile spoke of an ontology of the revolt? The
revolt is less in need of a metaphysics than metaphysi-
cians are in need of a revolt.

— Raoul Vaneigem,
*The Revolution of Everyday Life*

### Being in Need

Faced with the ubiquitous return of the question of being
in the field of political thought today, put into relief most
eloquently by the recent collection of essays *A Leftist
Ontology*, I am tempted to repeat Adorno's gesture from the
first part of his *Negative Dialectics*, when he explains, "ontology is understood and immanently criticized out of the need
for it, which is a problem of its own."[1] In keeping with this
model, I too want to ask in what way the answers arising out
of the recent ontological turn in self-anointed leftist circles

---

1  Theodor W. Adorno, *Negative Dialectics*, trans. E. B. Ashton
(London: Continuum, 1990), xx. See also Adorno, *The Jargon of
Authenticity*, trans. Knut Tarnowski and Frederic Will (Evanston:
Northwestern University Press, 1973).

may be "the recoil of the unfolded, transparent question," and to what extent these answers also "meet an emphatic need, a sign of something missed," even if that no longer corresponds to what Adorno sees as "a longing that Kant's verdict on a knowledge of the Absolute should not be the end of the matter."[2] We need not stoop to the level of Adorno's blunt and for this reason often ill-understood attacks on the then new fundamental ontologies in Germany (Heidegger's in particular) to raise again the question about the need for a leftist ontology today. This would mean asking not only: what are the uses and disadvantages of ontology for politics, and a leftist or communist one to boot? But also: where does this politico-ontological need stem from in the first place?

The initial task would consist in outlining the general form in which the ontological question of being is presented to us today in the context of political thought. As opposed to Adorno's claim, the way this happens is in my view no longer—if ever it was—through an appeal to a supposed substantiality, or to some version or other of the Absolute, surreptitiously brought back to life behind Kant's back. In fact, if there is a common presupposition shared by all present-day political ontologies, it is that ontology is not, cannot be, or must not be a question of substance or of the Absolute. It presupposes neither the presence of being nor the identity of being and thinking as a guide for acting. On the contrary, ontology nowadays, in a well-nigh uniform

---

2   Adorno, *Negative Dialectics*, 61–3.

fashion, tends to be qualified as spectral, nonidentical, and postfoundational. It tries to come to terms not with present beings, but with ghosts and phantasms; not with entities or things, but with events—whether with events in the plural, or, alternatively, with the singular event of the presencing of being as such, which should never be confounded with a given present, albeit a past or future one. Consequently, there can be no determinate politics, not even a democratic or radical-democratic one, not to mention communism, that would simply derive from ontology as a thoroughly desubstantialized field of investigation into being and/as event—even though most commentators are quick to add that democracy, often in the guise of direct democracy, radical democracy, or a democracy-to-come, rather than in any of its historical shapes, would be the only political formation or regime of power attuned to the horizon of ontology at the close of the metaphysical era. "This, then, is the argument: in the answers that they have traditionally brought to bear on the 'special' question 'What is to be done?' philosophers have relied, in one way or another, on some standard-setting first whose grounding function was assured by a 'general' doctrine, be it called ontology or something else. From this doctrine, theories of action received their patterns of thought as well as a great many of their answers," writes Reiner Schürmann, in one of the very first attempts at outlining the practical and political implications of a postfoundational, or properly an-archic, ontology, that is, an ontology without *arkhè*, without ground or first standard-setting principle. He continues:

"Now, the deconstruction of metaphysics situates historically what has been deemed to be a foundation. It thus closes the era of derivations between general and special metaphysics, between first philosophy and practical philosophy."[3] The specifically leftist nature of such an antifoundational proposal, however, is not always clear, except insofar as some prior criteria are assumed to be at our disposal by which to judge what is leftist and what is not.

## Between Deconstruction and Psychoanalysis

Heidegger and Lacan, often in bold rereadings or creative misreadings, no doubt represent the two dominant strands

---

3   Reiner Schürmann, *Heidegger on Being and Acting: From Principles to Anarchy*, trans. Christine-Marie Gros (Bloomington: Indiana University Press, 1990), 9. Schürmann himself, despite his insistence on a "necessary ignorance" as to Heidegger's question "how a political system, and what kind of one, can at all be coordinated with the technological age," does not fail to suggest that the experiences of direct democracy, no matter how short-lived, would after all be most attuned to an economy of being as the event of presencing and expropriating. See also a more recent formulation of the same agenda: "Democracy, as a particular political formation, is the *only* universalizable paradigm because it is capable of turning its own foundational principle against itself." Roland Végsö, "Deconstruction and Experience: The Politics of the Undeconstructible," in Carsten Strathausen, ed., *A Leftist Ontology: Beyond Relativism and Identity Politics* (Minneapolis: University of Minnesota Press, 2009), 140. For a critique of the political philosophy of radical democracy, see Chapter 8 of my *Badiou and Politics* (Durham: Duke University Press, 2011).

in this revival of the ontological question in a practical or political key, with added inflections taken from the work of Carl Schmitt and Walter Benjamin. Heidegger's centrality in this context goes without saying, even as the political consequences of his ontology remain a topic of hot dispute, to say the least: "Our epoch can be said to have been stamped and signed, in philosophy, by the return of the question of being. This is why it is dominated by Heidegger. He drew up the diagnosis and explicitly took as his subject the realignment, after a century of criticism and the phenomenological interlude, of thought with its primordial interrogation: what is to be understood by the being of beings?"[4] But even Lacan's psychoanalytical work is concerned with ontology, as his son-in-law and soon-to-become official executor of his intellectual legacy, Jacques-Alain Miller, perceived as early as 1964, when he asked Lacan about his ontology and the latter responded rather coyly: "I ought to have obtained from him [Miller] to begin with a more specific definition of what he means by the term ontology," only to go on to stress "that all too often forgotten characteristic—forgotten in a way that is not without significance—of the first emergence of the unconscious, namely, that it does not lend itself to ontology." And yet, just a few weeks later in the same seminar, Lacan would seemingly go on to contradict himself: "Precisely this

---

4    Alain Badiou, *Deleuze: The Clamor of Being*, trans. Louise Burchill (Minneapolis: University of Minnesota Press, 2000), 19 (translation modified).

gives me an opportunity to reply to someone that, of course, I have my ontology—why not?—like everyone else, however naïve or elaborate it may be."[5] Regardless of this ambiguous self-evaluation, we might conclude with one of Lacan's most astute contemporary readers that, "Ontology or not, psychoanalysis according to Lacan imposes a general rectification on philosophy, which touches upon nothing less than the way in which truth leans up against the real."[6]

Between Heidegger's destruction of the metaphysics of being as presence and Lacan's subversion of the ideology of the subject as ego, there lies a general framework in which we can situate those authors whose writings dominate most discussions arising out of the "ontological turn" in political thought today, namely, Jacques Derrida, Giorgio Agamben, Ernesto Laclau, Chantal Mouffe, Alain Badiou, and Slavoj Žižek. Aside from the overarching legacy of Marxism, the principal exception to this Heideggerian–Lacanian framework that immediately comes to mind would be the neo-Spinozist or Deleuzian ontology of substance as pure immanence, or of being as life

---

5    Jacques Lacan, *The Seminar of Jacques Lacan*, ed. Jacques-Alain Miller, *Book XI: The Four Fundamental Concepts of Psychoanalysis*, trans. Alan Sheridan (New York: W. W. Norton, 1981), 29, 72.

6    Alain Badiou, *Theory of the Subject*, trans. Bruno Bosteels (London: Continuum, 2009), 135. For a detailed account of Lacan's early ontological reflections, see François Balmès, *Ce que Lacan dit de l'être* (Paris: PUF, 1999). For Slavoj Žižek's elaborations on the ontology of Lacanian psychoanalysis, see Adrian Johnston, *Žižek's Ontology: A Transcendental Materialist Theory of Subjectivity* (Evanston: Northwestern University Press, 2008).

itself, which Toni Negri and Michael Hardt, among others, offer as their contribution to the communist Left in their three-volume masterpiece, *Empire*, *Multitude*, and *Commonwealth*. However, this vitalist ontology, which likewise claims to be an ontology of the event as well, is not only underrepresented in collections such as *A Leftist Ontology*, it also paradoxically comes under serious attack both for being dangerously ideal-ist, insofar as it would eschew the dimension of raw bodily materiality, and, at the same time, for being too confidently materialist, insofar as it would seek to exorcize the indeter-minacy of ghosts whose uncanny smile turns out to be irre-ducible, all good intentions notwithstanding, to any pre-estab-lished political program, be it communist or otherwise. Thus, one critic argues that "Although Hardt and Negri, citing Paul of Tarsus, argue for the 'power of the flesh' within the political economy of the present, this flesh appears to have a peculiarly ghostly existence"; while for others, by contrast, this existence is precisely not ghostly enough, or is so in too dependable and predictable a fashion: "The political has so far been entirely on the side of the specter, believing the specter to be depend-able, predictable, trustworthy. Ghosts, meanwhile, seem out of place, lingering in a no-man's-land betwixt and between places and times."[7] This is why melancholia, or a melancholic stance

7    See, respectively, the criticisms of Negri's work in Christopher Breu, "Signification and Substance: Toward a Leftist Ontology of the Present," in Strathausen, ed., *A Leftist Ontology*, 200; and Klaus Mladek and George Edmondson, "A Politics of Melancholia," in ibid., 226.

of fidelity haunted by anxiety-producing ghosts, rather than the familiar exorcism of communist specters, may be needed to subtract the plan for a leftist ontology from all illusions of mastery, movement, and militantism: "As opposed to Negri's vision of a robust, virile political agent enveloping the new in his embrace, the haunted subject is held in place, petrified, by the decision to hesitate, by a declaration of fidelity to the undead, the discarded, the unremembered—to all of those as yet unlisted in the account books of monumental history."[8] A communist political ontology, too, would have to be able to heed the call from these ghostly and hesitant beings. It would have to be able to do without alibis and reassurances, without the certainties of fulfillment and the guarantees of authenticity that supposedly tie the entire tradition of militant politics, from Marx to Negri, to the history of a certain metaphysics.

## Leftism in the Closure of Metaphysics

Today, in other words, ontology by and large is supposed to be postmetaphysical, if by metaphysics we understand the age-old discourse for which the principle holds that "the same, indeed, is thinking and being."[9] The problem with this

---

8    Mladek and Edmondson, "A Politics of Melancholia," 227. The authors are here responding to Negri's essay "The Specter's Smile," in Michael Sprinker, ed., *Ghostly Demarcations: A Symposium on Jacques Derrida's "Specters of Marx"* (London: Verso, 1999), 5–16.

9    Parmenides, fragment 3. In this context, Nietzsche can be said to inaugurate the closure of metaphysics when, in a note from

characterization of metaphysics, which otherwise seems to
me no worse than any other and which in any case has the
virtue of concision, is that it ignores the extent to which
not only Heidegger but also someone like Badiou—both of
whom are widely perceived to be models of so-called postfoundational thought—might ultimately subscribe to this
Parmenidean principle, even though Heidegger does so by
displacing metaphysics in the name of thinking, whereas
Badiou (like Deleuze and Negri, for that matter) openly
embraces the notion that his ontology and theory of the
subject signal a new metaphysics, bypassing as an utter
nonissue the whole debate regarding the end or closure of
metaphysics. Even so, it is hard to ignore the fact that today,
with very few exceptions, most radical ontological investigations would seem to start from the nonidentity of being
and thinking—we might even say from their alterity, in the
Levinasian sense according to which an ethics of the other
must disrupt the metaphysics of the same, or from their
subalternity, in the sense in which Gayatri Spivak argues
that "the subaltern is necessarily the absolute limit of the

---

1888, included in *The Will to Power*, he writes: "Parmenides said,
'one cannot think of what is not';—we are at the opposite extreme,
and say 'what can be thought of must certainly be a fiction.'"
Friedrich Nietzsche, *The Will to Power*, trans. Walter Kaufmann
and R. J. Hollingdale (New York: Vintage, 1967), aphorism 539.
For a commentary on the significance of this note, see Philippe
Lacoue-Labarthe, "La fable" (1970), in *Le sujet de la philosophie
(Typographies 1)* (Paris: Aubier-Flammarion, 1979), 7–30.

place where history is narrativized into logic."[10] Being and thinking, but also history and logic, thus become delinked or unhinged in ways that perhaps are no longer even dialectical in the older sense of the term. This has profound consequences for politics precisely insofar as what disappears is any necessary linkage connecting the paradigm for thinking of being to practical forms of acting. Instead, it is to the very delinking or unbinding of the social that a leftist ontology would have to attune itself. Whence also the stubborn, not to say hackneyed, insistence on motifs—here we can forego the mention of proper names—such as the indivisible remainder or reserve, the constitutive outside, the real that resists symbolization absolutely, the dialectic of lack and excess, or the necessary gap separating representation from presentation pure and simple.

It is not, then, ontology as such that is either leftist or rightist, either communist or reactionary, unless of course we were to ascribe a moral value—whether good or bad—to being qua being in a fashion that could more properly be called religious or theological, but rather the specific orientation given to the impasse or aporia that keeps the discourse of being qua being from ever achieving full closure. Badiou's distinction, explored in much of *Being and Event*, between

---

10    Gayatri Chakravorty Spivak, "Subaltern Studies: Deconstructing Historiography," in Ranajit Guha and Gayatri Chakravorty Spivak, eds., *Selected Subaltern Studies* (New York: Oxford University Press, 1988), 16.

three fundamental ontological orientations—constructivist, transcendent, and generic—should be helpful in this regard, especially insofar as it does not correspond neatly to a leftist, rightist, or centrist tripartite division, or to the distinction, also common in current debates on political ontology, between immanence, transcendence, and failed or incomplete transcendence-within-immanence (although in this case the similarities and overlaps are rather striking indeed). Briefly put, the constructivist orientation seeks to reduce the impasse by bringing it back into the fold of a well-formulated language; the transcendent orientation raises the impasse to the level of a quasi-mystical beyond; and the generic orientation postulates the existence of an indiscernible with which to interpret the impasse of being as the effect of an event within the situation at hand—thus neither collapsing the event into the sum total of its constructible preconditions nor elevating the impasse to the level of a miraculous or monstrous-sublime Thing taking the place once occupied by God.

Following Marx and Freud, whose doctrines take us beyond ontology in the strict sense and possibly open up a fourth, antiphilosophical option, we could furthermore argue that the generic or indiscernible orientation shows the extent to which the science of being, through its inherent deadlock or impasse, presupposes the retroactive clarification of an intervening subject without which the ontological impasse would not even be apparent to begin with. "Its hypothesis consists in saying that one can only *render justice* to injustice from the angle of the event and intervention. There is thus no need to be horrified by an un-binding of being, because it is in the undecidable occurrence of a supernumerary non-being that every truth procedure originates, including that of a truth whose stakes would be that very un-binding."[11] Indeed, it may very well be the case that the defining polemic behind the current ontological turn in political philosophy—what we might call its principal contradiction or its fundamental line of demarcation—depends not so much on the elaboration of a leftist ontology in one form or another as on the possibility of a leftist (or communist—which is not necessarily the same) theory of the subject. The latter, actually, turns out to be barred or blocked, put under erasure, or kept at the level of sheer virtuality, or of potentiality without actuality, by some of the most radical arguments for a leftist ontology today.

In any case, returning to a simpler alternative, the unspoken presupposition behind recent arguments in favor of the option of—if not the need for—a leftist ontology seems to be that a leftist orientation in ontology is one that acknowledges, exposes itself to, or attempts to come to terms with the inherent gap or ghostly remainder in the discourse of being qua being, whereas a rightist orientation would be one that disavows, represses, or displaces this gap or remainder. "A leftist ontology therefore recognizes that everyday political practice—and not just 'the political'—is defined by this daily struggle about the very nature of our world and its lines of communication, about who possesses the right and

---

11   Badiou, *Being and Event*, 284–5.

the power to delineate its borders and enforce its rules," as Carsten Strathausen, the editor of *A Leftist Ontology*, writes in his introduction. "However," he continues, "at stake is not just any ontology, but one that acknowledges and thinks through its paradoxical, antifoundational horizon."[12] This means that, perhaps against the author's wishes, even Adorno's own negative dialectics, which hinges upon the gap between the concept and nonconceptualities, might fit the profile of a leftist ontology. Adorno, after all, writes as if to enable this posthumous rereading: "Regarding the concrete utopian possibility, dialectics is the ontology of the wrong state of things. The right state of things would be free of it: neither a system nor a contradiction."[13] However, this does not free negative dialectics itself, as a reflection of and on nonidentity, from the charge of potentially hypostasizing its fundamental ontological principle—a charge that Adorno himself levels against Heidegger and that an Adornian approach could level against philosophies of difference coming from thinkers who try critically and responsibly to take up the Heideggerian legacy.

## Political Ontology and Its Discontents

Nevertheless, as I hinted at a moment ago, not everyone agrees that there is a need for an ontological grounding of

---

12   Carsten Strathausen, "Introduction: Thinking Outside In," in Strathausen, ed., *A Leftist Ontology*, xxvi.
13   Adorno, *Negative Dialectics*, 11.

politics—not even if, as is most often the case today, this grounding actually takes the form of an un-grounding, a de-grounding, or a precipitation into the abyss of an absent ground. Many contributors to the debate over the ontological turn in political theory thus raise doubts about the very standard or index that would allow us to gauge the leftist or rightist nature of any ontology whatsoever, insofar as the discourse of being qua being cannot but be subtracted from all empirical specifications, including political ones:

> The problem, or antinomy, is this: one cannot empirically commit to one "thing world" over another (say, socialism, whatever that might be, over liberalism) if there is no shared index of reality to decide between them. At the same time, a purely theoretical or normative commitment is empty as long as the choice is not proved on the practical level where the things in a chosen system have a self-evidence—what I will call apodictic force—that lets them serve as their own index of validity.[14]

This antinomy is constitutive of the very project of a leftist ontology. Indeed, speaking of the latter, we might ask what possible relation there could be between being qua being, which is presumably generic if not indeterminate, and the

---

14  Benjamin Robinson, "Is Socialism the Index of a Leftist Ontology?," in Strathausen, ed., *A Leftist Ontology*, 102.

particular seating plan of the 1791 French legislative assembly, which historically lies at the origin of our modern division of political ideologies into Left and Right? Expressing similar doubts, several authors in *A Leftist Ontology* wonder whether we should not reinstate a question mark at the end of their project's title. Almost all, finally, reject the simple derivation of a leftist politics from a postfoundational ontology as a non sequitur at best and a performative contradiction at worst. As Roland Végső usefully summarizes:

> Because one of the basic insights of deconstruction is that the primary ontological terrain of the constitution of subjectivity is that of radical undecidability, it is impossible to found politics on an ontology. That is, there is no logical move from radical undecidability to a leftist politics. This is why deconstructionist ontology (or hauntology) cannot be inherently leftist. Of course, it can be used for leftist purposes, but that use must be determined on a normative and not on an ontological level.[15]

Some authors, however, explicitly or implicitly take ontology to refer not so much to the science of being qua being in the strict sense as to the basic presuppositions behind a given politico-philosophical stance—what we might call the bedrock of its fundamental assumptions and unshakable commitments, never mind that the term "ontology" is perhaps

---

15   Végső, "Deconstruction and Experience," 143.

less suited to name this value-laden and affect-imbued dimension than "political anthropology" or even the good old "ideology" would be. William Rasch even goes so far as to reject the ontological need in politics altogether: "There is no Leftist ontology. Let me phrase this less ontologically. There *ought not* be a *Leftist* ontology."[16] Still, the same author does not for this reason abandon the call to clarify his basic underlying commitments, such as to the ontological primacy of conflict and violence over consensus and public deliberation.

Rasch's warning goes a long way in highlighting both the enchanting appeal and the real danger involved in radical ontological orientations of politics of the kind that can be found in the work of Benjamin or Agamben. In fact, the argument seems to be that the ontological need in political thinking today stems precisely from an eschatological, even catastrophic desire for radicalization—whether by arguing for a purified politics that would step wholly and completely out of the modern administered world or by seeking a turning point where danger and salvation coincide as the power of ambivalence—the famous zone of indistinction so often sought after by the author of *Homo Sacer*. "This, of course, is its danger, for the temptation becomes one of thinking the political precisely in theological, which is to say, in messianic and redemptive terms," says Rasch, who would rather plead along with Max Weber for a modest and decidedly more secular view of the political: "A political ethics that

---

16   William Rasch, "The Structure of the Political vs. the Politics of Hope," in Strathausen, ed., *A Leftist Ontology*, 3.

recognizes the ever-present possibility of violence, rather than its glorious self-immolation, is the ethics of the human being in an unredeemed, and unredeemable, fallen state. Civil peace, not civil perfection, is the goal of such politics."[17] Similarly, we should heed warnings against the entanglement of redemption and catastrophe that, in the case of Agamben's discussion of Auschwitz, "instrumentalizes the pseudo-eschatological figure of thought in a way that neither Adorno nor Heidegger were familiar with," even if Agamben may also have a remedy of his own to offer against this danger: "If the price for grounding politics in ontology is the perpetuation of the very kind of ambivalences that Agamben's own critical account of ambivalence helps to analyze, then we should forego any ontologization. It is quite possible to separate Agamben's ethical speculations in the Auschwitz book from his sober analyses of the sacred and his critique of the ambivalence theorem."[18]

The quest for a leftist ontology, in other words, risks producing an ontologization of leftism that is as radical as it is empty. Was not the young Marx himself fond of recalling that to be radical means literally to go to the root of things, which for him meant the essence of the human being? What, then, could be more radical than, in the name of contemporary ontological interrogations, to forego all humanist anthropologies so as to unconceal the uprootedness of the human essence that is

---

17 Ibid., 14.
18 Eva Geulen, "The Function of Ambivalence in Agamben's Reontologization of Politics," in Strathausen, ed., *A Leftist Ontology*, 28.

its absent ground? The price to be paid for this radicalization, however, is either the expulsion of the politics to come from the social realm altogether, or else its sinister and undialectical conflation, through a speculative figure of ambivalence, with world-historical horrors such as the Holocaust. This enormous risk can be avoided only by reinscribing politics—I would say once again dialectically—in the present situation. Instead of seeking a pure or purified form of politics or of the political, no matter how violent and catastrophic, what is needed then amounts to formulating some kind of ontology of actuality.

## Toward an Ontology of Actuality

When Michel Foucault, in his programmatic elaboration on Kant's "What Is Enlightenment?" essay, coined the expression "ontology of actuality" to designate the task of his life-long endeavor, as different from an "analytic of truth," he perhaps could not have predicted the enormous enthusiasm this coinage would generate among contemporary thinkers. Figures as widely different as Gianni Vattimo, Fredric Jameson, and Roberto Esposito have since come to classify the overall aim of their work—if not also more generally the task of theory and philosophy as such—under this umbrella term. And yet, beyond this unexpected success of Foucault's coinage, have we fully understood the paradox that is encapsulated in the very project for an ontology of actuality?

For Foucault, the task of a "historical ontology of ourselves" or a "critical ontology of the present" amounts above all to an archaeological and genealogical criticism of our modes of doing, thinking, and saying:

> Archaeological—and not transcendental—in the sense that it will not seek to identify the universal structures of all knowledge or of all possible moral action, but will seek to treat the instances of discourse that articulate what we think, say, and do as so many historical events. And this critique will be genealogical in the sense that it will not deduce from the form of what we are what it is impossible for us to do and to know; but it will separate out, from the contingency that has made us what we are, the possibility of no longer being, doing, or thinking what we are, do, or think.[19]

---

19   Michel Foucault, "What Is Enlightenment?" ("Qu'est-ce que les Lumières?"), in *The Foucault Reader*, ed. Paul Rabinow (New York: Pantheon Books, 1984), 45–6. See also Gianni Vattimo, "Postmodernity, Technology, Ontology," in *Nihilism and Emancipation: Ethics, Politics, and Law*, ed. Santiago Zabala, trans. William McCuaig (New York: Columbia University Press, 2004): "The expression is meant to be taken in its most literal sense: it does not simply indicate, as Foucault thought, a philosophy oriented primarily toward the consideration of existence and its historicity rather than toward epistemology and logic—that is, toward what would be called, in Foucault's terminology, an 'analytic of truth.' Rather, 'ontology of actuality' is used here to mean a discourse that attempts to clarify what Being signifies in the present situation" (3–4). Roberto Esposito goes so far as to speak of an "ontology of actu-ality" to describe the best of what *all* Italian philosophy has to offer: "Unlike the Anglo-Saxon analytic tradition or for that matter German hermeneutics and French deconstruction, the continual problem for

The task of criticism then ultimately no longer consists only in drawing up limits but also and above all in enabling one to pass beyond them. In this sense, the ontology of actuality is nothing less than the work of freedom in action: "Although Foucault also develops Heideggerian theory, he interprets it in positive terms whereby its historical ontologies or epistemes enable the subject to assert him or herself."[20] In Foucault's wake, however, the conjunction of these two terms—ontology and actuality—to describe the task at hand has become increasingly paradoxical, especially with the advent of the so-called postmodern condition and the rise of late or finance capitalism.

On the one hand, as I mentioned earlier, the most radical ontological investigations today all tend toward spectrality,

---

Italian philosophy has been thinking the relationship with the present day [*contemporaneità*], that which Foucault would have called 'the ontology of actuality,' which is to say an interrogation of the present interpreted in a substantially political key. Thinking above all of Vico or differently of Gramsci, history and politics have constituted the obligatory point of transition from which and through which the dimension of thought generally has been constituted in Italy." See Timothy Campbell's interview with Esposito in *diacritics: review of contemporary criticism* 36: 2 (2006): 49. Compare with Fredric Jameson, *A Singular Modernity: Essay on the Ontology of the Present* (London: Verso, 2002). Another forgotten figure in this context, aside from Italian "weak ontology," is Georg Lukács, who saw his magnum opus as moving in the direction of the "ontology of social being." See Georg Lukács, *Zur Ontologie des gesellschaftlichen Seins*, 2 vols., ed. Frank Benseler (Darmstadt: Luchterhand, 1984–86).

20    Philip Goldstein, "Marxist Theory: From Aesthetic Critique to Cultural Politics," in Strathausen, ed., *A Leftist Ontology*, 95.

virtuality, potentiality—and not toward actuality. "Higher than actuality stands possibility," so Heidegger notes in *Being and Time*, not unlike Agamben, who insists that the most radical potentiality is a potential not to become actual: "It is a potentiality that is not simply the potential to do this or that thing but potential to not-do, potential not to pass into actuality."[21] Going against the grain of these tendencies, there is thus something intrinsically uncanny, not to say oxymoronic, at least today, about an ontology of actuality, if we take into account the dominant orientations of postfoundational thinking. Foucault's provocation, in this sense, also consists in enabling an historical ontology of ourselves that would not have to shy away from speaking about the present situation in the name of some knee-jerk aversion to the metaphysics of presence.

On the other hand, there can be no doubt that the ontological themes of difference, multiplicity, event, becoming, and so on are the product of late capitalism as much as, if not more than, they are counteracting forces. Marx himself, after all, was always quite enthusiastic about the power of

---

21  Martin Heidegger, *Being and Time*, trans. John Macquarrie and Edward Robinson (New York: Harper & Row, 1962), 63; Giorgio Agamben, *Potentialities: Collected Essays in Philosophy*, trans. Daniel Heller-Roazen (Stanford: Stanford University Press, 1999), 179–80. For a more detailed discussion of this revalorization of potentiality beyond the Aristotelian framework of potentiality and actuality, see my "Logics of Change: From Potentiality to Inexistence," in Mark Potocnik, Frank Ruda, and Jan Völker, eds., *Beyond Potentialities? Politics Between the Possible and the Impossible* (Berlin: Diaphanes, 2011), 79–101.

capitalism to break down and dissolve old feudal, patriarchal, or idyllic bonds and hierarchies. "It is obviously the only thing we can and must welcome within Capital," Badiou comments, referring to those well-known passages from *The Communist Manifesto* in which all that is solid melts into air: "That this destitution operates in the most complete barbarity must not conceal its properly *ontological* virtue."[22] But if it is indeed capitalism itself that reveals all presence to be a mere semblance covering over random multiplicity, then this means that the categories of a postfoundational ontology are not only not necessarily leftist, they also might turn out to be little more than descriptive of, if not complicit with, the current status quo. "In this case, 'critical' thought is in fact precisely adequate to its moment, just not in the way it imagines itself to be. It reiterates, no doubt in sublimated or misrecognized form, accepted social structures and political presumptions—effectively canceling out real critical reflection," Nicholas Brown and Imre Szemán warn us; and, referring to what might well be the quintessential category or trope of the whole ontological turn, they conclude: "The primacy of 'difference' in fact outlines an identity—the unacknowledged frame of the monoculture, global capitalism."[23]

---

22   Alain Badiou, *Manifesto for Philosophy*, trans. Norman Madarasz (Albany: SUNY Press, 1999), 56–7. See Karl Marx and Friedrich Engels, *The Communist Manifesto* (London: Penguin, 1967), 82–3.
23   Nicholas Brown and Imre Szemán, "Twenty-five Theses on Philosophy in the Age of Finance Capital," in Strathausen, ed., *A Leftist Ontology*, 35 and 49.

Difference, multiplicity, or the primacy of events and becomings over subjects and objects, far from giving critical leverage, would thus define our given state of affairs under late capitalism and its attendant cultural logic.

Jeffrey T. Nealon, in an astute periodization of the 1980s in which he tries to update Jameson's "Periodizing the 60s," similarly wonders whether the familiar theoretical dramas opposing essentialism to constructivism, or stasis to flux, are not precisely a bad hangover from the 1960s: "At this point, we'd have to admit that privatized finance capital has all but obliterated the usefulness of this distinction: to insist on the hybridity and fluidity of $x$ or $y$ is the mantra of transnational capital whose normative state is the constant reconstitution of 'value'—so it can hardly function unproblematically as a bulwark against that logic."[24] Transnational finance capital desubstantializes ontology even more thoroughly than the nineteenth-century bourgeoisie could have dreamed. Flexibility, difference, and innovation are on the order of dumb facticity today. In these circumstances, which define our actuality, how radical can a postfoundational ontology claim to be? How leftist or communist can it be? Is it not rather the spontaneous ideology of late capitalism?

We could argue, though, that the return of the ontological

24 Jeffrey T. Nealon, "Periodizing the 80s: The Cultural Logic of Economic Privatization in the United States," in Strathausen, ed., *A Leftist Ontology*, 71. Compare with Fredric Jameson, "Periodizing the 60s," *Social Text* 9/10 (1984): 178–209.

question in political thought today is also, at least in part, an attempt to respond—by way of a retreat or a step back—to the complicity, which is easier to intuit than to undo, between the desacralizing tendencies within capitalism itself and the drive toward difference, multiplicity, or becoming in the critique or deconstruction of metaphysics. Frequently, such a response leads to the introduction of a conceptual split *within* the notion of politics, that is, a split between politics (*la politique* in French, or *die Politik* in German) and the political (*le politique* in French, or *das Politische* in German).

## Politics and the Political

Common to thinkers as diverse as Carl Schmitt and Hannah Arendt, the distinction between politics and the political has recently been championed as a common feature that would unite contemporary figures as disparate as Laclau, Mouffe, Nancy, Lacoue-Labarthe, Lefort, or Badiou into a form of "Left Heideggerianism."[25] The distinction in question thus

---

25  See, above all, Oliver Marchart, *Post-foundational Political Thought: Political Difference in Nancy, Lefort, Badiou and Laclau* (Edinburgh: Edinburgh University Press, 2007). For a devastating attack, with which I am overall in agreement, on "Left Heideggerianism" as a contradiction in terms, see Geoffrey Waite, "Lefebvre without Heidegger: 'Left-Heideggerianism' *qua contradictio in adiecto*," in Kanishka Goonewarda et al., eds., *Space, Difference, Everyday Life: Henri Lefebvre and Radical Urban Theory* (New York: Routledge, 2008), 146–81.

comes to be mapped onto the difference of beings and being, or of the ontic and the ontological. "With regard to current political theory, the conceptual difference between politics and the political, *as difference*, assumes the role of an indicator or symptom of society's absent ground," Laclau's student Oliver Marchart argues in *Post-foundational Political Thought*. "*As difference*, this difference presents nothing other than a paradigmatic split in the traditional idea of politics, where a new term (the political) had to be introduced in order to point at society's 'ontological' dimension, the dimension of the institution of society, while politics was kept as the term for the 'ontic' practices of conventional politics (the plural, particular and, eventually, unsuccessful attempts at grounding society)."[26] The search for a more radical or a more fundamental level or dimension of politics than the everyday administration of public order thus continues to be what grounds, re-grounds, and de-grounds the politico-ontological need.

This so-called political difference between the political and politics, modeled on the ontological difference between being and beings, should nonetheless be handled with certain reservations. "These reservations have to do mainly with the possible misconstrual of the distinction—its transformation into a rigid bifurcation between structure and superstructure, between foundation and derivations, or between noumenal and phenomenal spheres of analysis,"

---

26   Marchart, *Post-foundational Political Thought*, 5.

Fred Dallmayr writes in *The Other Heidegger*: "As can readily be seen, the distinction relates obliquely to Heidegger's
notion of the ontic-ontological difference—but with the
proviso that the ontic can never be a derivation or simple
application of the ontological dimension."[27] Above all, the
two terms are not external to one another, nor should one be
used all too hastily to denigrate the superficiality or inauthen-
ticity of the other. If this last risk cannot always be avoided,
Roland Végsö reminds us that Derrida already tackled the
possible misconstrual of Heidegger's own distinction, which
allegedly undergirds the difference between the political
and politics: "Derrida criticizes the very category of ontological difference, the absolute separation of the ontological
and the ontic, and the concomitant philosophical and political project of the recovery of an authentic and originary
temporality," to the point where each of the two terms must
be considered radically impure and mixed. As Sorin Radu-
Cucu concludes: "Thus, the difference between politics and
the political functions in analogy with the ontological difference, while the displacement caused by the logic of the trait
(by *différance*) suggests that nothing is pure—neither politics nor the political—and that these categories exist only
to have their identity threatened."[28] Even when subject to

---

27   Fred Dallmayr, *The Other Heidegger* (Ithaca: Cornell University
Press, 1993), 50–1.
28   Végsö, "Deconstruction and Experience," 136; and Sorin Radu-
Cucu, "Politics and the Fiction of the Political," in Strathausen, ed.,
*A Leftist Ontology*, 153.

constant cross-contamination, however, the retreat from politics into the political cannot fail to endow really existing political processes with a negative aura of being merely positivist, sociologist, empiricist, or ontic—that is to say, further examples of the ongoing oblivion of being now translated as the oblivion of the essence of the political.

The retreat of the political, in other words, is a welcome gesture in the face of banal reassertions according to which everything is politics and politics is everything. It is from this complete suture of politics to the social that the ontological turn seeks to release itself by taking a step back to delve into the founding moment of society, which is the moment of the political as such as radical dislocation or antagonistic institution. In so doing, however, the gesture of radicalization may very well have disabled in advance the pursuit of truly emancipatory actions, insofar as the latter will necessarily appear far less radical, not to say blind to their own quasi-transcendental conditions of possibility, which are also always already and predictably conditions of impossibility.

Ultimately, then, the question with which I would want to address the ontological need today concerns the fate of the various "others" of ontology, that is, those domains from which the ontological dimension splits off, including the ontic, the empirical, and the epistemological, but also the social, the dialectical, and the historical-materialist. How can a critical or leftist—let alone a communist—ontology of actuality be articulated with these others without denigrating them or condemning them to the dustbin of metaphysical (pre)history?

## Ontology or Theory of the Subject?

Perhaps the most fundamental tension in this debate, though, is the one that brings together or separates the project of a leftist ontology and a leftist or communist theory of the subject. On the one hand, there can be no doubt that a psychoanalytical approach to this question allows a theorization of the complex process of subjectivization, for example, through the notion of hegemonic articulation or identification, including at the level of ideological recognition and misrecognition. But on the other hand, it would seem as if the most radical deconstructive and even psychoanalytical inquiries had to come to the conclusion that no leftist or emancipatory agenda can be complete without also questioning the centrality of the category of the subject with all its metaphysical baggage.

Some might well conclude by suggesting the possibility of a deconstructive theory of the subject that would be compatible with a de-grounding of ontology: "Even if this theory does not yet exist, its outlines are readable within the Derridean corpus. And what these dim shapes suggest is not only that such a theory is possible but that it is also necessary."[29] Others, while equally writing from a post-

---

29  Végső, "Deconstruction and Experience," 143.

Heideggerian or Derridean point of view, seem to conclude that a radical leftist ontology would necessarily have to include a complete break with the paradigm of subjectivity altogether, in favor of something like what Alberto Moreiras calls the nonsubject. In fact, the Left is said to have clung for far too long to an idea of subjective militantism based on notions of fullness, affirmation, productivity, and life, without considering the extent to which these notions, tied as they are to centuries of mythic and religious violence, have been responsible for the sacrifice of innumerable victims among both friends and enemies. The interruption of this sacrificial history thus would require at the same time an interruption of the entire subjectivist paradigm of politics. "If subjective militancy is at the same time a condition and a result of ontology, to go beyond ontology, and that means, beyond the subjectivity of the subject as the current horizon of political thinking, is also a condition and a result of an ethical position where every possibility of a nonsacrificial politics is sheltered," Moreiras writes in an essay on the Spanish philosopher María Zambrano. But this is not possible without the nearly impossible task of approaching the legacy of history in an entirely new way, by disremembering, as it were, the forgotten and the vanquished: "The abandonment of subjectivity, the accomplishment of a thinking that abandons subjectivity, is not possible in the wake of the resolute acceptance of a historical legacy. Rather, it fundamentally presupposes a thought of unlegacy, a thought of disinheritance, of disheritage, a thinking of the forgetting of that which will not be remembered."[30] For sure, nothing could be further removed from the populist call for hegemonic or counterhegemonic articulation than this appeal to the disinherited and the subaltern. In fact, the paradigm of subjectivism is said to be so all-encompassing, ranging from liberal and communist militantism in the name of appropriation all the way to reactionary attachments to identity and loss, that little more can be offered by way of alternative than the announcement of a promise of another constitution of the political altogether outside of subjectivity.

Still others, finally, propose that for the sake of a theory of the nonsubject, what is needed is a bold reevaluation of melancholia and anxiety. They start by asking: "Is melancholia, as Freud suggests, nothing more than the index of a suffocated, crushed rebellion, followed by feelings of impotence and resignation? Or could there be an affirmative, even proud dimension to the melancholic state—a dimension that recognizes doom itself as the engine of rebellion—that diverges from a certain model of political activism grounded . . . in a leftist ontology of fullness and presence?"[31] If the answer to this question entails daring to affirm the second option, it is because melancholia, far from being the paradigm of a pathological incapacity to mourn and overcome an actual

---

30    Alberto Moreiras, "The Last God: María Zambrano's Life without Texture," in Strathausen, ed., *A Leftist Ontology*, 171 and 179. For a more detailed commentary, see Chapter 2 of this text.
31    Mladek and Edmondson, "A Politics of Melancholia," 210.

loss, can provide the model for an unerring fidelity to the part of those who have no part, to use Jacques Rancière's expression: "The scandal that the melancholic presents to a political activism rooted in the modes of the not-yet is that one cannot count on him. Melancholia disrupts the tally-taking done in the accounting books of history and politics. It cannot help but address the wrong done to no-counts—the essential miscount that, according to Rancière, lies at the bottom of the political."[32] Rancière himself would probably prefer not to follow Klaus Mladek and George Edmonson in their argument, drawn from Freud and Lacan, that what ultimately induces this miscount is the death drive. But they would all certainly agree that what is at stake now that the classical models of political activism and partisanship have entered into a profound crisis, closely tied to the crisis of the party-form of politics and the State, is finding new ways of relating to the primordial antagonism or nonrelation—that is, new ways of relating to the impossibility of relating. "What emerges is thus a decompleted subject without mastery or agency, fully exposed and appropriated to the event," which might even signal the occasion for a community of leftist melancholics: "The community of melancholic subjects is then held together by the abyss of nonsubjective subjectivity."[33] Fidelity to this rather strange and uncanny community requires that we refuse to give up on our desire,

32  Ibid., 215.
33  Ibid., 227.

that we refrain from the urge to move on, and instead stubbornly stick to the remembrance of the unmourned and the undead:

> This is not to presume to speak on their behalf; that would be to draw them into symbolic order in such a way as to silence them even further. Indeed, if there is anything that the melancholic cannot abide, it is this very act of speaking for others. We are striving instead to remain faithful to the no-count's particular status as the traumatic object of the political: that which has fallen out, and which continues to fall out, of any social and political calculation.[34]

Here then, it seems to me, is the great either/or question behind the ontological turn in political theory: Can emancipatory politics today still take the form of militant subjectivization, or should the deconstruction of metaphysics also include all theories of the subject among its targets? Is every subject necessarily enmeshed in the history of politics as a history of sacrificial violence, or can there be a form of subjective fidelity to the very traumas and anxieties that bear witness to those vanquished and sacrificed? And furthermore, can we even ask this concluding question without in turn sacrificing the radical nature of the question of being to one of the many "others" of ontology? If we cannot, then

---

34   Ibid., 229.

should we not also question the emphatic need for a left-ist ontology today as a sign of something missed, namely, a truly emancipatory politics for which communism might still serve as a name?

# 2

# Politics, Infrapolitics, and the Impolitical

Is politics always necessarily and in every case a politics of the subject?

— Alberto Moreiras, *Línea de sombra:*
*el no sujeto de lo político*

Can one think of a subject against power? Or is power [*potere*] the *absolute* verb of the subject?

— Roberto Esposito,
*Categorie dell'impolitico*

I remain convinced that every philosophy that eliminates the category of the subject becomes unable to serve a political process.

— Alain Badiou,
*The Concept of the Model*

## Politics and Its Prefixes

During times of decline and reaction in which an actual transformation of the prevailing political order seems ever more unlikely, language often comes to the rescue so as to allow one to revitalize, think anew, or at the very least re-delimit the concepts of "politics" or "the political" with the simple yet thought-provoking addition of a prefix. Thus, in response to the disaffected scene of "postpolitics," so widely discussed in the late 1980s and early 1990s, we obtain the triad of "archipolitics," "parapolitics," and "metapolitics" in the work of Jacques Rancière, particularly in his 1995 book *Disagreement: Politics and Philosophy*, a triad to which Slavoj Žižek in *The Ticklish Subject: The Absent Centre of Political Ontology* responds rather sympathetically before adding a fourth term, "ultrapolitics," supposedly of his own making. Around the same time, in 1994, Badiou proposes his own, rather different understanding of "metapolitics" in a collection of essays of the same title, while in a talk from two years earlier he finds an "archipolitics" at work in the radical philosophy, or rather antiphilosophy, of Friedrich Nietzsche, especially during the latter's downward spiral into madness in Turin. To this already quite complex conceptual constellation, Roberto Esposito and Alberto Moreiras, between the late 1980s and today, add their respective coinages of "the unpolitical" or, perhaps better, "the impolitical," and "infrapolitics."[1] These last neologisms are the ones I would

---

1  Whereas "infrapolitics" readily corresponds to the Spanish *infrapolítica* in Alberto Moreiras's work, "impolitical" in my view is preferable to "unpolitical" as a translation of the Italian *impolitico*, which Roberto Esposito draws from the German *unpolitische*, as in Thomas Mann's *Betrachtungen eines Unpolitischen* (Berlin: S. Fischer, 1918), translated into English as *Reflections of a Nonpolitical Man*, trans. Walter D. Morris (New York: F. Ungar, 1983), and

like to discuss in this chapter, both by teasing out the resonances between the two and by contrasting them with the
use of those other prefixes that have come to enrich and
revitalize a certain politico-philosophical scene over the past
three decades.

From the outset I should clarify that my aim here is not
to offer an exhaustive account of the ways in which these two
concepts function either in their own right or in relation to the
broader political and philosophical framework of the work of
each of their authors. Nor do I pretend to judge their validity
as though speaking from the safety of some higher tribunal—
whether of the traditional academic type or in an imaginary
people's court. If there comes a moment of judgment or dissen-
sion in what follows, and it would be a sign of bad faith to
deny this, I will nonetheless try to suspend this moment for as
long as possible so as first to follow the profound reorientation
that occurs within the realm of political thought, including the
realm of politics *as* thought, once it undergoes the unsettling,
tremor-like effects of infrapolitics and the impolitical.

---

already taken up in Italy in an important essay from 1978 by
Massimo Cacciari titled "Nietzsche and the Unpolitical," now available in Cacciari's *The Unpolitical: On the Radical Critique of Political
Reason*, trans. Massimo Verdicchio, ed. Alessandro Carrera (New
York: Fordham University Press, 2009), 92–103. Occasionally, in
the context of discussions about the "end of politics," Esposito also
invokes the category of "antipolitics," for example, in his essay "Fine
della politica?," in *Inoperosità della politica*, ed. Roberto Ciccarelli
(Rome: Derive Approdi, 1999), 24–31.

My aim in this chapter, then, is both more local and more generic than a systematic overview would require. More local, insofar as I will limit myself to tracing the sheer contours of the two notions of infrapolitics and the impolitical and their retroactive effects upon the category of politics as deployed in modern political philosophy. But also more generic, insofar as we are indeed dealing only with contours, figures, or profiles. Neither of these two notions, it seems to me, amounts to the status of a full-bodied speculative or theoretical concept, and perhaps their authors do not even wish to have them do so.

As Esposito says in an interview, looking back upon the contributions of his *Categorie dell'impolitico*, first published in 1988 and reissued in 1999 with a new preface in which the author also addresses some of the criticisms directed against the arguments of the first edition: "I prefer to call the impolitical, more so than a category, let us say, a perspective, a way of looking, a mode of seeing politics; and I do not call it a category because the latter already gives the idea of something complete and definite, something like a concept, whereas in this case it is in fact rather a question of a tonality, of a way of looking."[2] Thus, insofar as the original title of *Categorie dell'impolitico*, in addition to Thomas Mann's *Betrachtungen eines Unpolitischen*, also plays on *Le categorie del "Politico,"* which is how Schmitt's *The Concept of*

---

2    Roberto Esposito, "L'impolitico," in *Enciclopedia multimediale delle scienze filosofiche*; available on-line at www.emsf.rai.it

*the Political* is translated in Italian, there certainly would be much to be said for keeping this echo by rendering the title in English as *The Concept of the Impolitical*. Yet *Contours of the Impolitical* might also be an appropriate translation since this is all that Esposito ultimately seeks to offer: contours rather than concepts; a tonality rather than a closed set of theses; a figurative approximation rather than a formal axiomatic. After all, according to this author, only such an oblique or negative approach is able to think politics: "Politics cannot be conceptualized in positive form but only on the basis of that which draws its contours at its outer margin and which determines it negatively, constituting both its ground and its reverse side."[3]

Similarly, on the opening page of *Línea de sombra: El no sujeto de lo político* (*Line of Shadow: The Nonsubject of the Political*), the book in which he proposes the notion of infrapolitics together with a deconstruction of the politics of the subject in the name of the so-called "nonsubject," Moreiras writes:

It is therefore not a question of a theory or a typology of the nonsubject. The latter rather resists any will to theory and aspires to a certain dryness of the proposal. It seeks to expose, and thus also to expose itself. In the end it might be possible to think that there exists no

---

3    Roberto Esposito, *Categorie dell'impolitico* (Bologna: Il Mulino, 1999), 139.

satisfying knowledge [of the nonsubject] of any kind
to which to latch onto but perhaps this insinuates the
latent tremor of an obscure figure without which no
politics whatsoever can matter at all.[4]

Such a tremor, as the effect of the exposure of politics to its
own finitude, is what infrapolitics—no less than the impolitical—seeks to insinuate, if not provoke. Under the effect of
these prefixes, all existing figures of politics are made to trem-
ble and shake while at the same time there emerges, perhaps,
the latency of an as yet obscure mode of thinking politics.
Both Esposito and Moreiras, in fact, claim that the meaning of politics is not itself political and cannot be thought
except when refracted through their respective categories of
the impolitical and infrapolitics.

## Archipolitics, Parapolitics, Metapolitics

Before moving on to the two instances that form the actual
topic of this chapter, it might be useful briefly to go over
the meaning of those other prefixes and the way they are
deployed, for example, in the work of Rancière. This will also
allow me to problematize further the so-called "return of the
political" in European philosophy over the last few decades
by raising a set of questions that will recur in response to

---

4   Alberto Moreiras, *Línea de sombra. El no sujeto de lo político*
(Santiago: Palinodia, 2006), 9.

the work of Esposito and Moreiras, while postponing a fuller discussion of Rancière's politics to the next chapter.

For Rancière, archipolitics, parapolitics, and metapolitics name the three dominant figures of "political philosophy," or what he also calls "the politics of the philosophers," from Plato to Hobbes and from Marx to Bourdieu. Precisely what is at stake in this reflection is the very question of the relation between politics and philosophy, which is but one instance among others of the relation between the real and the thought of the real. For Rancière, as for all the other authors under discussion here, this relation is one that is fundamentally wrought with tensions and rivalries. Philosophy, in the guise of political philosophy, is in fact very much defined by an ongoing attempt to suppress the conflict inherent in all politics: "We will be testing the following hypothesis: that what is called 'political philosophy' might well be the set of reflective operations whereby philosophy tries to rid itself of politics, to suppress a scandal in thinking proper to the exercise of politics."[5]

Archipolitics, which Rancière associates with Plato and with modern-day republicanism, thus seeks to realize the "true" essence of the political community by returning to a proper *arkhê*, both as beginning or initial cause and as first principle of order, over and above the supposed anarchy of democratic politics in Athens. "Archipolitics, whose model

---

5   Jacques Rancière, *Disagreement: Politics and Philosophy*, trans. Julie Rose (Minneapolis: University of Minnesota Press, 1999), ix.

is supplied by Plato, reveals in all its radicality the project of a community based on the complete realization of the *arkhê* of community, on its integral sensibilization, replacing without any leftover the democratic configuration of politics."[6] In this ideal community, which the republic opposes to the unrest of democracy, people are (only) who they are and they do (only) what they are supposed to do. Such is the tautological truth of politics when it is reduced to archipolitics. Instead of the empty category of the people as *demos*, the philosopher proposes the fully particularized body of a community accomplishing its inner essence or character; instead of the power of paradoxical speech acts, in which the part of those who have no part claims to be equal to the whole, the philosopher proffers the truth of a discourse that claims to be seamlessly derived from an ideal cosmic nature; and instead of a polemical universality, the philosopher seeks to breathe life into particular ways of doing, speaking, and living as molded into the fragile bodies of each of the community's members.

Parapolitics, associated with Aristotle for ancient times and Hobbes for the modern era, while acknowledging the war between the parts or parties of the rich and poor, displaces and recenters the question of "politics" (Rancière speaks of *la politique* in French) onto "the political" (*le politique* in French), in the guise of different doctrines regarding the origin and distribution of power. "Such centering

---

6    Ibid., 65 (translation modified).

seems obvious to a modernity for whom the issue of politics is quite naturally one of power, of the principles that legitimize power, the forms in which power is distributed, and the types of personality specific to it," adds Rancière. "But it is important for us to see that it is a peculiar response to the specific paradox of politics, to the confrontation between the police logic of the distribution of parts and the political logic of the part of those who have no part. Aristotle displaces the singular knot that ties the effect of equality to the inegalitarian logic of social bodies, the knot that is proper to politics, toward *the political* as the specific place of institutions."[7] Hobbes, on the other hand, would seem to want to counteract the subversive potential hidden in the ancient version of parapolitics handed down to us from Aristotle. If people are all equally political animals by nature, and if all political constitutions are delivered over to popular judgment as to their capacity to match their norm, then ancient "political philosophy" paradoxically begins to look at once utopian and seditious. For Hobbes, consequently, the human being must not be said to be political by nature; instead, politics comes in second place, as the outcome of a decision in the face of a prior state of nature.

In terms of the actual content of its propositions, though, modern parapolitics still follows the path of its ancient forerunner. Politics continues to be defined in terms of power, except that now the fundamental question tends to revolve

---

7     Ibid., 73 (translation corrected).

around the enigma of the origins of power, legitimate or otherwise. Like all versions of political philosophy, this presentation of the problem of political power still serves to liquidate the paradoxical appearing of a part of those who have no part, which is the only practice that names the effectiveness of actual politics for Rancière. "The problematization of the 'origins' of power and the terms in which it is framed—the social contract, alienation, and sovereignty—declare first that there is no part of those who have no part. There are only individuals and the power of the state," writes Rancière: "Modern parapolitics begins by inventing a specific nature, an 'individuality,' strictly correlating to the absolute of a sovereign power that must exclude quarreling between fractions, quarreling between parts and parties. It begins by initially breaking down the people into individuals, which, in one go, exorcizes the class war of which politics consists, in the war of all against all."[8] The third and final figure of the politics of the philosophers, namely, the metapolitics associated with Marx and Marxism, will propose to undo this exorcism precisely in the name of the class struggle.

Emblematized with particular force by Marx's "On the Jewish Question," metapolitics serves both as an accompaniment to all existing forms of politics, which as a result can always be found wanting insofar as they hide the true content of the class struggle at the level of civil society, and as the programmatic anticipation of a true politics, which would

---

8   Ibid., 77–8.

also be a politics of truth, leading to the withering away of all classes under communism. "As the *truth* of the lie of politics, the concept of class thus becomes the central figure of a metapolitics conceived as a *beyond* of politics, in keeping with one of the two senses of the prefix. But metapolitics can be understood at the same time according to the other sense of the prefix, which indicates *a complement, an accompaniment*," writes Rancière. In the end, we obtain two distinct senses of the category of metapolitics:

> So metapolitics becomes the scientific accompaniment of politics, in which the reduction of political forms to the forces of the class struggle is initially equivalent to the *truth of the lie* or the truth of illusion. But it also becomes a "political" accompaniment of all forms of subjectivization, which posits as its hidden "political" truth the class struggle it underestimates and cannot not underestimate. Metapolitics can *seize* on any phenomenon as a demonstration of the truth of its falseness.[9]

To this diagnostic of archipolitics, parapolitics, and metapolitics, Žižek, in his critical rejoinder to Rancière and other fellow ex-Althusserians, proposes to add a fourth term, "ultrapolitics," which he claims is "not mentioned by Rancière" and by which he means to refer to "the attempt to

---

9   Ibid., 85 (translation modified).

depoliticize the conflict by bringing it to an extreme via the direct militarization of politics—by reformulating it as the *war* between 'Us' and 'Them,' our Enemy, where there is no common ground for symbolic conflict—it is deeply symptomatic that rather than class struggle the Radical Right speaks of class (or sexual) *warfare*."[10] The fact of the matter is that in *Disagreement* Rancière already mentions not only the term "ultrapolitics" or "suprapolitics" but also the "infrapolitics" that functions as the former's mirror image. Infrapolitics and ultra- or suprapolitics, to be more precise, are the twin outcomes of a Marxian metapolitics that submits real political practices to a double verdict: either of being mere "appearances" concealing the infrapolitical "truth" of the class struggle, or else of falling short of the realization of a "genuine" suprapolitics "beyond" politics, in which society would reach its true fulfillment that would also signal its immanent end. This double verdict applies in an exemplary manner to the Marxist concept of class, which can be seen socially as the true content of all political formations while politically class has no positive content whatsoever, being merely the empty operator of the communist withering away of all classes in the name of the proletarian nonclass. Perhaps, then, we are not so far removed as we might think from the logic of the nonsubject—not as an alternative subject but as the constitutive void of the whole paradigm of political subjectivism—with which

10    Slavoj Žižek, *The Ticklish Subject: The Absent Centre of Political Ontology* (London: Verso, 1999), 190.

infrapolitics, like the categorial horizon of the impolitical for Esposito, will come to accompany and mark off the closure of militant politics in the work of Moreiras. Besides, did not Esposito also publish an anthology of impolitical writings by Hannah Arendt, Georges Bataille, Elias Canetti, Simone Weil and others, significantly titled *Oltre la politica*, which from the impolitical seems to indicate the possibility of moving "beyond politics," if not "toward an ultrapolitics"?[11]

It is important to note, however, that Rancière's real goal in defining archipolitics, parapolitics, and metapolitics—with the latter in turn splitting off into suprapolitics and infra-politics—is almost diametrically opposed to that of Esposito's impolitical or Moreiras's own infrapolitics. Thus, whereas Rancière uses prefixes as devices to name the different mechanisms through which the specificity of politics tends to be erased, displaced, or given the lie, for Esposito and Moreiras it is the metaphysical illusions and totalitarian temptations involved in militant politics that can be avoided only through the minimal distance or gap introduced by the use of prefixes. Similarly, whereas Moreiras and Esposito seem to accept the displacement of politics onto the political, all the while proposing to take an additional step back into the infra- or impolitical, Rancière's critical diagnosis very much attempts to undo the prior move of defining the political, which according to him constitutes Aristotle's lasting contribution

---

11    Roberto Esposito, ed., *Oltre la politica. Antologia del pensiero "impolitico"* (Milan: Bruno Mondadori, 1996).

to the paradigm of political philosophy. The entire project of *Disagreement* thus seeks to capture the nature of politics as a process of subjectivization, without resorting to its suppression and/or realization in the name of a proper philosophical determination of the political. To formulate the discrepancy in yet another way, we can recall that Rancière, in the preface to *Les Scènes du peuple*—a recent collection of essays mostly published in their original form in the 1970s in the journal *Les Révoltes logiques*—still defends the use of "crude words" such as "the people" or "proletariat" all the while holding on to their "difference from themselves" and "the space of dissensual invention that this difference has to offer."[12] In contrast, Esposito and Moreiras would much rather agree with Simone Weil that all such terms, including "war," "revolution," "progress," and "democracy," have in the latter half of the twentieth century proven themselves to be even emptier than they already were at the origin: "We can take almost all the terms, all the expressions of our political dictionary, and upon opening them, at their center we will find the void."[13]

What we might call Rancière's attempt to think politics without prefixes and outside of all hitherto existing political philosophies nonetheless raises three important methodological questions that will also prove to be relevant in the

---

12   Jacques Rancière, *Les Scènes du peuple (Les Révoltes logiques, 1975/1985)* (Lyon: Horlieu, 2003), 16. Selections from this collection of essays are translated as *Staging the People: The Proletarian and His Double*, trans. David Fernbach (London: Verso, 2011).
13   Simone Weil quoted in Esposito, *Categorie dell'impolitico*, 227.

context of our discussion of infrapolitics and the impolitical. There is first of all the rather thorny question regarding the status of Rancière's own discourse. His outlook obviously cannot be yet another instance of the politics of the philosophers, but this does not mean that we are dealing with the real of politics as such, even though the reader might well be justified in drawing such a conclusion. In fact, toward the end of the chapter "From Archipolitics to Metapolitics" in *Disagreement*, to which I have been referring so far, Rancière himself all of a sudden draws a distinction between two possible readings of terms such as "class," "the social," or "the people": on the one hand, there is indeed what he calls the metapolitical reading, which again tends to oscillate between an infrapolitical and a suprapolitical outcome; but, on the other hand, there is also a strictly political reading of such terms. Consider, for example, the category of "proletarian": "From the metapolitical point of view, it designates the performer of the real movement of society who denounces the democratic appearances of politics and is supposed to cause them to be blown to smithereens," writes Rancière. "From the political point of view, proletarian is a specific occurrence of the demos, a democratic subject, performing a demonstration of its power in the construction of worlds of litigious community, universalizing the issue of the count of the uncounted, beyond any regulation, short of infinite wrong."[14] At this point, the author openly seems to allow for

14    Rancière, *Disagreement*, 90.

a certain amount of slippage in the use of the term "politics," both as the *act* of political intervention and as the *interpretation* of such an act. Or, rather, given the theatrical connotations of the term, any interpretation of the empty operativity of "class" or "the people" is already the act of politics as such. In other words, Rancière's own discourse, which constantly distances itself from "the politics, of the philosophers," somehow thrives on the suggestion that it coincides with a "political interpretation of politics," the well-nigh tautological authority of which depends on the supposition of a discourse capable of erasing the traces of its own separateness. In the case of Esposito and Moreiras, by contrast, the logic of separation between politics and the thinking of politics will acquire hyperbolic overtones, to the point where the gap between the two almost seems to take the place, in a strange kind of compensatory mimicry, of the political conflict itself.

In addition to the relation between the real of politics and the thinking of this real, a second question concerns the relation between politics and history. With archipolitics, parapolitics, and metapolitics, in fact, we are not dealing with three different forms of politics but rather with different ways in which philosophy obfuscates the nature of politics, which as such remains invariant. To be sure, linked to Plato, Hobbes, and Marx, all three figures appear roughly in chronological order, just as for each one there also appears to be an ancient and a modern variant, so that we can indeed speak of "eras" or "ages" that would be marked by archipolitics, parapolitics, and metapolitics. But, in reality, these are only the various figures taken by the negation, disavowal and/or suppression of the scandal of politics, a scandal that at bottom remains unchanged throughout the history of political philosophy. By contrast, what is still open is the question of the possible existence of different historical forms of doing politics and the specific character thereof.

This question, which is not even raised in *Disagreement*, no doubt Rancière's least historical work, receives a useful methodological framework in the work of someone like Sylvain Lazarus, who in his *Anthropologie du nom* speaks of various "historical modes of politics," such as the Jacobin mode, the Bolshevik mode, the Stalinist mode, the Maoist mode, or the capitalist-parliamentary mode. Each of these modes is defined by a name, a place, and a specific operativity of thought to think the real. Together these terms provide the categorial framework with which politics as a process is supposed to be intelligible. "The category pertaining to this thinkability is that of the historical mode of politics," as Badiou writes in a review of Lazarus's book: "The mode is defined as the relation of a politics to its thought, which may itself be apprehended through categories internal to political subjectivity (virtue and corruption for Saint-Just, revolutionary consciousness as a condition for Lenin, etc.)."[15] Badiou further specifies the place of philosophy in this context by

---

15    Alain Badiou, *Metapolitics*, trans. Jason Barker (London: Verso, 2005), 46.

arguing in favor of what he calls a "metapolitics," over and against Lazarus's own "anthropology of the name," which by contrast would provide a kind of intermediary discourse between politics and philosophy: "Accordingly, what is at stake here is what I name metapolitics, or what, in philosophy, carries a trace of a political condition which is neither an object nor what requires production in thought, but only a contemporaneity that produces philosophical *effects*."[16] Badiou's aim in *Metapolitics*, in this sense, is really no different from Rancière's in *Disagreement*, since both seek to extricate the thinking of politics from the operations with which "political philosophy" attempts to obscure, displace, or deny politics as such. As Badiou stipulates in the programmatic epigraph to the book: "By 'metapolitics' I understand the consequences that a philosophy can draw out in and for itself from the fact that true forms of politics are forms of thinking. Metapolitics is opposed to political philosophy, which claims that it belongs to the philosopher to think 'the political,' insofar as politics would not be a form of thinking in itself."[17] Thus, ironically, while these two thinkers share a similar understanding of emancipatory politics as both egalitarian and universalist, Rancière sees metapolitics as an obstacle that covers up the play of liberty and equality inherent in all such politics, which Badiou under the very same banner proposes to think through and set free.

---

16    Ibid., 55.
17    Ibid., xlix (translation modified).

A third question, finally, in some way supposes a complex articulation of the first two. That is, the relation of the real and thought, of historical modes of politics and the categorial apparatus devised to render them intelligible, must in turn be historicized alongside specific political experiences and the lessons drawn from them. To be sure, as Esposito and Moreiras both rightly insist, this last question cannot be phrased in terms of the immediate confrontation of a philosophical system and a political experience, nor can a politics be derived directly from a philosophical framework as its practical application. While all such solutions to the old problem of theory and practice may seem impossible or obsolete, however, the further question nonetheless remains as to why this is so, or why it appears to be the case with particular force today, for example, as a result of the previously discussed ontological turn in political philosophy. Which lessons of the last two or three centuries are implicitly or explicitly taken into account in this reformulation of the question of politics and thought? In his *Metapolitics*, Badiou proposes to rethink this question in terms of a relation of conditioning, rather than in the more traditional framework of direct causality and/or determinism. Each way of thinking politics, then, regardless of whether or not it accepts the label of political philosophy, is conditioned by a specific politics. "Thus, one can treat philosophy, from within itself, as a kind of recording apparatus of its own political condition. In particular, a new philosophical possibility might allow itself to be deciphered—albeit at the expense of a complex

'torsion'—as the intra-philosophical index of a real movement of the political condition," Badiou writes with reference
to the work of Louis Althusser: "What philosophy *is* able to
do is to record, in the unfolding of previously unseen philosophical possibilities, the sign of a renewed 'thinkability'
(as Lazarus says) of politics *conceived on the basis of its own
exercise*."[18] In a long endnote to *Logics of Worlds*, on the other
hand, Badiou expands this vocabulary of the condition and
the conditioned through more dangerously idealist notions
such as renaming, sublimation, and speculative formalization. If politics continues to be seen as a truth procedure, a
mode of universalist and egalitarian thought that conditions
philosophy from the outside, this also means that to evaluate
a given philosophy, including not just Badiou's own but any
other as well, we cannot treat the conditioned as though it
were the condition capable of producing a political truth of
its own. At most we can inquire into the degree of compat-
ibility between a given political experience, even one that
might still be to come, and certain conceptual or categorial
arrangements:

> In short, the relation of philosophy to other kinds of
> thought [such as politics] cannot be evaluated in terms
> of identity or contradiction, neither from its own point
> of view nor from that of these other kinds of thought.
> Rather, it is a matter of knowing what it is that—as an

---

18   Ibid., 61–2.

effect of the conceptual sublimations (or speculative formalizations)—remains essentially compatible with the philosophy in question, and what is instead organically alien to it.[19]

With respect to the period enclosed within the categorial horizon marked off by the twin notions of the impolitical and infrapolitics more specifically, useful elements for the historicization of the relation of politics and thought can be found in Domenico Losurdo's *L'ipocondria dell'impolitico*. Losurdo, best known as a Hegel scholar, allows us to place this whole debate in a much larger temporal frame by showing how the rise of a certain impolitical orientation tends to coincide with moments of crisis and disillusion that follow a previous moment of revolutionary fervor, as happens for example in the thought of Schelling and Schopenhauer in contrast to Hegel's allegedly undying commitment to the event of the French Revolution. "The good fortune currently enjoyed by the impolitical certainly is not unrelated to the disillusions and the crisis of rejection that have come after the hope and the enthusiasms of another great revolution," Losurdo writes in his preface:

Instead of being analyzed historically, the intricate unity of emancipation and horror on a gigantic scale that

19   Alain Badiou, *Logics of Worlds: Being and Event, 2*, trans. Alberto Toscano (London: Continuum, 2009), 521.

characterizes the sequence of events initiated in 1917 (if not already in 1789) becomes the occasion for fleeing the historical and political terrain and approaching an "impolitical" which can take on various configurations: an intimate and edifying discourse, a utopianism full of itself and disdainful of any confrontation with reality, or a problematicism that tends to see any ambitious project of political transformation as being generally condemned to failure.[20]

If, for Losurdo, Hegel offers the quintessential counterargument against this "hypochondria" or "listlessness" of the impolitical, then it should come as no surprise that, inversely, Hegel's dialectical philosophy in general, and his philosophy of history in particular, frequently serves as a shorthand notation for everything that would be wrong with the tradition of thinking politics and that for this reason is rejected by Moreiras and Esposito.

## The Impolitical

At first sight, Esposito's take on the impolitical as a categorial horizon may seem to share one of the basic premises behind Rancière's *Disagreement* and Badiou's *Metapolitics*, namely, the rejection of "political philosophy" as a tradition

---

20   Domenico Losurdo, *L'ipocondria dell'impolitico. La critica di Hegel ieri e oggi* (Lecce: Milella, 2001), ix.

of thought that in principle would be unable to think politics. In fact, there is a gaping abyss between politics and thought, which philosophy tries in vain to cover up: "As if politics denied itself to the experience of thought to the same degree to which thought proves itself incapable of thinking politics; and this despite the proliferation of political philosophies that also takes place in Italy today."[21] Esposito thus envisions the relation between philosophy and politics as an impossible dialogue, or what Rancière—before finding a style of near-tautological authority of his own—describes paradoxically as the (philosophical) misunderstanding of (political) misunderstanding. "This is because philosophy approaches politics by way of the question of *foundations*," writes Esposito: "From Plato (not only the famous Letter VII) to Heidegger (not only the Rectorial address), we can say that political philosophy has claimed to found politics precisely in philosophical terms: as if the task of philosophy consisted in 'realizing' itself politically and as if (political) reality needed to be 'educated' by philosophy."[22] Esposito's work, therefore, is better described as a form of political thought, or as a thinking of the political, rather than as political philosophy in any traditional disciplinary sense. "Political philosophy is the philosophy of the end of politics. But politics is the

---

21   Roberto Esposito, "Filosofía política o pensamiento sobre la política," trans. Isabel Vericat, in Martha Rivero, ed., *Pensar la política* (Mexico City: Instituto de Investigaciones Sociales, Universidad Nacional Autónoma de México, 1990), 95.

22   Ibid., 96.

end—or the impossibility—of political philosophy. What is possible—necessary—is by contrast the thought about politics. To think politics in terms of what the latter possesses that is irreducible to political philosophy is precisely the task of the impolitical," he writes: "The impolitical negates political philosophy as the (philosophical) foundation of politics on behalf of philosophy. It negates it in the double sense of considering it harmful and at the same time impossible."[23]

For Esposito, in the end, all hitherto existing political philosophies are defined by an impossible attempt to reduce the conflict that belongs to the essence of politics. The proposal to elaborate the figure of the unpolitical or impolitical well beyond Thomas Mann's original intent is, then, an attempt to think politics without passing through those usual schemes with which political philosophy seeks to reduce antagonism. To be more precise, it is an attempt to come to terms with the limits that are inherent in all such schemes— limits whose uncanny presence hollows out the whole tradition of modern political philosophy with the force of an immanent outside. If the conceptual language of philosophy is marked by a constitutive inability to think through the fact of conflict, and if this fact or facticity lies beyond the scope of conceptual representation, then the impolitical does nothing more than project the shadow of this unrepresentability back

23    Roberto Esposito, "Por un pensamiento de lo impolítico," in Paolo D'Arcais Flores et al., *Modernidad y política: Izquierda, individuo y democracia* (Caracas: Nueva Sociedad, 1995), 103–4.

upon the domain of politics. "Politics is not always aware of its own constitutive finitude. It is inherently meant to forget the latter," writes Esposito. "The impolitical does nothing more than to remind it of this. That is, it returns finitude to the very heart of the political."[24]

Following a recurrent distinction in all of his work, we could say that Esposito's thought simultaneously targets the paradigms of thinking politics as *transcendence* and as *immanence*. Eric Voegelin is quoted in *Categorie dell'impolitico* as remapping the battlefield of political thinking precisely in these terms: "The true dividing line in the current crisis does not run between liberals and totalitarians, but between religious and philosophical transcendentalists, on one hand, and liberal and totalitarian immanentists on the other."[25] Esposito, too, will frequently redefine the stakes of the debate in this way. This means not only to shift the argument from actual politics to the thinking of politics by translating the conflict in question into the philosophical terms of immanence and transcendence, but also and more importantly to subsume under one and the same category what otherwise would be two ideological extremes such as liberalism and totalitarianism. By cutting across this divide, the impolitical is at one and the same time able to present itself as a double refusal of any traditional definition of politics in terms of Left and Right.

---

24    Esposito, *Categorie dell'impolitico*, xvi.
25    Eric Voegelin, quoted in ibid., 83.

The principal virtue of the impolitical thus consists in tracing a diagonal that would avoid both the (Catholic, conservative, decisionistic) tradition of political theology and the alternative (modern, functionalist, or system-theoretical) argument of secularization (including the fashionable trends of a "new polytheism" or of "weak thinking"): "Impolitical is precisely that attitude or, if you prefer, that form of thought that even while rejecting the depoliticizing success of modern secularization, and rather situating itself at its antipodes—its intention being 'ultrapolitical' and not antipolitical—rejects at the same time all falling back on any theologico-political *repraesentatio*, any transcendent place for *grounding* the political."[26] These two traditions—political theology and the trend toward the complete depoliticization of society in the name of technical expertise and governmentality—are opposites only in appearance. According to Esposito, both in fact deny the conflict at the heart of politics: the first by subordinating conflict to the normative value of a transcendent idea; the second by diluting conflict in the total administration of society.

With the impolitical, however, it is not a question of proposing a value different from the alternatives of myth and modernity, decisionism and nihilism—much less a dialectical mediation between the two. "The impolitical rebels precisely against this combination of depoliticization and theology, of technique and value, of nihilism and apologetics.

---

26  Esposito, "Por un pensamiento de lo impolítico," 228.

We already stated that it is something other than representation, or better: *the* other, that which remains obstinately
outside of representation. But this unrepresentability is
not that of modern depoliticization," warns Esposito. "It is
not the refusal of the political. In this sense, it is radically
subtracted from Thomas Mann's semantics. It is not the
value that is opposed to the political. It is rather precisely
the contrary. It is the refusal of the political as value, of
any 'theological' valorization of the political."[27] Following a
logic of retreat sympathetic to the political seminar organized in the 1980s by Nancy and Lacoue-Labarthe—represented in collections such as *Rejouer le politique* (*Replaying
the Political*) and *Le retrait du politique* (*The Retreat of the
Political*), where *retrait* connotes both a "withdrawal" or
"retreat" and a "re-treatment" or "redrawing"—it is a matter
of sidestepping the necessity of the alternative itself, of void-
ing the obligation to choose, by means of a resolute decision
or a partisan commitment, either one side or the other.

The necessity of the either/or decision, as in the friend/
enemy distinction, is what finds expression in political theology, especially among Catholic thinkers such as Romano
Guardini or Carl Schmitt, the first authors to be discussed
in detail in *Categorie dell'impolitico*. In a sense rather different from Schmitt, Esposito defines "political theology" as
the articulation of power and value, or of representation and
idea. It is that which permits the transit from an idea to its

27    Esposito, *Categorie dell'impolitico*, 14.

enactment, and conversely, it is that which structures power in the name of a normative value or transcendent idea, which is precisely the representation of the good to be realized in politics. "This is in essence the meaning of the expression 'political theology' to which from now on I will refer," explains Esposito, namely, "the conception according to which the good would be politically representable and politics would be interpretable in terms of value."[28] All political theology thus presupposes a suturing of politics and ethics, while the impolitical, by postulating the unrepresentability of the value of the good, at the same time recognizes the radical incompatibility of political power and ethical ideas. "Power is neither a representation nor an emanation of the good, much less a dialectical mechanism capable of extracting it from evil, of translating evil into good," so that the two are henceforth separated by an insuperable abyss: "Between ethics and politics there opens an abyss that no theory of history can heal because history is precisely what continuously recreates it."[29]

Topologically, the result of the deconstruction of politics in the name of the impolitical draws the picture of a strange kind of immanent transcendence, or of an outside within. This is one reason why *impolitico*, at least in Esposito's case if not already for Cacciari, is better translated as "impolitical," as I have chosen to do here, rather than as "unpolitical,"

---

28   Esposito, "Por un pensamiento de lo impolítico," 236.
29   Esposito, *Categorie dell'impolitico*, xvii and 170.

as is the preferred option of Cacciari and Mann's English-language translators. This is because the Latin root of the prefix im- has both a negative connotation (as in the existing English term "impolitic," attested to for many centuries and meaning roughly what we would today call "politically incorrect" or "tactless") and a more positive one (as in "immanence," from the Latin for "staying or standing inside," "remaining within"). Throughout *Categorie dell'impolitico*, Esposito multiplies the spatial and audiovisual figures that convey the presence of the impolitical, not as some position safely outside of the political, much less as the "good" pole of reserve opposite the "evil" pole of militant politics, but as the hollow void, the inverted echo, the silent unthought, or the negative reverse of the political. Time and again, the point is that one arrives at the impolitical not by a stark either/or choice or a decisionistic breakthrough but rather by a radicalization of the very premises behind all Western politics, the excessive accomplishment of which at one and the same time entails their critical implosion.

From Hermann Broch to Georges Bataille, by way of Elias Canetti, Hannah Arendt, and Simone Weil, all the authors who comprise the impolitical tradition according to the trajectory painstakingly traced between Esposito's *Categorie dell'impolitico* and the anthology *Oltre la politica* share this attempt to follow the contours of politics from the extreme limit of a constitutive outside. "Ultimately, the whole process of elaboration to which the category of the impolitical has been subjected over the years has been oriented toward an ever more explicit interiorization of exteriority, of the outside, the confines," Esposito explains, referring to Bataille's paradoxical idea of "inner experience" as an experience of the outside: "Transcendence—but this element is already largely present in the last chapter of *Categorie*—is not the contrary of immanence but its interruption, or its exposition, to its own outside. It is transcendence, or better the transcending, *of* immanence, not *from* immanence."[30] As the constitutive outside of politics, or its immanent transcending, the impolitical therefore cannot be seen as yet another value, external to political valorization, because there is neither a secure interior nor a safe exterior to politics from which the latter might be accomplished or criticized. "As this book tries to argue through 'its' authors, for the impolitical there exists no entity, force, or power that could be opposed to politics from within its own language. But neither is there an outside, for this 'exteriority' does not exist except as an ideological, mythical, self-legitimating projection of the political itself once it reaches the stage of 'civil war' with its twin the antipolitical."[31] Rather than an external or dialectical relation of contradiction, we could say that between politics and the impolitical there exists a relation of anamorphosis. Through a slight shift of perspective, a pushing to the extreme confines of the premises of the one, we arrive at the hidden, unspoken, forgotten dimension of the other.

---

30    Ibid., xxviii–xxix.
31    Ibid., xiv.

As Esposito reiterates with reference to Weil: "We are situated at the limit, on the threshold that separates the political from its unrepresentable ground and that from this ground throws new light onto the reality of the only thing that exists: 'bordering upon' (*côtoyer*) politics, Simone will say in 1942, referring to her previous experience."[32] This is precisely the limit or threshold, bordering upon the void at the heart of politics, where the thought of the impolitical seeks to dwell.

In the end, the impolitical is not only not antipolitical, it also seeks to extricate itself from all confusion with the apolitical as well as with a certain complacency toward the "weak" or "depoliticizing" effects of modernity and postmodernity. This is an aspect to which I will return below, that is, the desire that the impolitical may provide a unique reference point, if not the only one, for an extreme radicalization of politics: "For this reason, the impolitical is not simply the negation of the political. It is also, looked at from a perspective shifted by 180 degrees, its maximal intensification. Or again, its extreme 'projection' through a lexical displacement to its external limits at a time when any affirmative (not critical) political theory can only lapse back into politico-theological monotheism (in the final instance, into the philosophy of history)."[33] The ambition, in a certain sense, is neither apolitical nor antipolitical but rather ultrapolitical: more radically political, in any event, than any really existing

---

32  Ibid., 228.
33  Esposito, "Por un pensamiento de lo impolítico," 228–9.

mode of politics, whether communist or fascist, liberal or anarchist.

Paradoxically, this radicalization is enabled by the very same impasse from which the impolitical seeks to escape, namely, the fact that due to the so-called increasing differentiation between politics and thought, politics as such can no longer be thought, if ever this was possible in the first place, from within politics. To the contrary, what is needed to think politics is a minimal distance, a step back: precisely the step marked by the added prefix. Esposito thus can speak of "the dialectic between 'political' and 'impolitical,' whereby 'impolitical' means neither an apolitical nor antipolitical attitude but rather the space of a form of thinking from where alone, by contrast, the sphere of politics could be thought," for indeed, "the place from where to think politics cannot itself be political. It must remain separate and delayed with regard to real politics, and it must be safeguarded as such, in its 'modern impoliticity,' especially in critical situations such as the present, as Hannah Arendt herself underlined with great intensity in her final and 'impolitical' writings."[34] In *Categorie dell'impolitico*, Esposito explains this last reference, which at least implicitly begins to answer the final of the three questions mentioned above in the context of my discussion of Rancière's *Disagreement*: "The impolitical does not consist simply in the absence of 'political relevance' but in the politicity that this absence assumes in those 'particular

---

34    Esposito, "¿Retorno al ágora?," in *Modernidad y política*, 209.

situations of exception' that Arendt defines with an expression from Karl Jaspers as 'limit-situations,' that is, in an absence that becomes presence, or a presence that silently resounds in an absence, or better yet, that transcends itself into an absence."[35] Here, in other words, we begin to grasp the peculiar timeliness that the impolitical claims for itself. Ours would be a limit-situation in which the impolitical becomes not only desirable but urgent as well. In fact, what at first sight appears to be a purely axiomatic assumption, namely, the unrepresentability of the value of the good that would have to be empowered within the realm of politics, in retrospect acquires the almost militant (or rather, as we will see, antimilitant) urgency of a task that cannot be postponed except at the risk of the worst. As we can also read in *Categorie dell'impolitico*: "Thus, paradoxically, when the political situation becomes critical, that is to say, 'when all let themselves be carried away without reflection by that which others believe and do,' the innovative function of the political finds refuge in the impolitical realm of thought, which in this way assumes a role of control and substitution with regard to the temporarily dulled and degraded active faculties."[36] This explains why Arendt's shift of attention in her later writings from the actor to the spectator, from the active to the contemplative faculties, or from practical reason to aesthetic judgment in the Kantian sense—a shift that for

35   Esposito, *Categorie dell'impolitico*, 120.
36   Ibid., 126.

Badiou's *Metapolitics* exemplifies everything that is wrong with "political philosophy"—in the eyes of Esposito must be understood as providing a much-needed distance from blind praxis, including the Marxist and certainly any communist philosophy of praxis.

## Infrapolitics

Except for the brief discussion in Rancière's *Disagreement* and even briefer mentions in texts such as Badiou's *Theory of the Subject*, as a concept or categorial horizon infrapolitics, as far as I know, has almost no antecedents prior to Moreiras's *Línea de sombra: El no sujeto de lo político*. There are, without a doubt, plenty of echoes and resonances between infrapolitics and the impolitical, beginning with the negative reference to political theology or, more generally speaking, to any political philosophy or philosophy of history based on the militant subject of the sovereign decision, whether this subject is called a "person," as the sacred bearer of inalienable rights, or a "victim" of the infraction of these same rights, all the way to the images or figures of "retreat," "passive decision," the "neûtral," and the "impersonal," not as values that are the opposite of politics but as "delimitations," that is, as limit-concepts, or as "determinations," in the nondialectical sense of a taking-to-their-final-terms the premises of politics in its theological and metaphysical essence.

Like Esposito's impolitical, Moreiras's infrapolitics does not seek to oppose another valorization to the tradition of political theology but rather to avoid the disjunction itself. "My goal," writes Moreiras, "is not to deny the importance of the determination of the political on the basis of the friend/ enemy division, but to show that there can be a beyond of this division, not in an antipolitical or postpolitical sense, but in an alternative political sense": "The exodus from the alternative: infrapolitics is nothing but the search for a non-biopolitical exodus from such a conjuncture."[37] Infrapolitics, then, introduces into the logic of politics as subjective militancy a kind of intimate fracture, a de-domestication, or a point of internal exodus. What Moreiras describes with the thought-images of *éxodo* ("exodus"), *ajuste* ("adjustment") or *desalojo* ("ousting" or "expulsion"), among others, corresponds quite closely to the *scarto* ("gap" or "distancing"), *arretramento* ("withdrawing") or *ritiro* ("retreat") in Esposito. It is what creates a minimal distance and produces an "unworking" (along the lines of the *désoeuvrement* that runs from Bataille to Foucault to Nancy) of politics in its theological and metaphysical sense.

The perspective of infrapolitics, aside from the fact that it shares many authors—even negative ones such as Schmitt— with the tradition of the impolitical, and aside from the fact that it now seems to move in the direction of an even greater proximity through authors such as Weil or Arendt, also has the advantage of centering the debate on the sore point that is the theory of the subject. That is to say, infrapolitics

37    Moreiras, *Línea de sombra*, 74 and 238.

fundamentally seeks to delink the thinking of the political from all affiliations with the metaphysical, politico-theological, or more properly onto-politico-theological tradition of the subject as a militant, partisan, even messianic figure: "The question then is whether, given the reshuffling of sovereignty, including democratic sovereignty, it is possible today to develop a conception of antipartisan and antimilitant political practice of a democratic nature; and one that would also be antimessianic or at least antimessianist in nature," since the messianic, or at least all existing messianisms, would still run the risk of falling into the trap of a certain version—in this case a catastrophic but for this reason no less redemptive one—of subjective militancy:

> What does the messianic without messianism in sum promise? The crucial question here concerns the determination of a practical understanding of the political beyond all messianic illusion. The messianic illusion—the hoax—converts all politics into a kind of ultrapolitics whose effectiveness oscillates between the void and the catastrophic. Or the alternate question: Is ontotheological politics the only possible politics of our time?[38]

Moreiras's principal claim in *Línea de sombra* is that the "hoax" of political theology is inseparable from what he calls

---

38    Ibid., 266.

the "plague" of subjectivism, based on a humanist-metaphysical understanding of the subject, and that the first cannot be avoided without at the same time dismantling the second. Moreiras, in this regard, sides with Althusser, who sees the subject purely and simply as the effect of an ideological process. "In the face of so many attempts to make of the 'subject' the very possibility of political resistance, a real plague of contemporary thought, there are worse things to do than to return to the old Althusser essay on ideology," he writes. "Subjectivism is just a step away from identitarianism, which from my earliest years I have always considered the most obvious contemporary reconciliation of messy nihilism and pious humanism in all its forms, from nationalism to sexuality and gender, without forgetting the schizoidentitarianism fashionable among North American Deleuzians (though they do not call it that)."[39]

Already toward the end of *Categorie dell'impolitico*, Esposito had arrived at the conclusion that only a nonsubjective understanding of politics could keep one at a distance from what Simone Weil would call "idolatry." This is because the subject as such is through and through marked by power, or by a will to power in its common pejorative sense. "There is no real alternative to power, no *subject* of antipower, for the basic reason that the subject is *already* constitutively power. Or, in other words, because power is by nature inherent in the dimension of the subject in the sense that power is precisely

---

39    Ibid., 12 and 74.

*its* verb," writes Esposito, playing on the active verbal sense of *potere* or *posse* as a power-to-act, or as the capacity of the subject to do this or that: "For this reason, the conclusion to be extracted from this, not only according to Canetti but according to the whole tradition of impolitical thought, from Broch to Kafka and Simone Weil—the latter with a blinding clarity—is that the only mode of containing power is by reducing the subject."[40] Moreiras's proposal for thinking the political on the basis of what he calls the "nonsubject," then, renders explicit what is already understood to lie at the core of *Categorie dell'impolitico* and turns it against the politics of the subject. Referring more specifically to Žižek and Badiou's

---

40  Esposito, *Categorie dell'impolitico*, 20–1. In his following book, *Communitas: The Origin and Destiny of Community*, Esposito also speaks of nonsubjects or not-subjects: "*Not* subjects. Or subjects of their own proper lack, of the lack of the proper. Subjects of radical impropriety that coincides with an absolute contingency or just simply 'coincides,' that falls together." See Roberto Esposito, *Communitas: The Origin and Destiny of Community*, trans. Timothy Campbell (Stanford: Stanford University Press, 2010), 6. The fact that Moreiras recently devoted a lengthy essay to Esposito's book *Terza persona: Politica della vita e filosofia dell'impersonale* (*Third Person: Politics of Life and Philosophy of the Impersonal*) only further highlights this confluence of interest around the issues of subjectivity and personhood, which these thinkers seek to deconstruct in the name of the nonsubject and the impersonal. See Roberto Esposito, *Terza persona. Politica della vita e filosofia dell'impersonale* (Milan: Einaudi, 2007); and Alberto Moreiras, "La vertigine della vita: Su *Terza persona* di Roberto Esposito," trans. Davide Tarizzo, in Laura Bazzicalupo, ed., *L'impersonale. In dialogo con Roberto Esposito* (Milan: Mimesis, 2008), 117–49.

notion of subjectivization as fidelity to the event, as in the case of Saint Paul's proposition of "love," "faith," and "hope" as the principal virtues of the militant Christian subject, Moreiras raises the question of the sacrificial cost of all such processes of fidelity: "How does an event of truth relate to that which it leaves behind? If the political is based on the event, what happens with what is not tied to the event, with the neutral, with the nonsubject?"[41] The question of the nonsubject, in other words, is not a search for an alternative—marginal, minoritarian or counterhegemonic—subject but an attempt to unravel the very logic of all subject-based politics from the point of view of the enigmatic remainder that it necessarily produces and excludes at the same time.

Once again, we end up with a topology of the constitutive outside, of the excluded other that is inherent in the subject's self-identity: "The permanence of the nonsubject within the subject (the nonsubject: all that which struggles in fidelity against fidelity, all that which resists conviction, certainty, love)," Moreiras summarizes. "The nonsubject is that which the subject must constantly subtract in a kind of self-foundation that extends into virtue (a virtue that the catechism not coincidentally names or named 'theological': faith, love, and hope are the necessary and sufficient conditions of the absolute subject of political life, which is also the absolute subject of spiritual life)," so that the task of infrapolitics would amount to a thorough de-theologization of politics: "In other words,

---

41    Moreiras, *Línea de sombra*, 115.

what is at stake is the radical possibility of a de-theologized theory of the political."[42] The real difficulty of this task stems from the fact that the nonsubject is not an alternative entity that can be made to appear; it is not a remainder or leftover waiting to be embraced and incorporated into a new collective identity. Only negatively, or by way of oblique figures, can the remainder of all militant subjectivism be brought to bear upon the definition of the political. "Such a thinking, merely indicative with regard to the notion of the enigmatic remainder, is both deconstructive and subalternist: that is to say, its conflictive and polemical virtuality cannot give itself in the positivity of a new proposal of community, no new proposal of translative mediation, no new proposal of hegemonic or counterhegemonic articulation."[43] Through the notion of the nonsubject, infrapolitics thus puts us on the threshold of a nonhegemonic perspective whose line of shadow necessarily falls over all subjectivized politics.

The ultimate target of infrapolitics is, then, none other than the subject as the foundation for a politics of militancy. Both communism and liberalism, as dominant ideologies of the past century and a half, are here considered mere variants of one and the same politics of subjectivization. "The promise of liberalism is the promise of the antipolitical constitution of a full subject of humanity, without enemies. Such is also the promise of communism, as the historical extension

42  Ibid., 134.
43  Ibid., 150.

of liberalism. The unlimited continuum of modern tempo-rality closes in on the fissureless constitution of a unique subject—*the* subject."[44] To this metaphysical understanding of the subject as appropriating plenitude, it is not enough to oppose even a Derridean politics of friendship. "Thus, a politics of the nonsubject, of the enigmatic remainder, committed to the redemption of the part of those who have no part, is no longer a politics of friendship, which is only another name for a politics of hegemony."[45] Rather, and more unexpectedly, given the radical critique of subjectivization, infrapolitics claims to be compatible with the kind of poli-tics that, in Rancière's view, no longer requires any prefixes: "The part of those who have no part, the part that is not, is always the enigmatic remainder, the radical outside of every possible subject of humanity or for humanity, and thus the very possibility of a politics beyond the subject—a politics of the nonsubject that is, perhaps even for Rancière though not explicitly, the only possible formulation proper to politics."[46]

## Against Militancy

We can thus come back to the questions raised in the context of my reading of Rancière's *Disagreement* and ask ourselves

44    Ibid., 76–7.
45    Ibid., 84; see also a similar rejection of the Derridean poli-tics of friendship as insufficiently impolitical, in Esposito, *Categorie dell'impolitico*, xxix.
46    Moreiras, *Línea de sombra*, 63.

in the first place whether infrapolitics and the impolitical mark—or open the path to—new forms of politics, or if they rather constitute new perspectives, new frames of thought, for approaching the definition of the political. In other words, are we dealing with new historical forms of politics or with new attempts to think the essence of politics? If the latter, then which historical lessons are taken into account in such attempts? And do the new frames or perspectives also pretend to open up new forms of politics to come? Or does the radicalism of the step back toward the political with its additional prefixes guarantee in advance that any actual form of politics will be judged a subjectivist illusion, a case of idolatry or, worse, a hoax? In the end, what possibilities remain open when we must at all costs avoid the sacrificial price of politics as subjective militancy?

To respond to these questions, we can turn to the essay on María Zambrano in which Moreiras appears to extend the infrapolitical conclusions of his book *Línea de sombra* into a truly devastating judgment upon the entire spectrum of political possibilities from the present and recent past. The article distinguishes between two types of subjectivity, both of them considered equally treacherous and metaphysical. The first type is a militancy of immanence and plenitude, which in turns includes two versions, one liberal and the other communist:

> Subjective militancy is ontotheological militancy. There are two primary ways of it in modernity. In the first way, the militant—formal subject of a practice of

the will—seeks the exhaustive exploitation of being, the thorough appropriation of being to militant practice. The subject, as a singular absolute, works on the remainder of its autistic immanence, thinks of the world as the infinitely reducible, and affirms its own apotheosis in the closure of world into subject and subject into world. This is the figure of the liberal subject, which is also the communist subject: a progressive subject, a subject beyond the shadow of its own impossibility.[47]

With the second type of subjectivized politics, on the other hand, we would seem to be approaching a partial self-criticism, since here notions of lack, loss, and even, at least implicitly, subalternity are addressed in ways that seem to refer back to earlier writings by the same author, even though all such notions are now equated with identity politics:

In the second way of ontotheological militancy, the militant emphasizes distance, dwells on the loss through which the subject finds its bliss through open,

---

47    Alberto Moreiras, "The Last God: María Zambrano's Life without Texture," in Carsten Strathausen, ed., *A Leftist Ontology: Beyond Relativism and Identity Politics* (Minneapolis: University of Minnesota Press, 2009), 181. For a similar critique of communism, largely referring to the metaphysical or mytho-poietic humanism attributed to Marx's *Economic and Philosophic Manuscripts of 1844*, see Roberto Esposito, "Mito," in *Nove pensieri sulla politica* (Bologna: Il Mulino, 1993), 113–36.

painful deconstitution. The subject is here pierced by its own insufficiency, and must affirm a blind transcendence from that which, upon giving itself, is lost: from that which gives itself as loss. This is the reactionary subject, which is also the subject of personal identity.[48]

Appearances to the contrary notwithstanding, both types of militancy, the liberal-communist and the reactionary-identitarian, are equally considered paradigmatic cases of a subjectivist tradition of political theology, from which the infrapolitical orientation seeks to subtract itself. To do so, however, infrapolitics obviously cannot claim to have access to a more resolute or originary subject, since this would put us back in the midst of political theology. In this sense, we might also say that what Moreiras proposes is a political atheology, which is not the same as a negative or reactive political theology:

In both cases, through both ways, the ontotheological ground of militancy is a *ground* because the world appears as an entity regarding which one must either insist or resist. Through the first militancy, insistence is a will for saturation: the world will reach proper totality, will be the One-All as it coalesces with a subject only upon which a world is possible. In the second

48    Moreiras, "The Last God," 181.

militancy, the world is always already One-All, and the subject experiences it as it experiences its own expulsion towards nothingness. The world is experienced as possible through its very withdrawal, appears as an always vanishing horizon, and it is through this very vanishing that the subject can exercise its own overwhelming presence: the subject is nothing but a resistance against nothing, hence the subject is all.[49]

Infrapolitics and the impolitical in sum propose a double distancing *both* from political theology with its transcendent norm for representation *and* from the full immanentism of the subject in the total biopolitical administration of social identities and their excluded others, the victims and vanquished of history. "Double distance—a distance from reactionary militancy, and a distance from progressive militantism, a distance from the insistence of subject/world and resistance to its loss," writes Moreiras, "cannot form a new subject of the political, but it is the site for the appearance of that which dwells in the unthought of modern subjectivity. It is the promise of another constitution of the political."[50] The promise, that is, of a constitution of the political, or of a thinking of the political, which at last would no longer be sacrificial, militant, identitarian, subjectivized, or partisan.

---

49  Ibid., 181–2; cf. Esposito, *Categorie dell'impolitico*, 298–9.
50  Moreiras, "The Last God," 182.

## Grand Politics?

If it is difficult to conceive of the passage from the philosophical orientations of the impolitical and infrapolitics toward a
new constitution of politics, this is because it seems that all
the really existing and presently imaginable historical modalities remain locked within the horizon of categories marked
by subjectivization, militancy, decisionism, or representation. This is at the same time the strength and the weakness
of the orientations in question. If I may be allowed to play on
the last names of Esposito and Moreiras, we could say that
infrapolitics and the impolitical leave politics "abandoned"
and "exposed" to its own finitude while letting the subject
"die" or "dwell" in its mortality. By contrast, any attempt actually to transform what is thus exposed and delimited falls
necessarily into the trap of a metaphysical illusion regarding
the infinite powers of the subject. What is more, any objection—such as my own—against the limited practicality of
the respective proposals of infrapolitics and the impolitical is
always already preemptively taken into account and refuted,
insofar as the aim of these proposals is precisely to render
inoperative all such criteria of practicality, regardless of their
ideological orientation. In *L'origine della politica* (*The Origin
of Politics*), Esposito draws a fine distinction in this respect
between Arendt and Weil. Whereas the former still hopes to
revitalize an alternative origin for politics, that is, other than
its perceived enmeshment with the factuality of power and
war, for the latter politics and war are inseparable so that the

thing to do is not dialectically to overcome war by means of a regrounded politics but rather to reinterpret politics from the impolitical perspective of its shadowy reverse. "No longer to reconstruct the devastated space of politics but to uncover its hidden 'impolitical' soul," suggests Esposito. And if Weil on rare occasions seems to be optimistic about the possibility of an alternative art of the political, this does not mean that the impolitical perspective becomes practicable: "Even in these cases, however, the positive evaluation of politics is always conditioned by its being rooted in a point that is external and transcendent to it—thus altogether 'inoperative.'"[51]

And yet, curiously, the arguments for thinking the inoperativity of the political in the name of finitude—even if the latter does not amount to a new value and despite the apparent reserve in the style of argumentation—never cease to invoke some proximity with the Nietzschean idea of a "grand politics" or with an almost "ultrapolitical" radicalism. This is the case, most obviously, in Cacciari's original essay on "Nietzsche and the Unpolitical," but Esposito, too, not only in *Categorie dell'impolitico* but also and even more explicitly in *Bíos: Biopolitics and Philosophy*, offers what we might call an impolitical transvaluation of "great" or "grand politics."[52]

---

51   Roberto Esposito, *L'origine della politica. Hannah Arendt o Simone Weil?* (Rome: Donzelli, 1996), 16. On the idea of inoperativity, see also the essays collected in Ciccarelli, ed., *Inoperosità della politica.*
52   Roberto Esposito, *Bíos. Biopolitics and Philosophy*, trans. Timothy C. Campbell (Minneapolis: University of Minnesota Press,

How then do we move from infrapolitics and the impolitical to *die grosse Politik* in Nietzsche's sense? Or, conversely, how, by what interpretive sleight of hand, can a Nietzschean-styled grand politics possibly be read as being already impolitical or infrapolitical rather than ultra- or overpolitical, as after all we might have expected, coming from the philosopher of the *Übermensch*?

The key to understanding this move consists in grasping the point at which Nietzsche's radical critique of all hitherto existing politics, far from implying the affirmation of an alternative value, is actually said to presuppose the complete emptying out of all political valorization. "The unpolitical does not represent the value that frees itself from the nonvalue of the political, but the radical critique of the political as invested with value. The unpolitical is the reversal of value. And only this reversal can liberate the will to power in the direction of politics on a grand scale," writes Cacciari. "Grand politics are not possible there where the critique of the unpolitical is limited to affirming the necessity of politicization. This affirmation is still historicism, tradition. Grand politics is a critique of the values that still form the basis of this politicization."[53] Nietzsche's grand politics, according to

---

2008), 78–109. Moreiras, in the announcement for the conference "New Paths in Political Philosophy" at the University of Buffalo, where I first presented some of the ideas for this chapter, also expresses the hope that "the notion of a 'grand' academic politics in the Nietzschean sense might be allowed here."

53   Cacciari, "Nietzsche and the Unpolitical," 95.

this account, is not the heroic moment following the nihilistic disenchantment of all hitherto existing values; rather, the moment of nihilistic destruction already coincides with grand politics itself once the latter is read in an unpolitical or impolitical key: "The unpolitical brings the political back to the acknowledgement of its intrinsic nihilism. This key direction opens up, above all, by attacking the concepts, the forms, and the conducts that are the substance of the political as value. But this very same *pars destruens* is already a construction of grand politics insofar as it is a nihilistic devaluation."[54] Paradoxically, therefore, it is not so much the will to power or the affirmation of the eternal return but a certain measure of inaction that defines Nietzsche as an impolitical philosopher. "If it turns out to be impossible to interpret Nietzsche because his primary feature is precisely to de-ground or make flounder any possible hermeneutic in its own subtraction from all meaning, it is much more unthinkable to attempt a 'realization' of his thought, because he contains no theory of action whatsoever and even presents himself provocatively as a theory or rather a practice of inaction," writes Esposito, who in this regard seems to be in complete agreement with Cacciari: "Nietzsche the philosopher of inaction is *the* philosopher of the impolitical."[55]

---

54  Ibid., 96.
55  Esposito, *Categorie dell'impolitico*, 282. Any attempt, including the impolitical one, to recuperate the philosopher of the overman for the sake of a self-proclaimed progressive or leftist agenda must come to terms with Geoff Waite's forceful indictment of

Badiou, interestingly enough, offers a very different reading of Nietzsche's grand politics, one that can furthermore serve as a useful contrast for the framing of our overarching questions about the relation between politics and thought, on one hand, and between philosophy and history, on the other. Badiou first of all proposes to link the idea of grand politics to concrete historico-political events such as the French Revolution and the Paris Commune. Nietzsche relates to these events according to a logic of rivalry and mimeticism. To be more precise, he absorbs the explosive energy of the historico-political revolution into the realm of the philosophical act, which as a result comes to operate as an antiphilosophical act as well. "The philosophical act is in fact represented by Nietzsche as an *amplified mimetics of the revolutionary event*," Badiou claims. "Nietzsche adopts with regard to the revolutionary act a rapport of formal fascination and substantive repulsion. He proposes for himself to render formally equivalent the philosophical act as an act of thought and the apparent explosive power of the politico-historical revolution."[56] The result is a philosophical appropriation of the revolutionary act, which can present itself

---

"Left-Nietzscheanism" as a contradiction in terms that is at least as harmful as "Left-Heideggerianism," if not more so due to its all-pervasiveness. See Geoff Waite, *Nietzsche's Corps/e: Aesthetics, Politics, Prophecy, or, the Spectacular Technoculture of Everyday Life* (Durham: Duke University Press, 1995).

56   Alain Badiou, *Casser en deux l'histoire du monde?* (Paris: Les Conférences du Perroquet, 1992), 10–11.

not only as capable of breaking the history of humankind into two, like dynamite with a before and an after, but also as being far more radical than any really existing revolutionary process. This is why Nietzsche's grand politics, rather than receiving an impolitical or unpolitical slant, can be seen as an example of what Badiou calls archipolitics, which is also different from the way this term is defined in Rancière. "The philosophical act is, I would say, *archipolitical*, in that it proposes itself to revolutionize all of humanity on a more radical level than that of the calculations of politics," Badiou explains. "It is the philosophical act itself that is archipolitical, in the sense that its historical explosion will show, retroactively, that the political revolution properly speaking has not been truthful, or has not been authentic."[57] Badiou's reading of Nietzsche thus restores not only a certain historicity but also a profound ambivalence to the peculiar articulation of thought and politics that goes by the name of grand politics. Far from merely devaluing politics, this articulation both validates and depreciates what we have come to understand under this term. Most importantly, by absorbing the violent break of revolutionary politics into the characterization of the philosophical act proper, archipolitics allows the philosopher of the overman to portray himself as infinitely more radical than any existing politics.

Could we not conclude that the points of view of infrapolitics and the impolitical are also archipolitical in the sense

----

57    Ibid., 11.

outlined in Badiou's reading of Nietzsche? This would be confirmed by a long quotation from Karl Jaspers via Georges Bataille in Esposito's *Categorie dell'impolitico*, according to which Nietzsche's interest in grand politics, though inspired and conditioned by concrete empirical activities, at the same time can claim to operate at an ontological level that will always be more originary than any given political event. This is because the explosive event produced by politics in the grand style is aimed at the totality of being, and not just at the mere administration of public affairs. Jaspers as quoted by Bataille, in a French translation most likely due to Pierre Klossowski, writes the following about Nietzsche:

> He establishes the origin of the political event, without plunging methodically into the concrete particular realities of political activity, such as it manifests itself every day in the struggle among powers and peoples. He wants to engender a movement that would awaken the last foundations (the final causes) of the human being and with his thinking force those who listen and understand him to enter into this movement, without the content of this movement having received any statist, populist or sociological determination whatsoever. The content that determines all judgments is rather for Nietzsche the "integral" attitude with regard to the totality of *being*; it is no longer only politics but philosophy by means of which, in the abundance of the possible and without rational principle, the contrary

and contradictory can be attempted—in an attempt that obeys only the principle of salvation and gradation of the human condition.[58]

Similarly, I would argue, infrapolitics and the impolitical can lay claims to being forms of grand politics because they too absorb the radicality of the historico-political break, now rendered inoperative, into the realm of philosophy—into the thought of the political. Thus, the category of the impolitical can even acquire the virtue of the incorruptible usually reserved for revolutionary politics, only to turn it back against the allegedly necessary betrayal of the ideals of the French Revolution. As Esposito writes: "Before an effective politics—and nothing is more irrevocably effective than a triumphant revolution—which *must* betray its own idea of justice, the only possible solution is protected by the ineffective incorruptibility of the impolitical."[59] Is this not the greatest example of the attitude of the beautiful soul relying

---

58  Karl Jaspers, quoted in Esposito, *Categorie dell'impolitico*, 283–4. In English, the passage can be found in Jaspers, *Nietzsche: An Introduction to the Understanding of His Philosophical Activity*, trans. Charles F. Wallraff and Frederick J. Schmitz (Tucson: University of Arizona Press, 1965), 252–3 (translation modified). Badiou's understanding of Nietzsche's "grand politics," by contrast, seems more inspired by Pierre Klossowski's reading of the posthumous fragments from the last ten years of Nietzsche's life, in his *Nietzsche and the Vicious Circle*, trans. Daniel W. Smith (Chicago: University of Chicago Press, 1998).

59  Esposito, *Categorie dell'impolitico*, 155–6.

on its ineffectiveness as proof of its moral superiority over and above all politics as usual?

More generally, in fact, through the notions of the impolitical and infrapolitics the very impossibility of the dialogue between politics and philosophy, or between the real and the thought of the real, which would be due to the unrepresentability of conflict within political philosophy, seems to take the place otherwise occupied by conflict as it traditionally operates in the realm of politics. What such a substitution gains in terms of philosophical radicality, it gives up in terms of political effectiveness. For Esposito and Moreiras, however, this does not signal a loss or a defeat so much as it is the inevitable outcome of a willful act of renunciation: a will not to will. In the end, theirs is a strange kind of passive decision, or a decision in favor of passivity and inaction, this being the only remedy against the deafening calls for political effectiveness and activism.

# 3

## *Leftism and Its Discontents*

"Communism" is the name of the possible that opens up each time and in every place where appropriation runs aground—on a wildcat strike, a ravaged planet or an ecstatic feminism. This shows that the sentiment of disaster that haunts us stems first of all from the difficulty we face in finding a passage, in forging a language, in embracing the barrenness from where we might seize onto a completely different possibility of existence. This also goes to show that communism is scarcely an affair of hypotheses or Ideas, but a terribly practical question, essentially local and perfectly sensorial.

> — Cover blurb for Tiqqun,
> *Tout a failli, vive le communisme!*

### Rancière's Lesson

If Esposito and Moreiras remit us to the impolitical and infrapolitical horizon of a politics without actuality, does Rancière have a lesson to teach to us about actual politics—perhaps even about the actuality of communist politics? This opening question may seem incongruous for the simple reason that all of Rancière's work is meant to break with the normative claim and hierarchical pretense implicit in the notion that any one person or class of persons would indeed have a lesson to teach to any other person or class. Beginning with the ferocious indictment of his former teacher, who for a long time served as the very model of the master-thinker, in *Althusser's Lesson*, all the way to the no less unforgiving rebuttal of Pierre Bourdieu's sociology as captured in particular in the latter's speech upon entering the Collège de France, a speech significantly titled *Lesson on the Lesson*, the whole pedagogical hierarchy supporting the very idea of teaching someone a lesson—a *leçon de choses* ("show") no less than a *leçon de mots* ("tell")—always presupposes a distance between the teacher and the taught subjects and objects, between knowledge and non-knowledge, or between the knowing master and the ignorant masses: "The master's secret is to know how to recognize the distance between the taught material and the person being instructed, the distance also between learning and understanding."[1] But through a new and special kind of knowledge that is neither strictly philosophical nor purely historical insofar as it seeks to do without all figures of mastery still associated with the disciplines of philosophy and history, we also know that this is the distance most stubbornly and systematically meant to

---

1    Jacques Rancière, *The Ignorant Schoolmaster: Five Lessons in Intellectual Emancipation*, trans. Kristin Ross (Stanford: Stanford University Press, 1991), 5.

be crossed in the writings of Rancière. In fact, in an interview with Peter Hallward, he tries to avoid the description of himself as a teacher and instead compares himself to the well-known image of the eternal student: "I am, in the first instance, a student. I am one of those people who is a perpetual student and whose professional fate, as a consequence, is to teach others."[2] Rancière's professional fate may well have been to turn from student into teacher, but this does not mean that he has a lesson to teach to us, in the old pedagogical sense of the expression.

And yet, at the center of this body of work, we also find the fascinating description of Joseph Jacotot, in *The Ignorant Schoolmaster*, perhaps Rancière's most luminous and in my eyes certainly his most passionate book. Subtitled *Five Lessons in Intellectual Emancipation*, this book also offers an emancipatory reconfiguration of the idea of the lesson itself: a different "lesson on the lesson," not one to be confused with that of Bourdieu. "*La Leçon de l'ignorant*," or "The Ignorant One's Lesson," is how Rancière describes this radical alternative in the second chapter of his book. *La Leçon de Rancière*, or "Rancière's lesson," is how I would translate this, before asking myself—in a pun that has been much exploited of late by both

---

2    Jacques Rancière, "Politics and Aesthetics: An Interview," in *The One or the Other: French Philosophy Today*, special issue edited by Peter Hallward, *Angelaki: Journal of the Theoretical Humanities* 8 (2003): 194. With thanks to my friend Peter Hallward for giving me a copy of the original transcription of this interview, held in Paris, August 29, 2002.

Badiou and Žižek—whether there is more to the expression than the mere rhyme with *La Leçon d'Althusser*. In fact, already in the four chapters of this latter book, as we move from "A Lesson in Orthodoxy," through "A Lesson in Politics" and "A Lesson in Self-criticism," all the way to "A History Lesson," we can see a subtle and profound shift in the very concept of the lesson and its uses. Thus, the implied teacher of the final lesson does not quite seem to be the same as the one responsible for the first. As a matter of fact, it turns out that Rancière is the one who ends up teaching his former teacher a history lesson so as better to unmask both the profound apoliticism hidden behind Althusser's dogmatic lesson in orthodoxy and the revisionism of his botched attempt at self-criticism.

Rancière, however, is no Jacotot. Despite the brilliant use of the free indirect style of speech, his is not exactly the role of the ignorant schoolmaster, nor did he ever have to teach French, as Jacotot did, to the Flemish youth of my native Louvain. Rancière, rather, presents himself anachronistically as one of Jacotot's imaginary long-term students whose professional fate is to teach us a few lessons about the lesson of this ignorant schoolmaster. Jacotot thus serves as a kind of anti-Althusser for Rancière, following the example of Engels' *Anti-Dühring*.

## The Double Operation

The difficulty inherent in the notion of Rancière's lesson is intimately tied to a second difficulty, which comes down to deciding whether he is a philosopher or a historian, an antiphilosopher or an archivist of popular struggles. Here too it must be said that Rancière's work introduces an irreparable disturbance in the fixed demarcation of disciplines with their boundaries between the sayable and the unsayable, the proper and the improper, the legitimate and the illegitimate. Precisely by introducing some play in the interval between various discourses, the aim of this work is always to derail the regimes of thought that would assign certain ways of doing, speaking, and seeing to a stable set of competences, qualities, or properties.

If it is out of the question to think the singularity of Rancière's work in disciplinary terms, perhaps a better approach consists in interrogating his *modus operandi*. I am thinking in particular of the following description, which comes toward the end of *Althusser's Lesson*, when the author by way of conclusion seeks to explain the method he has just followed throughout the book, perhaps even with an eye on a future program of studies:

> I have tried to apply a double operation on an exemplary discourse: I have made an effort to reinsert it in its history, in the system of practical and discursive constraints that make it enunciable. I have sought to surprise its articulations by forcing it to respond to other questions than those of the partners of complacency that it had chosen for itself, by reinscribing its argumentation in those chains of words in which the

necessities of oppression and the hopes of liberation formulated themselves and continue to formulate themselves. Not a refutation, because it serves no point to refute dogmatisms. Rather a mise-en-scène aiming to deregulate the functioning of one of those wise Marxist discourses that occupy our theoretical space in order to make readable the consecration of the existing order in the discourse of the revolution. By doing so I would like simply to echo that which, in the disparity of the struggles and interrogations of our present, seeks to express itself in terms of a newfound liberty.[3]

For Rancière, I would argue, the purpose of thought always lies in following this double procedure: to reinsert (a discourse, a practice, a regime of doing, seeing or speaking into its system of constraints) and to derange (this system of constraints itself). These two operations, of course, stand in a precarious balance to each other, since they are always on the verge of tilting over into the hypostasis of only one of them, according to their corresponding objects or concepts: on one hand, the system of constraints, which results from the act of reinscription, and, on the other, the promise of liberty, which is the principle of derangement and which a second time comes to constrain the previously established

---

3   Jacques Rancière, *La Leçon d'Althusser* (Paris: Gallimard, 1974), 226.

practical and discursive constraints by finding undesirable
or at least unexpected bedfellows for them. In a sense that is
rather close to Foucault, liberty thus responds to the structure of constraints with the surprise of an unpredictable
reinscription, just as the hopes of liberation make themselves heard as soon as the machine of necessity and oppression is ever so slightly displaced or brought to a screeching
halt.

This double operation, moreover, may help us appreciate the force and originality of any mode of thinking whatsoever, including Rancière's own. He himself writes in the
*avant-propos* to *The Philosopher and His Poor* that one of the
presuppositions behind his readings of the philosophers from
Plato to Bourdieu, far from keeping with the habit "not to ask
an author any questions except for those that he had asked
himself," consists precisely in understanding that "the power
of a mode of thinking has to do above all with its capacity to
be displaced, just as the power of a piece of music may derive
from its capacity to be played on different instruments."[4] Is
this not how Rancière himself always approaches the work
of his interlocutors?

---

4    Jacques Rancière, *The Philosopher and His Poor*, ed. and with
an introduction by Andrew Parker, trans. John Drury, Corinne
Oster, and Andrew Parker (Durham: Duke University Press, 2003),
xxviii.

## A Restricted Nominalism

Actually, with regard to this double operation that to this day seems to me to define the work of Rancière, I want to draw attention to the presence of a profound asymmetry in his treatment of art and politics. Indeed, it seems to me that art and politics are not just two domains, two fields, or two territories that otherwise would receive one and the same treatment in Rancière's readings. Rather, we should understand how art and politics lead to two distinct approaches or to two tendencies that are deeply unequal and asymmetrical. Despite the appearance of a strict homology between them, in many ways the two actually appear almost as polar opposites.

Thus, if art is treated according to the vaguely historical order of three regimes of identification (the ethical regime, the representative regime, and the aesthetic regime), without there being any essence "proper" to art in itself, the same does not apply to politics. Especially in *Disagreement*, as I began discussing in the previous chapter, it seems perfectly possible to define what is specific to politics—a specificity that certainly marks a "proper" that, even if it is constitutively "improper" (whence the commonly assumed homology with art, most notably under the aesthetic regime), for this reason is no less universally identifiable or separable as such. Thus, the political triad (archipolitics, parapolitics, and metapolitics), though also historical in appearance insofar as it is originally associated with the successive proper names of

Plato, Aristotle and Marx, does not function in the same way as the three regimes of identification of art (ethical, representational, and aesthetic). Rather, if we stick to the theses of *Disagreement* there exists after all a stable essence or a rational kernel of politics as such, which subsequently would have been covered up, denied, repressed or obscurely designated in the three dominant forms of political philosophy.

The result is an insurmountable *plurality* of regimes to identify art, with the pluralization itself being the effect of *one* historical regime among others, namely, the aesthetic regime, whereas politics enables the establishment of a *unique* kernel of politicity properly speaking that, while never natural, remains so to speak *invariant* throughout history because in the end it is the nonhistorical and apolitical condition of politics itself, namely, that which is hidden in the *different* forms of all hitherto existing political philosophy. Besides, as far as I know, Rancière never calls these three forms of identifying politics "regimes" and we can easily understand why: this is one more sign, or perhaps a symptom, of the asymmetry between art and politics, namely, the profuse invocation of the term "regime" for the first domain and its relative absence from the treatment of the second, for which the term no doubt is too closely tied to the destiny of the form of the political State.

It is worth dwelling for a moment longer on this asymmetry, both to contextualize the question of method and to underscore the singularity of politics (or of its treatment) in comparison to art (and its treatment) in Rancière's work.

Indeed, following the first half of what I have described as his double operation, Rancière has always been admirably consistent in stating that there is no such thing as *the* science, or *the* people, or *the* Marxism with an emphatically used definite article but only at best a variable series of practical and discursive constraints, or, in terms of his more recent vocabulary, a series of regimes of visibility and intelligibility that allow certain modes of doing, saying, and seeing, all the while excluding others. This is what I would call the principle of nominalism at work in Rancière's thought, which could be summed up in the following formula: the universal exists only in the plurality of its particular modes, places, and operations.

Let me recall a few examples of this nominalist tendency in Rancière—a tendency that, though perhaps badly named, he shares with the likes of Althusser and above all Foucault.[5] All these examples are drawn from *Althusser's Lesson* and

---

5  I am thinking not only of Althusser's famous statement according to which Marx would have taught him that "nominalism is the royal road to materialism, in truth it is a road that leads only to itself, and I do not know of any more profound *form* of materialism than nominalism," but also of the captivating analysis of Foucault's nominalism by Etienne Balibar, "Foucault et Marx: L'enjeu du nominalisme," in *Michel Foucault philosophe* (Paris: Seuil, 1989), 54–76. For Althusser's affirmation, see *L'avenir dure longtemps* (Paris: Stock/IMEC, 1992), 243; and compare with Warren Montag's careful analysis, "Althusser's Nominalism: Structure and Singularity (1962–6)," *Rethinking Marxism* 10 (1998): 64–73.

from the extremely useful collection of essays *Les Scènes du peuple*, soon to be translated into English.

First, with regard to Man:

> It is not Man who makes history, but men, that is to say, concrete individuals, those who produce their means of existence, those who fight the battle in the class struggle. Marx goes no further in the critique of Feuerbach.[6]

Then, about science:

> There is no "pure" scientific practice; the latter has its forms of existence in a system of social relationships of which propositions, logical chains, and experiments (on the basis of which *the ideal of science* is constituted) are only elements.[7]

Or again, in a clear rebuttal of Althusser's canonical opposition of science and ideology, neither of which can be understood apart from the modalities of their ongoing differentiation:

> Science does not appear opposite of ideology as its other; it appears in institutions and in forms of

---

6   Rancière, *La Leçon d'Althusser*, 26–7.
7   Ibid., 254 n.

transmission in which the ideological domination of the bourgeoisie manifests itself.[8]

Further, about the category of time:

Time [*Le temps*] does not exist but only several temporalities [*des temps*], each of which is always itself a way of linking a plurality of lines of time, plural forms of temporality.[9]

And, coming closer to the question of politics that sits at the center of our interrogation of Rancière's work, the famous voice of the people:

History as practiced in *Les Révoltes logiques* will have repeated this: there is not one voice of the people. There are shattered, polemical voices, dividing at each time the identity they put on stage.[10]

Only to arrive in the end at the question of Marxism itself:

The Marxism of the camps is neither a vain adornment nor a deviation that would leave untouched the

---

8   Ibid., 250.
9   Jacques Rancière, "Préface: Les gros mots," *Les Scènes du peuple (Les Révoltes logiques, 1975/1985)* (Lyon: Horlieu, 2003), 7.
10   Ibid., 11.

pure essence of Marxism. Sure, but this also means that there is no pure essence of Marxism but there are Marxisms, determinate montages of theoretical and practical schemes of power; it means that there is no fatality to Marxism that would globally account for the forms of subservience produced by certain Marxist powers or justified by certain Marxist discourses.[11]

In sum, not only is there always *a logic to the revolt*, in contrast to the official dogma of Marxism-Leninism according to which the revolt is merely ephemeral spontaneity as long as it is not concentrated and organized into revolutionary discipline thanks to the vanguard party, but there is also always *a revolt among various logics* in Rancière's thought, in contrast to the dogma according to which there only ever exists a single just line, surrounded by deviations. As we read in *Althusser's Lesson*, there exists always a "plurality of conceptualities" or, to use an expression from *Disagreement*, referring to politics in the age of militantism, "a multiplicity of modes and places, from the street to the factory to the university."[12] It is no doubt this taste for the plurality of practices, discourses, and stagings that explains

---

11  Rancière, "La bergère au Goulag," *Les Scènes du peuple*, 314. With regard to this recurrent gesture of nominalistic pluralization, I am tempted to quote the expression of doubt coming from Rancière himself: "One doesn't change the nature of a concept by putting it in the plural. At best one masks it" (*La Leçon d'Althusser*, 261).

12  Rancière, *La Leçon d'Althusser*, 154.

the frequent use of the figure of the "banquet" as the place of the mixed and the confused for Rancière. In addition to the chapter on Plato in *The Philosopher and His Poor* where we read: "The order established by the banquet is the order of mixture. If the city began with the clearcut distribution of useful workers, politics begins with the motley crowd of the unuseful who, coming together into a mass of 'workers,' cater to a new range of needs—from painters and musicians to tutors and chambermaids; from actors and rhapsodists to hairdressers and cooks; from the makers of luxury articles to swineherds and butchers," Rancière gives this motley principle an eloquent formulation in his text on André Glucksmann for *Les Révoltes logiques* reprinted in *Les Scènes du peuple*: "The discourse of revolutionary intellectuals is always a Harlequin dress, sewn together with different logics."[13]

That being said, when it comes to politics, particularly in *Disagreement*, we seem to hit upon a point of exception to this generalized nominalism. Here Rancière all of a sudden exchanges the revolutionary intellectual's Harlequin coat for the monochrome appeal of a dark-grey suit—or perhaps it is still a collarless Mao shirt. Together with *On the Shores of Politics*, which in many ways serves as its perfect companion piece, the approach to politics in *Disagreement* in this sense undoubtedly presents an anomaly in Rancière's work. Here, a

---

13   Rancière, *The Philosopher and His Poor*, 9–10; "La bergère au Goulag," 317.

thinker who has elevated a certain shyness into a methodological principle suddenly seems to experience no reticence whatsoever before the axiomatic enunciation of "politics" (*la politique*) properly speaking and even, albeit only briefly and to a much lesser extent, before the definition of "the political" (*le politique*) as the terrain defined by the encounter between politics and the "police" (*la police*, also incidentally a near-homonym of the Greek *polis*).

Many of these statements, of course, are well known. If I quote a large number of them, it is only to enable the reader to appreciate the "special effect" of the repetitions that, as if in a profane litany, run through the pages of *Disagreement*:

> There is politics—and not just domination—because there is a wrong count of the parts of the whole.[14]

> There is politics when there is a part of those who have no part, a part or party of the poor.[15]

> Politics exists when the natural order of domination is interrupted by the institution of a part of those who have no part.[16]

---

14  Jacques Rancière, *Disagreement: Politics and Philosophy*, trans. Julie Rose (Minneapolis: University of Minnesota Press, 1999), 10.
15  Ibid., 11.
16  Ibid.

Now, politics comes about solely through interruption, the initial twist that institutes politics as the deployment of a wrong or of a fundamental dispute.[17]

Politics exists simply because no social order is based on nature, no divine law regulates human society.[18]

Politics occurs because, or when, the natural order of the shepherd kings, the warlords, or property owners is interrupted by a freedom that crops up and makes real the ultimate equality on which any social order rests.[19]

There is politics when the supposedly natural logic of domination is crossed by the effect of this equality. This means that politics doesn't always happen—it actually happens very little or rarely.[20]

Politics occurs when the egalitarian contingency disrupts the natural pecking order as the "freedom" of the people, when this disruption produces a specific mechanism: the dividing of society into parts that are not "true" parts; the setting-up of one part as equal to

---

17   Ibid., 13. Rancière plays with the echoes between *torsion*, here translated as "twist," and *tort*, "wrong."
18   Ibid., 16.
19   Ibid.
20   Ibid., 17 (the English translation skips the first sentence in this quotation).

the whole in the name of a "property" that is not its own, and of a "common" that is the community of a dispute.[21]

Politics exists because those who have no right to be counted as speaking beings make themselves of some account, setting up a community by the fact of placing in common a wrong that is nothing more than this very confrontation, the contradiction of two worlds in a single world: the world where they are and the world where they are not, the world where there is something "between" them and those who do not acknowledge them as speaking beings who count and the world where there is nothing.[22]

Politics occurs by reason of a single universal that takes the specific shape of wrong. Wrong institutes a singular universal, a polemical universal, by tying the presentation of equality, as the part of those who have no part, to the conflict between parts of society.[23]

To recapitulate: politics exists wherever the count of parts and parties of society is disturbed by the inscription of a part of those who have no part.[24]

---

21  Ibid., 18.
22  Ibid., 27.
23  Ibid., 39.
24  Ibid., 123.

In addition to the formulae "there is politics because ..." or "politics exists when ..." the reader can also find another recurrent formulation, "politics begins when ..." though this time the formula is less prone to incantatory effects:

> Politics begins precisely when one stops balancing profits and losses and worries instead about distributing *common* lots and evening out communal shares and entitlements to these shares, the *axiai* entitling one to community.[25]

> Politics begins with a major wrong: the gap created by the empty freedom of the people between the arithmetical order and the geometric order.[26]

> The only city is a political one and politics begins with egalitarian contingency.[27]

> The reign of the "humanitarian" begins, on the other hand, wherever human rights are cut off from any capacity for polemical particularization of their universality, where the egalitarian phrase ceases to be

---

25   Ibid., 5 (translation modified to keep "politics" for *la politique*).
26   Ibid., 19.
27   Ibid., 71.

phrased, interpreted in the arguing of a wrong that manifests its litigious effectiveness.[28]

Of course, *Disagreement*, like almost all of Rancière's books according to the author himself, is also a conjunctural intervention, tied in this particular case to the dominant model of consensus from which he seeks to free himself without for this reason lapsing into the other extreme, which would posit the absolute anteriority of the unrepresentable, or of the sublime. To maintain himself "equally far removed from the consensual discussion and from the absolute wrong," such is the task of the logic of disagreement according to the blurb on the back cover of Rancière's *Disagreement*. Or, to put some name tags on this: the task is to maintain himself at an equal remove from Jürgen Habermas and from Jean-François Lyotard. Only to note that this operation is another constant in Rancière's work, namely, his tendency to occupy the space or nonplace in between two positions according to the well-known formula *neither/nor*, which at the same time entails a categorical refusal of the *either/or* as a false dilemma. "Struggle on two fronts," people used to say not so long ago: neither left-wing nor right-wing opportunism; neither anarchic adventurism nor orthodox dogmatism; or again, a few years later: neither apocalyptic nor integrated. It is within the structure of such a struggle on two fronts that I would situate the peculiar antinominalist use of the category of politics in *Disagreement*.

---

28   Ibid., 125–6.

In criticizing this use of politics or the political, my aim is not to chasten the philosopher in the name of some knee-jerk form of anti-essentialism. Nor am I taking issue with the axiomatic allure of the formalization per se. I merely wish to interrogate some of the consequences, for politics as a thought-practice, of the style "there is politics when . . ." or "politics begins there where . . ." Besides, this last formula recalls another of Rancière's favorites, the one that precisely opens the first chapter of *Disagreement* under the title "The Beginning of Politics": "Let's begin at the beginning."[29] My sole question concerns the exact status of this "there is" or of this "beginning": Is it a theoretical principle or a historical fact? A logical presupposition or a chronological start? A transcendental condition of possibility or a haphazard empirical event? Or, and this would be a tempting last possibility, can we hold on to all these interpretations at once in a singular mixture—another banquet, this time methodological—that could very well be constitutive of the style of thinking of all of Rancière's work?

---

29   Ibid., 1. The expression is actually quite common throughout Rancière's work. See also "L'éthique de la sociologie," in *Les Scènes du peuple*: "Let us begin from the beginning: the dissimulation of politics that Durkheim produced to ensure the acceptance of sociology in the university" (355). Or the beginning of *The Philosopher and His Poor*: "In the beginning there would be four persons" (3). Or, again, more recently: "Let us start from the beginning," in Jacques Rancière, *The Future of the Image*, trans. Gregory Elliott (London: Verso, 2007), 1.

## Politics and the Police

I want to tackle this larger question by interrogating just one of the possible effects of Rancière's restricted nominalism, namely the risk of falling into what the author himself, in *Althusser's Lesson*—that is to say, almost twenty years before the reemergence of the same expression in Badiou's meditation "The Intervention" from *Being and Event*—calls "speculative leftism."[30] Indeed, I fear that the definition of politics in *Disagreement*, most notably when formulated from within the opposition of politics and the police, is all too easily assimilated to the leftist scheme that in earlier times used to oppose, for example, the plebes and the State. This risk is all the more striking, and the objection may seem all the more unfair, insofar as it has been Rancière himself who has given us many of the tools necessary to dismantle the narrow schematism and conceptual reductionism of this very presentation.

Let us look at a last series of quotations, this time taken from "La bergère au Goulag," the lengthy review of Glucksmann's *La cuisinière et le mangeur d'hommes* reprinted in *Les Scènes du peuple*. According to Rancière, this important book by one of the foremost New Philosophers in France proposes only a "purified" version of contradictions, without respecting their dialectical complexity: "The whole book is an organized effect based on a purification of the

---

30   See my discussion above in the Introduction.

contradiction: on one hand, power and the discourse of the masters (philosophers, kings, Jacobins, Marxists . . .) organized according to the rules of state constraint; on the other, the class of nonpower, the plebs, pure generosity, whose discourse expresses the sole desire of not being oppressed."[31] It belongs to Lenin, among the first, to have denounced the false dialectic of this kind of dualist opposition: "'On the one hand, and on the other,' 'the one and the other.' That is eclecticism. Dialectics requires an all-round consideration of relationships in their concrete development but not a patchwork of bits and pieces."[32] Rancière, for his part, proposes several refutations of this false image of the dialectical contradiction:

> Everything would be simple for sure if we could move in this purged contradiction: the revolt of the "wretched of the earth" against a state power represented by social-fascism. But reality is not like this.[33]

> Reality: that there is no principle of subversion drawn from anything other than practices of resistance, that there is nothing beyond the distribution [*partage*] of servitude and of refusal, which is always and for everyone renewed; no movement of history, no ruse of

---

31   Rancière, "La bergère au Goulag," 317–18.
32   V. I. Lenin, "Dialectics and Eclecticism," *Collected Works*, vol. 32 (Moscow: Progress, 1960), 93.
33   Rancière, "La bergère au Goulag," 322.

reason that can ever *justify* oppression and servitude. Myth: the incarnation of this division [*partage*] in the pure opposition of power and the plebes.[34]

The plebs: those excluded from power? But who is ever totally excluded from power? . . . Such a division [*partage*] is possible only at the expense of simply identifying the reality of power with the visible face of the state apparatus.[35]

Nowhere the conflict of power and nonpower plays itself out. Everywhere the task of the state stumbles upon, not the plebs but classes, corporations, collectives and their rules, their forms of recognition and democracy, but also of exclusion and even oppression.[36]

The discourses from below are still discourses of power and it is from the point of view of this reality that we can think the position of a discourse such as Marx's.[37]

Here we are back at the heart of the matter. Once he arrives at the core of his critique of the discourse of the New Philosophers exemplified by Glucksmann, Rancière

---

34   Ibid., 329.
35   Ibid., 318.
36   Ibid., 319.
37   Ibid.

himself indeed proposes a lesson, after all, in which we must again and always hear echoes from Marx's thought: "Lesson perhaps of this confrontation: that there is never any pure discourse of proletarian power nor any pure discourse of its nonpower; neither consciousness from below that would suffice for itself nor science that could be imported . . . The force of Marx's thought—but perhaps also its untenable character—resides no doubt in the effort to hold these contradictions together, stripped bare since then in the police fictions of proletarian powers or the pastoral dreams of plebeian nonpower."[38] Instead of purifying the contradiction, the task would thus lie in maintaining its open-endedness, even if this may turn out to be untenable. The lesson to be learned lies in defining the knot between power and resistance, between power and nonpower, between the State and the plebes. Otherwise, if this knot is allowed to unravel into stark dualisms, we would quickly fall back into the trap of speculative leftism, according to a Manichaean scheme that is as radical and profound as it is inoperative.

I wonder, though, to what extent the author of *Disagreement* himself might have forgotten this lesson. Does not the opposition between the police, as ordered partitioning of the sensible, and politics, as inscription of a part of those who have no part, come dangerously close to the "purification" of the contradiction that would be characteristic of speculative leftism? Whether or not this is due to its assertive

---

38    Ibid.

style or to its tactical goals, *Disagreement* remains to a large extent caught in the nets of a contradiction stripped down to the *police fictions* of the existing distribution of power, on the one hand, and the *political dreams* of the part of those who have no part, on the other.

Rancière's essay on Glucksmann is not the only conceptual tool at our disposal to reconstruct what I would call a "critique of pure leftist reason." Even within the logic of *Disagreement*, we can admittedly find arguments that enable us to pinpoint and criticize this leftist reading. First of all, the police is never identified with the state apparatus pure and simple. Second, the police is not the night in which all cows are black: "There is a worse and a better police."[39] Finally, the antagonism between politics and the police, as two heterogeneous logics of being-together, is far from being the last word in the book. Rancière insists at least as much on the need of a bind, an encounter, or an intertwining of both logics, without which politics would not have any effect whatsoever on the original situation. In other words, even if we wanted to hold on to these two terms, which the author is the first to problematize, there must be a reciprocal inscription, or at the very least the verification of a retroactive effect of politics back upon the police. "We should not forget that if politics implements a logic entirely heterogeneous to that of the police, it is always bound up with the latter," writes Rancière. "Politics acts on the police.

---

39    Rancière, *Disagreement*, 30–1.

It acts in the places and with the words that are common to both, even if it means reshaping those places and changing the status of those words."[40] In fact, to posit the radical exteriority and strangeness of these two logics—the political-egalitarian and the social-policing—without ever letting them tie a knot that would not be treacherous or illusory, would have been the gravest limitation, for example, of the endeavor associated with Jacotot.

A fundamental ambiguity nonetheless continues to run through the pages of *Disagreement*. The book may very well refuse the purely external opposition between politics and the police that would bring it closer to speculative leftism. One thus continues to divide into two for this former Maoist—whence the insistence on the motifs of the originary scission and the torsion; whence, also, the recourse to the double meaning of *partage*, as both community and separation, both sharing and dividing. This would mean that, in the final instance, what matters is to hold the untenable, to measure the common between two incommensurables, to think together the *rapport* and the *non-rapport*. Consider, for instance, the way in which Rancière, in a familiar recourse to his nominalist principle, refuses to oppose the pure ideality of doctrine and the impure mixture of reality: "There is not on the one hand the ideal people of the founding texts and, on the other, the real people of the workshops and suburbs. There is a place where the power of the people is inscribed

---

40    Ibid., 32–3.

and places where this power is reputedly ineffective."[41] To think politics, then, always entails having to follow these types of retroactive and twisted effects—or, as the case may be, the absence thereof.

All this may seem perfectly compatible with the nominalist principle mentioned above. Instead of thinking in purified oppositions such as *the* people against *the* power structures, the task would be to study the places where one paradoxically divides and inscribes itself in the other, as well as to investigate the historical modalities of this inscription. But this does not take away the fact that in other fragments of the same book, precisely with regard to politics and the police as two logics of being-together, it is once again the purification, not to say the Manichaeism, that takes priority over and above the sharing and the intertwining: "On the one hand, there is the logic that simply counts the lots of the parties, that distributes the bodies within the space of their visibility or their invisibility and aligns ways of being, ways of doing, and ways of saying appropriate to each. And there is the other logic, the logic that disrupts this harmony through the mere fact of achieving the contingency of the equality, neither arithmetical nor geometric, of any speaking beings whatsoever."[42] Clearly, we are far from being done with the temptations of a certain speculative leftism and its dual oppositions. Perhaps this is the price to be paid if we

---

41  Ibid., 88.
42  Ibid., 28.

wish to maintain a polemical edge in the discussion against the democratic idyll of Habermas's "consensus" and the absolute wrong of Lyotard's "*differend*", an idyll and a wrong whose noisy celebrations and sublime demonstrations, as I mentioned earlier, *Disagreement* seeks to interrupt with the affirmation of politics as an invariant process of emancipatory thought-practice.

## Legends of Leftism

In any case, given the extent of Rancière's long-term engagement with the history of the Left, from *Althusser's Lesson* to *Hatred of Democracy*, it would be an act of bad faith to remain at the level of a mere critique of speculative leftism. Far more important is something along the lines of what Jacques Rancière himself, in an article co-authored with Danielle Rancière, calls "the traversing of leftism," historically and genealogically speaking, so as to come to terms with the "legend of the philosophers."

What Jacques and Danielle Rancière suggest in their article for *Les Révoltes logiques* is that the New Philosophers should not be allowed to define the stakes for contemporary thinking except in the extent to which they provoke an "occultation of the militant history" of May '68 and its long aftermath in the 1970s. It is this "occultation" or "liquidation" of history that the authors propose to deactivate by trying to learn a few lessons in the history of politics:

The stakes for us lie in this occultation of the militant history that the discourse on the Gulag has produced: occultation of the conjunction of student and popular struggles, of the encounter of militant intellectuals and the masses, attempts to throw into doubt the mechanism of representation: instead the figure of a *plebs* appears whom the intellectual represents just as yesterday he represented the proletariat, but in a way that precisely denies representation, the plebs means both and at the same time all the positivity of suffering and popular laughter and the part of refusal, of negativity, that each carries with them, realizing the immediate unity of the intellectual and the people; liquidation by simple denial of the objectives and aspirations of the struggles as well as of the problems they came across . . .[43]

Now, for the more recent era, could we not hope for a historical and conceptual analysis similar to the one Danielle and Jacques Rancière present in "La légende des philosophes"? Here I only express my desire that one day we will be able to read the "legend," now also in the positive sense of what is truly "to be read," concerning the long and sinuous trajectory that leads from *The Nights of Labor* to *Les Révoltes logiques*

---

43  Rancière (with Danielle Rancière), "La légende des philosophes. Les intellectuels et la traversée du gauchisme," *Les Scènes du peuple*, 307–8.

all the way to *Disagreement*. However, such a labor of theoretical and historical apprenticeship, which by and large still
remains to be accomplished for the post-leftist age, also poses
a problem of a methodological and philosophical nature. As I
suggested before, this problem concerns the exact status of the
"there is," the status also of the "beginning" and of the "end,"
whether in art or in politics, such as they are captured—not
without considerable scandal—inside philosophy.

This problem regarding the relation between politics
or art and the historicity of their concepts and practices is
certainly not unique to Rancière's work, and it seems to me
at least an equally burning issue for someone like Badiou.
This also means that in their mutual attacks, the one by
Badiou in *Metapolitics* against Rancière's "apoliticism," and
the one by Rancière in *Aesthetics and Its Discontents* against
Badiou's modernist "aestheticism," what remains hidden or
unsaid concerns precisely the other pole of the debate, insofar as art or the aesthetic regime for Rancière and politics
for Badiou, respectively, are the conditions of truth, or the
regimes of thinking, for which each has proven himself capable of setting up a new configuration of historicity, otherwise
absent or at least insufficiently elaborated on the opposite
side of the polemical chiasmus between the two.[44]

44 See Alain Badiou, *Metapolitics*, trans. Jason Barker
(London: Verso, 2005), 107–23; Jacques Rancière, *Aesthetics and
Its Discontents*, trans. Steven Corcoran (Cambridge: Polity, 2009),
63–87.

With respect to art and aesthetics, I would like to give a brief example of this new configuration and of the tasks it imposes on us by referring to the case of Mallarmé. The principal task in this regard consists in coming to an understanding of the double valence of Mallarmé's case, not only as a poet-thinker of the event in and of itself, but also and at the same time as a groundbreaking innovator within French post-romantic poetry.

For Badiou, the first half of this reading seems to take away much of the interest of the second half. "Mallarmé is a thinker of the event-drama," Badiou writes in *Being and Event*. He explains: "A cast of dice joins the emblem of chance to that of necessity, the erratic multiple of the event to the legible retroaction of the count. The event in question in *A Cast of Dice* . . . is therefore that of the production of an absolute symbol of the event. The stakes of casting dice 'from the bottom of a shipwreck' are those of making an event out of the thought of the event."[45] However, if it is also a matter of understanding the link between this poetry-thought of the event-like nature of the event, on the one hand, and the function of this poetry as an event among others in the history of modern post-Hugolian poetry, on the other, it must be said that readers will find very little information about this link if they limit their search to *Being and Event*.

---

45  Alain Badiou, *Being and Event*, trans. Oliver Feltham (London: Continuum, 2005), 191 and 193.

By contrast, it is the second half of the question that receives much greater attention in Rancière's brilliant short book on Mallarmé. The latter remains without a doubt the great poet of the event-like nature of the event, emblematized by the sirens: "Mallarmé transforms them into emblems of the poem itself, power of a song that is capable both of making itself heard and of transforming itself into silence."[46] But we should immediately add that according to this reading, the event-like nature of the poem is inseparable from the equally singular relation it establishes with the place and time of its appearance: "The poem escapes the abyss that awaits it because it modifies the very mode of fiction, substituting the song of a vanishing siren for the great epic of Ulysses. What the siren metaphorizes, what the poem renders effective, then, is precisely the event and the calculated risk of the poem in an era and a 'mental environment' that are not yet ready to welcome it."[47] Rancière understands these two aspects—the event and its relation to an era and an environment not yet ready for it—as part of one and the same question.

Based on indications such as these, we can begin to see the consequences of an important theoretical and methodological decision that is equally applicable to the domain of politics. I mean the decision to understand the value of affirming the "there is" of Mallarméan poetry, like that of the "there is" in

---

46   Jacques Rancière, *Mallarmé. La politique de la sirène* (Paris: Hachette, 1996), 24.
47   Ibid., 25.

the case of politics, as being inseparably structural *and* evental, transcendental *and* historical. Each time there is an event, in politics perhaps no less than in poetry, we witness a breakdown of principle that at the same time allows a reconstruction of its links with history. As in the double game of liberty and constraints, one thing certainly does not exclude but rather presupposes the other. Otherwise, in the absence of such an articulation, which I would gladly call "dialectical" in a new and perhaps untimely sense, we would fall back once again on *either* the flights of fancy of unconstrained liberty *or* the inevitability of practical and discursive constraints, which would lead us straight into the scheme of speculative leftism all over again.

When it comes to politics, however, it is Badiou, paradoxically, who in his recent work has contributed more elements to reconstitute the links between history and politics than Rancière. I am thinking in particular of the talks on the Paris Commune and on the Chinese Cultural Revolution, both strongly marked by the category of the "historical mode of politics," proposed by Lazarus in his book *Anthropologie du nom*.[48] Such a history of different "modes" of doing politics

48    Alain Badiou, *La Révolution culturelle: La dernière révolution?* (Paris: Les Conférences du Rouge-Gorge, 2002) and *La Commune de Paris: Une déclaration politique sur la politique* (Paris: Les Conférences du Rouge-Gorge, 2003). Both conferences have now been translated as Part Three, "Historicity of Politics: Lessons of Two Revolutions," in Alain Badiou, *Polemics*, trans. Steve Corcoran (London: Verso, 2006), 257–328. For my own translation of the first conference as well as a wider bibliography related to Badiou's Maoist inflection

would evidently be hard to come by if we limited ourselves to the axiomatic theses of *Disagreement*. In this latter book, there certainly are "ages" or "eras" such as "the Marxist age" or "the nihilist age," just as the article written with Danielle for *Les Révoltes logiques* speaks of "the post-leftist age," but in the final instance, history's role seems limited to determining the successive eras of the covering-up of an invariant form of politics, to which the book with the utmost rigor seeks to restitute the "improper property" that is also "the ultimate secret of any social order," namely, "the pure and simple equality of anyone and everyone," which serves as "the basis and original gulf of the community order."[49]

Earlier, I mentioned Rancière's tactic of situating himself in the space or nonplace in between two previously given extremes. For *Althusser's Lesson*, it was a matter of keeping the sharp edge of his master's voice while falling *neither* into pure "theoreticism" *nor* into "cultural gossip."[50] Similarly, for *Disagreement*, it is a question of being *neither* on the side of communicative reason *nor* on the side of sublime unrepresentability; of falling for *neither* the ready-to-wear sociologism *nor* the hyperbole of the pure event. Now, even if the place of

---

of the relation between politics and history, see the special issue on "Badiou and Cultural Revolution," *positions: east asia culture critique* 13.3 (2005), that includes my contribution "Post-Maoism: Badiou and Politics" (576–634); and Chapter 3, "One Divides into Two," in my *Badiou and Politics* (Durham: Duke University Press, 2011).

49    Rancière, *Disagreement*, 79.
50    Rancière, *La Leçon d'Althusser*, 205.

the missing "third," as in the "third people" between the police and politics, is a nonplace, in order for this "third way" to be tenable it seems to me that the question of the historicity of politics and thought can no longer be postponed. Thus, we must come to understand what it means to think today under the condition of certain transformations in politics or in art. Not only: What does it mean to think in the present of our actuality? But also and above all: What does it mean to think in the present under the condition of certain events from the past, whether in the long or in the short run?[51]

---

51  The figure who best sums up the stakes of this question of course is Michel Foucault. For a long time the very model of work for Rancière, Foucault is also mentioned in "La légende des philosophes" as one of the intellectuals responsible, perhaps unwittingly, for the "liquidation" of militant history in France. "If, among the thinkers of my generation, there was one I was quite close to at one point, it was Foucault. Something of Foucault's archaeological project—the will to think the conditions of possibility of such and such a form of statement or such and such an object's constitution— has stuck with me," Rancière says in his interview with Hallward ("Politics and Aesthetics: An Interview," 209), but after the New Philosophers this influence may seem suspicious: "Now, it is first of all Foucault's discourse and intervention that serve as support today for the new magisterial and prophetic figures of the intellectual: it is as application of a general theory of knowledge/power that the analysis of the Soviet concentrationary system as accomplishment of the knowledge of master-thinkers presents itself. And it is similarly based on Foucault's analyses that others prophesize the coming of the Angel, the cultural revolution freed by the vanishing of the old knowledge of Man or the barbarism of a power coextensive with the social order" (Rancière, "La légende des philosophes," 300–1).

The risk involved in giving too quick an answer to these questions should be clear enough: the radical historicity of politics and art would be reduced to mere historicism, the event would be realigned with the system of constraints that made it possible, and the novelty of the disruption would end up getting diluted in the proverbial water under the bridge. And yet, it is possible that the price to be paid for not taking these questions into account is even higher: a radicalism pivoting on its own emptiness, a thinking of the pure "there is" of art and politics cut off from any inscription in a specific place and time and according to specific historical modes, and, finally, the relapse into the false appeal of a certain speculative leftism that our age—the nihilist age of the ethical turn and postpolitics—had flattered itself for having been able to do without.

## The Inactuality of Communism?

Directly responding to some of my criticisms, Rancière has recently admitted that his treatment of art and politics is indeed asymmetrical, as discussed above: "I have insisted on the historicity of the regimes of art, while my discussion of politics often tended to skip over centuries and societies, from Plato to the latest social movements or the latest statements on the return or the end of politics." He quickly goes on to deny, though, that this asymmetry would in any way lead to a dismissal of the historicity of politics or to an ontologization of its founding categories: "But this does not mean that I dismiss the existence of historical forms of politics, as Bruno Bosteels suspects."[52] All that Rancière seems prepared to offer to help us overcome this suspicion, however, amounts to an abstract statement of principles followed by a repetition of the now-familiar scheme of an invariable kernel of politics covered up by the three figures of political philosophy:

There is a history of the political, which is a history of the forms of confrontation—and also the forms of confusion—between politics and the police. Politics does not come out of the blue. It is articulated with a certain form of the police order, which means a certain balance of the possibilities and impossibilities that this order defines. Nor does politics ever go alone. A historical form of politics is always more or less entangled with forms of archi-politics, para-politics, or meta-politics, as I defined them in *Disagreement*.[53]

---

52   Jacques Rancière, "Afterword. The Method of Equality: An Answer to Some Questions," in Gabriel Rockhill and Philip Watts, eds., *Jacques Rancière: History, Politics, Aesthetics* (Durham: Duke University Press, 2009), 287.

53   Ibid. In an earlier version of this rebuttal, Rancière also insists on the conjunctural, tactical or strategic nature of his mode of arguing in *Disagreement*: "I underscored this in my answer to Bruno Bosteels: the commentary on Plato and Aristotle is no less actual, no less engaged with the present political issues than the historical works or the polemical articles of *Les Révoltes logiques*.

More broadly speaking, Rancière responds to this charge of ahistoricism by insisting on the political efficacy of a certain untimeliness. His proposed method of studying the politics of equality would thus counteract the relativism inherent in traditional historiography, in which each subject or event is retrofitted into its proper time and place: "This is why the method of equality must implement, at the same time, a principle of historicization and a principle of untimeliness, a principle of contextualization and a principle of de-contextualization."[54] And yet, while this critique of historicism is quite forceful, I also wonder whether the alternative principle of untimeliness, when applied to the politics of communism, does not risk privileging once again inactuality

---

To come back to the 'origins' of 'political philosophy' is one way of answering to a context marked by the practices of consensus and the simultaneous and complicit theorizations of the 'return' and 'end' of politics,'" he writes, before proposing an eloquent articulation of history and the untimely: "Time, here understood as a form of historicizing and periodizing, appears once more as the operator that is indissociably conceptual and sensory, a priori and de facto, which serves to put the condition under condition. The question 'What is politics?' in *Disagreement* is then a way of unraveling the link between the condition and its condition, different from the one that follows the spiral of the 'night' of labor but equivalent in its aim." See Jacques Rancière, "La méthode de l'égalité," in Laurence Cornu and Patrice Vermeren, eds., *La Philosophie déplacée: Autour de Jacques Rancière* (Lyon: Horlieu, 2006), 520–1.

54   Rancière, "Afterword. The Method of Equality: An Answer to Some Questions," 282.

over actuality, whereby we would lapse back into the kind of speculative leftism associated with the ontological turn in contemporary political philosophy.

Rancière is indeed wary of the claim that communism would somehow already be actual and immanent within the current conditions of capitalist production: "The syntagm of the 'actuality of communism' means that communism is not only desirable—as a response to the violence, injustice or irrationality of capitalism—but that, in a certain sense, it already exists. Communism's actuality is not only a task; it is also a process."[55] Today, he adds, this view typically finds support in arguments regarding the sensory community of the multitude's increasingly immaterial, collective, and inseparable forms of labor. For Rancière, however, no such relations of reversibility or transitivity exist between the regimes of capitalist and communist production. "For this reason, it pays to turn the problem around and to start out from the *inactuality* of communism," he suggests, alluding to the Nietzschean notion of the inactual as untimely or intempestive. Rancière explains:

> To be *intempestive* means at once that you do and do not belong to a time, just as to be *a-topian* means that

---

55 Jacques Rancière, "Communism: From Actuality to Inactuality," in *Dissensus: On Politics and Aesthetics*, ed. and trans. Steve Corcoran (London: Continuum, 2010), 76.

you do and do not belong to a place. Being intempestive and a-topian communists means being thinkers and actors of the unconditional equality of anybody and everybody, but this can only happen in a world in which communism has no actuality bar the network framed by our communistic thoughts and actions themselves. There is no such thing as an "objective" communism already at work in the forms of capitalist production or able to be anticipated in the logic of capitalism.[56]

Far from enabling the actualization of communism in a straightforward manner, we would thus always have to pass through the detour of a prior critique of the notion of actuality itself. "The 'actuality' of communism, in fact, is the actuality of its critique," adds Rancière. "It is the actuality of the critique of the very notion of actuality insofar as the latter presumes that capitalism contains an inherent communist power. The idea of communism cannot and has not escaped the quandary that Marx wanted to sweep aside: communism can be a process or a programme but not both."[57] And yet, does this defense of the inactuality of communism not simply push the question ahead to the next level of having to decide when and where the element of the inactual as such has an emancipatory bearing on our actuality? Does this not

---

56   Ibid., 82.
57   Ibid., 83

force us to go in search of the act or the enactment of this intempestive and a-topian communism? These are the questions that I propose to answer in the next chapter by turning to the work of Slavoj Žižek.

# 4

## *In Search of the Act*

The one available act, forever and alone, is to understand the relations, in the meantime, few or many;
according to some interior state that one wishes to
extend, in order to simplify the world.

— Stéphane Mallarmé, *Divagations*

The awareness that the power of a proper act is to
retroactively create its own conditions of possibility
should not make us afraid to embrace what, prior to
the act, appears as impossible. Only in this way will our
act touch the real.

— Slavoj Žižek, Foreword to Molly Anne
Rothenberg, *The Excessive Subject*

### Žižek for Dummies

If they were honest, most readers of Žižek's work would no
doubt confess to having indulged in any or all of the typical
charges leveled against him on the grounds that he publishes
too much, that he publishes too much of the same argument
over and over again, or that his argument is too much indebted
to the legacy of a certain dogmatic Hegelo-Lacanianism.

What these criticisms with their ugly mixture of fascination and repulsion fail to recognize, though, is the extent to which the so-called giant of Ljubljana is actually his own best critic. Being the quintessential theorist of the role of too-muchness in the libidinal economy of late capitalism, not only does he lay the groundwork for an analysis of the attacks against him that all share this feature, but the harshness of these attacks also finds a striking counterpart in the way Žižek, too, frequently takes aggressive stabs at "standard" arguments for multiculturalism and New Age obscurantism, or at "stereotypical" deconstructionist misunderstandings of Hegel or Lacan. Aimed at vague generic opponents whose names are mentioned only rarely, if at all, perhaps with the not-so-honorable exceptions of Derrida (or some stand-in of Derrideanism such as Rodolphe Gasché) and Laclau (or disciples of his such as Yannis Stavrakakis), these rebuttals are usually introduced by the rhetorical catchphrase "The crucial point not to be missed here is . . ." Aside from just taking perverse pleasure in them, however, perhaps we have yet to pick up on all the implications of the fact that these cheap potshots at the eclectic poststructuralist-deconstructionist-respect-for-the-other-multiculturalist consensus of today can also be read as ongoing and barely disguised self-criticisms, or as criticisms of the way in which Žižek feels his work has been misread, or still risks being misread, for example, in Anglo-American cultural studies.

Much of Žižek's work in this sense offers a sustained self-criticism, if not a self-analysis, in which many of those opponents who are said to represent either simplistic versions or standard misinterpretations of the truly Hegelian dialectic or properly Lacanian psychoanalysis, on closer inspection turn out to offer a portrait of the author at an earlier stage of his thinking. In fact, the same reason that explains why for Žižek there is actually no such thing as self-analysis, namely, the impossibility of a discourse not mediated through some third, may also help us gain insight into his repeated tactic of bouncing off possible self-criticisms from the work of others with whom he openly enters into a polemical dialogue. When we as readers are left to wonder who could possibly be the total idiot responsible for this or that blatant misunderstanding of a crucial point in Hegel or Lacan, the key methodological trick consists in transposing this idiocy first onto ourselves and then onto the author: "The idiot for whom I attempt to formulate a theoretical point as clearly as possible is ultimately myself."[1] There is thus nothing offensive about the claim that Žižek is our much-needed global village idiot. Quite the contrary, when I once made this claim at a book presentation of *The Puppet and the Dwarf: The Perverse Core of Christianity*, I took it to be the highest form of praise. What Žižek places at the center of the discussion about philosophy, politics, and psychoanalysis is precisely an ineradicable kernel of idiotic egotistical enjoyment that we all share in common. Idiotic, then, is the unique pathological stain that sticks to any universal claim to truth;

---

1    Žižek, *The Metastases of Enjoyment: Six Essays on Woman and Causality* (London: Verso, 1994), 175.

it is the kernel that keeps such a claim from ever achieving complete consistency in a formal structure. As Žižek writes in *The Indivisible Remainder*: "We are dealing here with the inherent constituent of the emergence of a formal structure—in short, with the *condition of the structure's consistency*: but for this exclusive base in a One—but for this partiality and distortion sustained by a minimum of Egotism—the structure disintegrates, loses its consistency in the dispersed plurality."[2] Only beautiful souls would maintain that the idiot is always the dummy sitting next to them whereas in actual fact, far from placing us at a safe distance from the toxicity of our neighbor, the line of demarcation between truth and idiocy is part of the truth itself—at least when seen through the prism of Žižek's Lacano-Hegelianism.

For instance, to the question *Did Somebody Say Totalitarianism?* as in the eponymous book subtitled *Five Interventions in the (Mis)Use of a Notion*, the answer should be: Yes, of course, it was Žižek himself who (mis)used this notion, especially in *The Sublime Object of Ideology*, the book that launched his career in the English-speaking world and that derived much of its impetus from the deployment of a psychoanalytical theory of "totalitarian" ideology and the hopes for a "radical democratic" alternative! But this is precisely the kind of thinking—the defense of democracy as the only political regime capable of assuming the empty

2    Slavoj Žižek, *The Indivisible Remainder: An Essay on Schelling and Related Matters* (London, Verso, 1996), 76.

place of power as opposed to the totalitarian filling of this void in the name of the people, race, or the charismatic leader—against which Žižek now increasingly proposes a return to the communist hypothesis, whereas the politics of radical democracy, which he himself at one point adopted via Laclau from a strong Lacanian rereading of Claude Lefort, is then seen as an overly limited version of social democracy. As he confesses about *The Sublime Object of Ideology* in the new foreword to *For They Know Not What They Do*: "It took me years of hard work to identify and liquidate these dangerous residues of bourgeois ideology clearly at three interconnected levels: the clarification of my Lacanian reading of Hegel; the elaboration of the concept of act; and a palpable critical distance towards the very notion of democracy."[3]

In several endnotes to other recent books of his, as if openly to invite a retroactive interpretation of his entire work along the same lines, Žižek draws attention to further elements of self-criticism. "At least concerning cultural studies," he writes in a note to *The Ticklish Subject*, "I speak here not from a condescending position of a critic assuming the safe position of an external observer, but as someone who has participated in cultural studies—I, as it were, 'include myself out.'"[4] Similarly, the small volume *On Belief* is described in

3   Slavoj Žižek, "Foreword to the Second Edition: Enjoyment Within the Limits of Reason Alone," *For They Know Not What They Do: Enjoyment as Political Factor* (London: Verso, 2002), xi.

4   Slavoj Žižek, *The Ticklish Subject: The Absent Centre of Political Ontology* (London: Verso, 1999), 396.

another note as a reflection that "prolongs, often in a self-critical mood, the analyses of my *The Fragile Absolute: Or, Why Is the Christian Legacy Worth Fighting For.*"[5] Following the logic behind brief remarks such as these, then, I want to explore one instance of self-criticism in particular, namely, the dramatic redefinition of the Lacanian notion of the act that appears to take place throughout much of Žižek's work.

Lacan himself, of course, had attempted to formalize this notion in his seminar on *The Psychoanalytical Act*, which began in 1967 at the École normale supérieure in rue d'Ulm, where Lacan had moved upon Althusser's invitation, only to be cut short before the end of the academic year, perhaps quite aptly or symptomatically, by the events of May 1968: "It is well-known that I introduced the psychoanalytical act, and I take it that it was not by accident that the upheaval of May should have prevented me from reaching its end."[6] Žižek's return to this notion of the act, on the other hand, serves primarily to shift our understanding of the concept of the real from that which is impossible to symbolize to that which transforms the very criteria by which what is possible or impossible is defined in the first place. More so than with stages in a linear development, we are dealing here with what I am tempted to call different intonations of the act, in the sense in which Jorge Luis Borges talks about the different

5    Slavoj Žižek, *On Belief* (London: Routledge, 2001), 152.

6    Jacques Lacan, "Radiophonie," *Autres écrits* (Paris: Seuil, 2001), 427.

intonations of the theme of infinity, from Giordano Bruno's exultation to Blaise Pascal's despair: "In that jaded century the absolute space that inspired the hexameters of Lucretius, the absolute space that had been a liberation for Bruno, was a labyrinth and an abyss for Pascal."[7] A similar interpretive principle, according to which perhaps universal history is the history of the diverse intonation of a few metaphors, should be applied to the notion of the act. As Žižek himself writes—again, I would argue, in part self-critically—in *On Belief*: "From 'impossible TO happen' we thus pass to 'the impossible HAPPENS'—this, and not the structural obstacle forever deferring the final resolution, is the most difficult thing to accept: 'We'd forgotten how to be in readiness even for miracles to happen.'"[8] Ultimately, what is at stake in this ongoing redefinition of the act is nothing less than the possibility of a radical political transformation of the existing state of things. This explains why the act proper, which earlier might have seemed part of an agenda of radical democracy that he briefly shared with the likes of Laclau and Mouffe, becomes in Žižek's most recent writings increasingly linked to the actuality of communism.

Like his friend and colleague Alenka Zupančič, moreover, Žižek also claims that there is a close proximity, if not a

---

7   Jorge Luis Borges, "Pascal's Sphere," *Other Inquisitions, 1937–1952*, trans. Ruth L. C. Simms (Austin: University of Texas Press, 1993), 8.
8   Žižek, *On Belief*, 84.

complete interchangeability, between the Lacanian notion of the "act" and the idea of the "event" as elaborated by Badiou in an explicit dialogue with Lacan. This comparison immediately raises a series of secondary questions: What does an act really entail to begin with, whether it is qualified as analytical, ethical or political? How is this similar to, or different from, an event? What do these concepts of act and event have in common? What figures of the subject respond to each of these concepts, if they are to be distinguished at all? Where should we look for examples, or instances, of such acts or events? [9]

Studying the reworking of Lacan's original notion of the act by focusing on the thought of Slavoj Žižek may help us answer some of these questions. As an added bonus, it might also lift some of the burden of common criticisms of this work in favor of a more systematic account of the place and function of Žižek's discourse in contemporary debates regarding

---

9   In recent years, the secondary literature on Žižek's work has grown exponentially at a speed that almost matches the proliferation of primary sources. With regard to the definition of the act, specifically, the most insightful commentaries can be found in Sarah Kay, "Politics, or, The Art of the Impossible," in *Žižek: A Critical Introduction* (Cambridge: Polity, 2003), 128–57; Rex Butler, "What is an Act?" in *Slavoj Žižek: Live Theory* (London: Continuum, 2005), 66–94; Adrian Johnston, *Žižek's Ontology: A Transcendental Materialist Theory of Subjectivity* (Evanston: Northwestern University Press, 2008); and Molly Anne Rothenberg, "Žižek's Political Act," in *The Excessive Subject: A New Theory of Social Change* (Cambridge: Polity, 2010), 153–90.

the fields of psychoanalysis, philosophy, and the actuality of communist politics. After all, there is no actuality without act, nor any communism without an understanding of the conditions of its possible enactment. "Empirically, communism is only possible as the act [*Tat*] of the dominant peoples 'all at once' and simultaneously, which presupposes the universal development of productive forces and the world intercourse bound up with them," Marx and Engels had also written in *The German Ideology*. But this presupposes another, perhaps prior act by which we might once again be able to simplify the world: "Without this, 1) communism could only exist as a local phenomenon; 2) the *forces* of intercourse themselves could not have developed as *universal*, hence unendurable powers: they would have remained home-bred 'conditions' surrounded by superstition; and 3) each extension of intercourse would abolish local communism."[10]

## Traversing the Fantasy

A useful working definition of the act in the early stages of Žižek's work can be found in *The Sublime Object of Ideology*. Even while interpreting the concept from a resolutely political and ideological standpoint, this definition

---

10  Karl Marx and Friedrich Engels, *Die deutsche Ideologie* in *Werke*, vol. 3 (Berlin: Dietz Verlag, 1962), 35; *The German Ideology*, *Collected Works* (New York: International Publishers, 1976), vol. 5, 49.

is also the one that is most strictly in keeping with Lacan's own views as expressed in his unpublished seminar on *The Psychoanalytical Act.*

For Žižek, the act in this first intonation entails above all a radical destitution of the subject, a self-divestiture that immediately coincides with an assumption of the fundamental gap or inconsistency in the symbolic order. This gesture of self-destitution requires that the subject not only traverse his or her fundamental fantasy by somehow coming to grips with the fact that fantasy is merely a scenario that fills out a central void—the gap or fissure that "is" the subject. Beyond the traversing of fantasy, the act that comes at the end of analysis also leaves the subject no other option than to identify with the leftovers of this process of symbolization—to occupy the place of the little piece of the real that sticks out and stands in for the emptiness at the core of the symbolic order itself. According to Lacan, in the analytical situation the role of this piece of the real imbued with idiotic enjoyment, which is the only thing that the act produces as a kind of surplus dropping, is assumed by the analyst at the very point where the analysand breaks through the transferential illusion of the subject who is supposed to know. This readiness to undergo a process of being reduced to a piece of shit is after all what makes the analyst into a modern-day saint.

Žižek himself, however, does not usually speak as an analyst, nor does his experience as an analysand serve him in any formal way to present his work as a kind of didactic analysis. Rather, as a result of the nonclinical place from where he speaks, in these early approximations he almost seems forced to scan the surface of art, politics, and popular culture in search of adequate examples of this momentous apparition of the real that is the act. And it is of course Antigone in the Sophoclean tragedy who, among many other examples, appears as the tragic heroine of the act in this first intonation, in the sense that her uncompromising insistence on the proper burial rites for her brother at the same time reveals the barbaric tautology and terrorizing superego injunction that support the regime of law and order under Creon. Whether we take Antigone or even Lacan himself as an example of the Žižekian act in this first sense, though, for the moment does not matter much. More important to note is how the act transcends the realm of the analytical situation and comes to coincide with the fundamental task in the critique of ideology. The act thus signals a sudden change of perspective, or anamorphosis, whereby what at first appears to be the supreme ideological guarantee of meaningfulness and order abruptly reveals its flipside that consists of the utter nonsense of obscene and idiotic enjoyment. On the part of the subject or critic, this entails a purely formal act of conversion, through which something that previously counted as a subjective failure or impotence all of a sudden can be shown to mark an objective impossibility or fissure of the whole symbolic structure as such. "What a moment ago evoked in us a mixture of fear and respect is now experienced as a rather different mixture of ridiculous imposture and brutal, illegitimate display of force," Žižek further explains in *Tarrying with the Negative*. "It is clear, therefore, how this shift is of a purely symbolic nature: it designates neither a change in social reality (there, the balance of power remains exactly the same) nor a 'psychological' change, but a shift in the symbolic texture which constitutes the social bond."[11]

On one hand, then, the act consists in the subject's assuming responsibility for what has already happened anyway. As Žižek writes, "the 'subject' is precisely a name for this 'empty gesture' which changes nothing at the level of positive content (at this level, everything has already happened) but must nevertheless be added for the 'content' itself to achieve its full effectivity." He adds: "We can literally say that this 'empty gesture' *posits the big Other, makes it exist*: the purely formal conversion which constitutes this gesture is simply the conversion of the pre-symbolic Real into the symbolized reality—into the Real caught in the web of signifier's network. In other words, through this 'empty gesture' the subject *presupposes the existence of the big Other*."[12] Along the lines of Lacan's early work, the act thus would seem to operate as a near-synonym for symbolization. It is the act qua symbolic inscription: "This tautological gesture is 'empty' in the precise sense that it does not contribute anything new, it only retroactively ascertains that the thing in question

---

11 Slavoj Žižek, *Tarrying with the Negative: Kant, Hegel, and the Critique of Ideology* (Durham: Duke University Press, 1993), 234–5.
12 Slavoj Žižek, *The Sublime Object of Ideology* (London: Verso, 1989), 221 and 230.

*is already present in its conditions*, i.e., that the totality of these conditions *is* the actuality of the thing. Such an empty gesture provides us with the most elementary definition of the *symbolic act*."[13] On the other hand, the act also imposes a step beyond the mere gesture of symbolic inscription. It is indeed not enough for the subject to posit as his or her own activity what is supposed to be given, but this act of positing must in turn be presupposed and, more specifically, it must be presupposed as inherently blocked. This additional step involves the radical experience of divesting oneself from the position of every available subject supposed to know. Beyond the measure of interpretive success for the inscription of a traumatic kernel of experience into the symbolic order, the criteria for evaluating the act proper thus also include the assumption of an element of necessary failure, by which the subject is divested of the ability to rely on the guarantee of the symbolic, or of the big Other. "What is at stake in this 'destitution' is precisely the fact that *the subject no longer presupposes himself as subject*; by accomplishing this, he annuls, so to speak, the effects of the act of formal conversion," Žižek concludes on the last pages of *The Sublime Object of Ideology*: "In other words, he assumes not the existence but the *nonexistence* of the big Other; he accepts the Real in its utter, meaningless idiocy; he keeps open the gap between the Real and its symbolization."[14]

---

13    Žižek, *Tarrying with the Negative*, 148–9.
14    Žižek, *The Sublime Object of Ideology*, 230–1.

Even from this quick summary, it should be clear that the first intonation of the act consists in a fleeting apparition of the real—the real not as some forbidden positive realm that would lie beyond or outside the symbolic order but as the intrinsic impossibility that keeps this order from ever achieving closure as an organic whole to begin with. In several formulations Žižek almost equates the two—the real and the act—all the while suggesting that the end of ideology critique, like the end of analysis, ought to lie in the assumption of this traumatic kernel of the real that in the final instance is nothing but the circulation of pure death drive. An ethical or political act (the two aspects, ethics and politics, being reciprocally implicated at this point in the theory of the act) operates as a kind of vanishing mediator, briefly revealing the inconsistency of our ideological edifice only to see how such fleeting encounters with the real, more often than not, tend almost instantly to be reabsorbed into the existing order of things. From the point of view of the first understanding of the act, no real transformation of this order itself seems possible—let alone an overcoming of the condition of human alienation—except at the cost of restoring all the ideological smokescreens concealing the traumatic fact that, psychoanalytically speaking, is inscribed in the impossibility of the sexual relationship as full enjoyment and, politically, in the impossibility of society as a transparent organic totality. Communism, therefore, from this first point of view, appears to be based on a mistaken belief in the possibility of some other space or new social order: "Marx's fundamental mistake was to conclude, from these insights, that a new, higher order (Communism) is possible."[15]

## The Art of the Impossible

In subsequent works, however, Žižek dramatically shifts his definition of the act to account for the possibility of true change, which will also be a radical change in what counts as true, as good, as possible or as impossible. Opposing what he calls "the act proper" to other modalities such as the hysterical *acting out*, the psychotic *passage à l'acte*, and the *symbolic act* of purely formal self-assertion, he writes in *On Belief*: "In contrast to all these three modes, the act proper is the only one which restructures the very symbolic coordinates of the agent's situation: it is an intervention in the course of which the agent's identity itself is radically changed."[16] To be sure, this is not another act but another presentation of the same underlying notion of the act. Instead of primarily assuming or recognizing the radical impossibility which alone gives some precarious consistency to the symbolic structure, and far from merely identifying with the symptomatic piece of the real that most stubbornly embodies this impossibility, the subject of the ethical or political act proper is now seen as capable of transforming the very symbolic structure of his or

---

15   Slavoj Žižek, *The Fragile Absolute: Or, Why the Christian Legacy is Worth Fighting For* (London: Verso, 2000), 17.
16   Žižek, *On Belief*, 85.

her own situation. Where previously the law of the symbolic seemed to be an overdetermining instance to the exclusion of the possibility of anything essentially new, genuine novelty is now miraculously allowed to emerge in a provocative redefinition or new intonation of the act. As Žižek claims in a chapter from *Did Somebody Say Totalitarianism?* in which he distances himself from other conceptions of the act in a series of negative statements that once again are best understood as self-criticisms, or as criticisms of the ways in which the author believes himself to have been misunderstood based on his earlier work: "One can now precisely locate the ethical act—or, rather, the act *as such*—with respect to the reign of the 'reality principle': an ethical act is not only 'beyond the reality principle' (in the sense of 'running against the current,' of insisting on its Cause-Thing without regard to reality); rather, it designates an intervention that *changes the very co-ordinates of the 'reality principle.'*" In other words, "an act is not only a gesture that 'does the impossible,' but an intervention in social reality which changes the very co-ordinates of what is perceived as 'possible'; it is not only 'beyond the Good,' it redefines what counts as 'Good.'"[17]

In the same key chapter from *Did Somebody Say Totalitarianism?*, titled precisely "Melancholy and the Act," Žižek once more seems to have no trouble finding perfect examples of such an ethical act proper. This proliferation of

---

17    Slavoj Žižek, *Did Somebody Say Totalitarianism? Five Essays in the (Mis)use of a Notion* (London: Verso, 2002), 167.

examples incidentally is an interesting problem in its own right. If we live in an atonal world, marked by postpolitics as the mere administration of society or of the political, then how come there exists such a flurry of instances of the miraculous courage of the act? Unlike Badiou or Rancière, who constantly insist on the rarity of the event or the intermittence of politics, and unlike Esposito's emphatic claim about the unrepresentability of politics within philosophy, Žižek freely accumulates perfect illustrations of the act proper ad nauseam. A closer look at these examples, however, reveals new and unexpected facets in the understanding of the act. As a matter of fact, a third intonation begins to make itself heard as if to mediate between the act as symbolic inscription and self-divestiture and the act of making the impossible possible.

Initially, Antigone takes us back to the understanding of the act of fully assuming the nonexistence of the big Other. By momentarily suspending the rules that govern what is accepted as social reality, she drives home the radical incompleteness of that reality: "The act involves the acceptance of this double impossibility/limit: although our empirical universe is incomplete, this does not mean that there is *another* 'true' reality that sustains it. Although we cannot fully integrate ourselves into our reality, there is no Other Place in which we would be 'truly at home.'"[18] Not only are we back in the dominant tonality of impossibility, but from the point of

---

18   Ibid., 175.

view of the latter any hope of overcoming the inconsistency and incompleteness of our universe must be dismissed as an ideological fantasy, the dream of superseding the ontological destituteness that is our human condition. Indeed, at this point we do well to remember how, in *The Sublime Object of Ideology*, the death drive appears as an insuperable obstacle to any old-style act of dis-alienation: "In this perspective, the 'death drive,' this dimension of radical negativity, cannot be reduced to an expression of alienated social conditions, it defines *la condition humaine* as such: there is no solution, no escape from it; the thing to do is not to 'overcome,' to 'abolish' it, but to come to terms with it, to learn to recognize it in its terrifying dimension and then, on the basis of this fundamental recognition, to try to articulate a *modus vivendi* with it."[19] Soon after the invocation of Antigone in the chapter "Melancholy and the Act" from *Did Somebody Say Totalitarianism?*, however, Žižek also illustrates the notion of the act with the example of the Pope, whose principled stance on abortion he contrasts with the liberal tolerance and permissiveness that Westerners believe they can find in the figure of the Dalai Lama. "One can now understand why the Dalai Lama is much more appropriate for our postmodern permissive times: he presents us with a vague feel-good spiritualism without any specific obligations," Žižek suggests. "The Pope, in contrast, reminds us that there *is* a price to pay for a proper ethical attitude—it is his very stubborn clinging

---

19    Žižek, *The Sublime Object of Ideology*, 5.

to 'old values,' his ignoring the 'realistic' attitudes of our time even when the arguments seem 'obvious' (as in the case of the raped nun), that makes him an authentic ethical figure."[20] In other words, what defines the act in this last sense, regardless of the political or ideological content, is a strict fidelity to principles. Bill Clinton's stance on healthcare would thus be as good an example of the ethical act proper as the views on abortion or anticonception of the Pope.

## Fidelity to Principles

If in this light we now turn for a moment to recent books such as *In Defense of Lost Causes*, we see that the three into-nations of the act, after having made their appearance in a chronologically staggered way, logically speaking should be seen as occupying a single plane of consistency. To perceive this consistency all the while respecting the internal differ-ences requires that the reader pay attention to seemingly minute details and shifts in emphasis. New connotations are constantly being added, to be sure, but always in the name of the concept's relentlessly proclaimed self-sameness. Here, in other words, we should draw an important lesson from the art of writing, as defined in terms of esotericism by Leo Strauss, so as to learn from it how to read Žižek: "From the Freudian perspective, the key strategy of the 'art of writing' under conditions of persecution is that of *repetition*: when

20    Ibid., 182.

a writer apparently just repeats or recapitulates a content he previously deployed or took from a classical text, the clues are small, barely discernible, changes in the repeated content—a feature added, a feature left out, a changed order of features."[21] *This*, I believe, and not the vulgar psychological explanations for the impression of too-muchness, is the key to understanding the element of repetition in all of Žižek's writing, including as far as his changing views on the subject of the act are concerned.

Let us consider, for example, the following definition of the act: "The true courage of an act is always the courage to accept the inexistence of the big Other, that is, to attack the existing order at the point of its symptomal knot."[22] Here, in the seemingly neutral comment clause meant to explain the first half of the sentence, we actually slide from the act as the acceptance or assumption of a structural impossibility to the notion of the act as a transformative intervention, by way of an attack, into the existing state of things. At the same time, as the point about the symptomal knot makes clear, our frame of reference is being shifted from a broadly understood Lacanian perspective to one dominated by Badiou's event, which is in fact situated in a given situation via the eventual site that is symptomatic of the situation as a whole and that

21    Slavoj Žižek, *Iraq: The Borrowed Kettle* (London: Verso, 2004), 169. Interesting guidelines for "How to Read Žižek?" can also be found in Butler, *Slavoj Žižek: Live Theory*, 12–17.
22    Slavoj Žižek, *In Defense of Lost Causes* (London: Verso, 2009), 152.

as such concentrates its specific historicity. In fact, once we grasp the shift from Lacan to Badiou that is involved in this redefinition of the act, we also understand that, already in the first half of the sentence, the notion of courage is greatly indebted to the author of *Being and Event*.

Based on such slight but crucial shifts in perspective, hidden behind the necessary appearance of an unchanged conceptual apparatus, Žižek can then refute those critics who blame him, on one hand, for elevating the act into an absolutized and miraculous occurrence outside of history. "Such an act is not only rooted in its contingent conditions, these very conditions make it into an act: the same gesture, performed at a wrong moment (too early or too late), is no longer an act," Žižek protests in a staunch rebuttal of Stavrakakis. But, on the other hand, this does not mean either that the act can be reduced purely and simply to its determining conditions; instead, an act emerges precisely from within the interstices that render visible the inexistence of the big Other: "The link between the situation and the act is thus clear: far from being determined by the situation (or from intervening in it from a mysterious outside), acts are possible on account of the ontological non-closure, inconsistency, gaps, in a situation."[23] Slowly but surely, the different versions of the act begin reciprocally to support and interact with one another. They expand and contract as if in a spiral, sometimes returning to an earlier conclusion as though nothing had changed and at

---

23    Ibid., 309.

other times passing off an entirely new feature as though it had been part of the original concept all along. We are thus told that an act can truly transform the existing situation only if and when it is anchored in the gaps in the symbolic order. But, at the same time, going back to the earliest understanding of the act, these gaps become visible only if and when the subject traverses his or her fundamental fantasy and assumes the nonexistence of the big Other. And, finally, between these two aspects or moments of the act, in an order that is not chronological but logical, the only possible mediation seems to be a stubborn fidelity to principles regardless of all consequences. The most difficult task is to come to the point where the act proper can be understood as a move in which these three intonations—assumption of impossibility, possibility of the impossible, fidelity to principles—strictly speaking, overlap.

The following fragment from *Iraq: The Borrowed Kettle* in which Žižek continues to counter Stavrakakis's arguments, brings together these different intonations of the act, all the while referring them back—in the midst of yet another self-critique or at the very least a critical self-clarification—to the supposedly stable authority of Lacan:

> "Acts" in Lacan's sense precisely suspend the gap between the impossible injunction and the positive intervention—they are "impossible" not in the sense of "it is impossible that they might happen," but in the sense of the impossible that *did happen*. This is why

Antigone was of interest to me: her act is not a strategic intervention which maintains the gap towards the impossible Void; rather, it tends to enact the impossible "absolutely." I am well aware of the "lure" of such an act—but I claim that, in Lacan's later versions of the act, this moment of "madness" beyond strategic intervention remains. In this precise sense, the notion of the act not only does not contradict the "lack in the Other" which, according to Stavrakakis, I overlook—it directly presupposes it: it is only through an act that I effectively assume the big Other's nonexistence, that is, I enact the impossible: namely, what appears as impossible within the co-ordinates of the existing socio-symbolic order.[24]

While we might be tempted to draw strict conceptual lines of demarcation between these different definitions of the act, such an approach would completely debilitate Žižek's work, which constantly refuses to make such distinctions. Part of the appeal of this work, I believe, stems precisely from the fact that its author holds on to a single concept or technical term (such as the ethical or political act proper) or to a single theoretical framework (such as the strictly Hegelian dialectic or the properly Lacanian understanding of the subject) all the while modifying them or transcoding them substantially along the way. And yet, even if there is a

---

24   Žižek, *Iraq*, 80.

myriad of tiny variations and intonations, these are all tied, in the final instance, to a stable category supposed to remain unchanged. This supposition constitutes a conscious methodological principle. What Žižek writes about Schelling in this sense is perfectly applicable to his own work: "Schelling often continues to use the same terms with totally changed, sometimes even directly opposed meanings," but, as in the case of the act, the recognition of these differences in meaning should not be mistaken for a defense of pluralism:

> On a somewhat higher, more "spiritual" level, one usually fails to take note of how a free play of our theoretical imagination is possible only against the background of a firmly established set of "dogmatic" conceptual constraints: our intellectual creativity can be "set free" only within the confines of some imposed notional framework in which, precisely, we are able to "move freely"—the lack of this imposed framework is necessarily experienced as an unbearable burden, since it compels us to focus constantly on how to respond to every particular empirical situation in which we find ourselves.[25]

So what would happen if we were to enumerate and keep separate the different categories of the act? We might be tempted to conclude that either things are relative in

---

25  Žižek, *The Indivisible Remainder*, 40, 25.

the good old nominalistic fashion (there is not *the* act but a *multiplicity* of different acts), or else that things in some obscure pseudodialectical fashion are self-contradictory (there is a blind spot, an unsuspected incompatibility, or an unacknowledged discrepancy *between* the different acts). But the fact of the matter is that what allows Žižek to break with this generalized perspectivalism is precisely his reference to a dogmatic stopping point that is not contradictory. We are expected to make sense of the opposing intonations of the act all at once and simultaneously; to move from one to the other and never to give in to the smug self-satisfaction of having outsmarted the latest idiot-author. In other words, the proclamation of doctrinal consistency is what keeps the system together and avoids the slippery slope of postmodern relativism. And the same goes for the so-called dogmatic references to Hegel or Lacan: were we to take away these halting points, Žižek's ruminations on our contemporary social order would collapse into a jumble of half-journalistic and half-conceptual jottings; more importantly, he would not be able to dislocate the expectations of his readers or provoke an internal shift or displacement of our current ideological framework, since he would just be adding a few more sound bites to the liberal-ironic conversation of humanity.

## Toward a New Social Order

The logical time of the act thus follows a strange loop or bootstrap mechanism whereby an intervention retroactively changes the conditions that make this intervention possible in the first place. "An act proper is not just a strategic intervention into a situation, bound by its conditions—it retroactively creates its own conditions," Žižek concludes in his *In Defense of Lost Causes*. Or, in an even more forceful expanded formulation from the same book:

> This, perhaps, is the most succinct definition of what an authentic *act* is: in our ordinary activity, we effectively follow the (virtual-fantasmatic) coordinates of our identity, while an act proper is the paradox of an actual move which (retroactively) changes the very virtual "transcendental" coordinates of its agent's being—or, in Freudian terms, which not only changes the actuality of our world, but also "rouses its infernal regions." We have thus a kind of reflexive "folding back of the condition onto the given it was the condition for": while the pure past is the transcendental condition for our acts, our acts not only create an actual new reality, they also retroactively change this very condition.[26]

Instead of an act of recognition and/or renunciation of the symbolic network that guarantees the minimal consistency of our everyday reality, we thus obtain a radical recasting of the notion of the act as the creation of a new reality. Instead of a fleeting apparition of the real as a vanishing

---

26    Žižek, *In Defense of Lost Causes*, 311 and 315.

act, we obtain an act engaged in making possible and giving lasting consistency to what prior to this act appeared as a formidable impossibility. And, finally, the criteria for assessing the authenticity and/or the betrayal of an act, which, in the process, becomes increasingly synonymous with the act of political emancipation rather than with the purely ethical realm, are not limited either to the symbolic inscription of some traumatic experience or to the sublimity of the encounter with the real. "The key test of every radical emancipatory movement is, on the contrary, to what extent it transforms on a daily basis the *practico-inert* institutional practices which gain the upper hand once the fervor of the struggle is over and people return to business as usual," Žižek writes in "The Communist Hypothesis," once again, I would argue, in a partial self-criticism: "The success of a revolution should not be measured by the sublime awe of its ecstatic moments, but by the changes the big Event leaves at the level of the everyday, the day after the insurrection."[27]

Indeed, one of the most important effects of this gradual transcoding of the notion of the act concerns the changed assessment of the place of communism in Žižek's ideology critique. Where previously, in the first intonation of the act, communism was judged part and parcel of Marx's fundamental mistake of assuming the existence of some other, higher social order, particularly one that would stem from

---

27   Slavoj Žižek, "The Communist Hypothesis," in *First as Tragedy, Then as Farce* (London: Verso, 2009), 154.

the removal of the inherent obstacles of capitalist production as just so many fetters, Žižek now considers it to be
the task of communism, beyond the short-lived appeal of
what we have called speculative leftism, to actually enforce a
new order: "There is an unexpected conclusion to be drawn
from this: insofar as (Badiou emphasizes this point again
and again) a true Event is not merely a negative gesture,
but opens up a positive dimension of the New, an Event *is*
the imposition of a new world, of a new Master-Signifier
(a new Naming, as Badiou puts it, or, what Lacan called
"*vers un nouveau signifiant*"). The true evental change is the
passage from the old to the new world."[28] Where previously
the ideological consistency of the existing state of things
had to be pulverized in the name of the radical negativity
of some point of the real, the task of politics today must
be to counter the endless flux of global capitalism with the
lasting possibility of ordering and simplifying the world in
the name of communism. Even the hypothesis of the existence of Another Space, or of an Other of the Other (Lacan's
teachings notwithstanding), must no longer be excluded as
a sheer ideological fantasy, for "it should also be clear that
the necessity of renunciation inherent to the notion of act in
no way entails that every utopian imagination gets caught
in the trap of inherent transgression: when we abandon
the fantasmatic Otherness which makes life in constrained
social reality bearable, we catch a glimpse of Another Space

---

28   Žižek, *In Defense of Lost Causes*, 397.

which can no longer be dismissed as a fantasmatic supplement to social reality."[29]

If the study of the ontological turn in contemporary political philosophy taught us anything, it is that flux, difference, and becoming—far from being subversive answers to a dominant ideology of stability, identity, and being—are rather the spontaneous forms of appearance of the underlying sameness of late capitalism. "This is why the focus on capitalism is crucial if we want to reactualize the communist Idea: contemporary 'world-less' capitalism radically changes the very coordinates of the communist struggle— the enemy is no longer the state to be undermined from its point of symptomal torsion, but a flux of permanent self-revolutionizing," Žižek warns us in *First as Tragedy, Then as Farce*. "My suggestion is rather this: what if today's global capitalism, precisely insofar as it is 'world-less,' involving a constant disruption of all fixed orders, opens up the space for a revolution which will break the vicious cycle of revolt and its reinscription, which will, in other words, no longer follow the pattern of an evental explosion followed by a return to normality, but will instead assume the task of a *new "ordering" against the global capitalist disorder*? Out of revolt we should shamelessly pass to enforcing a new order."[30] Short-lived and intermittent spectacles of revolt and contestation, in the style of what Žižek perceives in Rancière's politics of

---

29   Žižek, *The Fragile Absolute*, 158.
30   Žižek, "The Communist Hypothesis," 130.

disagreement, can easily by quarantined or co-opted, so that in the end the task of the political act proper must also lie elsewhere: "The true task lies not in momentary democratic explosions which undermine the established 'police' order, but in the dimension designated by Badiou as that of 'fidelity' to the Event: translating/inscribing the democratic explosion into the positive 'police' order, imposing on social reality a *new* lasting order."[31]

## The Act Before the Act

This does not mean, however, that the association of the authentic political act with the enforcing of a new social order would be Žižek's last word on the subject, since we still have to consider a fourth understanding of the act, one that furthermore can always be relied on for being more originary than all the others. This is what we might call the primordial arch-act involved in the real genesis or coming into being of the subject: not the act of this or that already-constituted subject but the unconscious act that is constitutive of self-consciousness and subjectivity as such. At the highest level of speculation, this act will appear as a strange repetition of the answer to that quintessential philosophical—or theological—problem, namely, the coming into being of something out of nothing, as in the creation of the cosmos out of pure, indeterminate chaos.

---

31   Žižek, *In Defense of Lost Causes*, 418–19.

The context for this additional shift of emphasis in the concept of the act is partly philosophical and partly political. Continuing his habit of presenting likely self-criticisms as criticisms of standard misconceptions, Žižek on the one hand wishes to correct what he calls "the predominant 'philosophical' reading of Lacan," which leads to "all the false poetry of 'castration,' of some primordial act of sacrifice and renunciation, of *jouissance* as impossible; the notion that, at the end of the psychoanalytic cure, the analysand has to assume symbolic castration, to accept a fundamental, constitutive loss or lack; and so on."[32] Žižek is careful enough to admit that, far from being a simple misreading, there are evidently numerous elements that point in this direction in Lacanian theory—and, I would add, in his own theory as well, including a kind of "heroism of the lack" that can then be illustrated or lambasted based on the example of Antigone's tragic sublimity. Yet he also insists that this is "an 'idealist' distortion of Lacan," which is once more closer to Kant than to Hegel: "What is lurking in the background, of course, is the Kantian distinction between the constitutive and the regulative aspect: the Thing (freedom, for example) has to remain a regulative ideal—any attempt at its full realization can lead only to the most terrifying tyranny. (It is easy to discern here the contours of Kant's criticism of the perversion of the French Revolution in the revolutionary terror

---

32   Žižek, *The Indivisible Remainder*, 93.

of the Jacobins).'[33] Philosophically, to undo the idealism of this reading means to find alternatives to the analytic of finitude with its unsurpassable (because formal-transcendental) horizon of thrownness and guilt, which has become a dogmatic commonplace from Kant through Heidegger to (early) Lacan, and elements of which arguably persist to this day even in Žižek's own work.[34]

Politically, on the other hand, the criticism is meant to steer us away from pure outbursts of a real that merely flashes up in short-lived traumatic encounters and subversive gestures. Žižek's own notion of ideology critique, of course, frequently limits itself to momentarily rendering visible the fragility of power, the nonexistence of the symbolic order, and so on, but now, he writes, "perhaps the moment has come to leave behind the old Leftist obsession with ways and means to 'subvert' or 'undermine' the Other, and to focus on the opposite question—on what, following Ernesto Laclau, we can call the 'ordering of the Order': not how can we undermine the existing order, but *how does an Order emerge out of disorder in the first place*?"[35] Only this prior question about the origin

---

33   Ibid., 96–7.

34   See my "The Jargon of Finitude, or, Materialism Today," *Radical Philosophy* 155 (2009): 41–7.

35   Žižek, *The Indivisible Remainder*, 3. Žižek not only relies on Laclau for this distinction between the *being* of order and its *coming-into-being* or *becoming*, he also compares it to the so-called political difference discussed above, in Chapter 1: "In political theory, the French distinction between *le politique* (the political)

of order out of disorder would enable us subsequently to envision the enforcing of a new order. Žižek thematizes this problematic under the heading of what he calls the "morning after," not just in psychoanalysis but also in politics, and for which neither the (Kantian-Heideggerian-early Lacanian) analytic of finitude and lack nor the (Spinozian-Nietzschean-Deleuzian) vitalism of desire and plenitude can provide a satisfactory solution. "At stake here is probably the most radical of all philosophical questions: is the alternative of *desire* and *drive*, of *lack* and *positivity*—the alternative between, on the one hand, remaining within the constraints of the negative ontology of lack, of man's constitutive 'out-of-jointedness,' and so on, and, on the other, yielding to the pure positivity of drive qua the eternal return of the will which wills its object for ever—truly the ultimate, unavoidable alternative to our lives?," asks Žižek. His answer, summarizing what may well be the rational kernel of his entire oeuvre for which all the rest is only the mystical or pop-cultural shell, is that there exists in fact a mediating third option, which can be found in German Idealism:

Our premiss, of course, is that the *Grundoperation* of German Idealism points towards a *tertium datur*; and,

---

and *la politique* (politics) plays the same structural role: the 'political' designates the process of becoming (of 'ordering') of a political order, its 'invention,' its generative movement; whereas 'politics' refers to a constituted domain of social being" (*The Indivisible Remainder*, 84 n.36).

furthermore, that it is only this third position which enables us to confront the key problem of "the morning after": what happens—not at the end of the psychoanalytic cure, but *afterwards*, once the cure is over? That is to say: it is easy to suspend the big Other by means of the act qua real, to experience the "nonexistence of the big Other" in a momentary flash—however, what do we do *after* we have traversed the fantasy? Is it not necessary to resort again to some kind of big Other? How are we to avoid the painful conclusion that the experience of the nonexistence of the big Other, of the act *qua* real, is merely a fleeting "vanishing mediator" between two Orders, an enthusiastic intermediate moment necessarily followed by a sobering relapse into the reign of the big Other? What corresponds to it in the domain of politics is the resigned conservative notion of revolution as a transitory moment of liberation, the suspension of social authority, which unavoidably gives rise to the backlash of an even more oppressive power.[36]

In yet another strange loop, however, the question of the morning after finds an answer only in a highly speculative return to the earliest dawn of human history and even to the origin of the world as such. To envision a new positive order beyond the present horizon thus requires that we take

---

36   Žižek, *The Indivisible Remainder*, 133.

a step back to grasp the moment of genesis of order out of disorder. "In the end, the alternative here is between idealism and materialism: is the 'big Other' (the ideal symbolic order) always already here as a kind of insurmountable horizon, or is it possible to deploy its 'genesis' out of the dispersed 'non-all' network of contingent material singularities?" Žižek also asks, before answering his own question in the positive: "The answer is a definite 'yes'—it is contained in Lacan's unexpected vindication of the notion of creativity at its most radical, that is, as *creatio ex nihilo*: by means of reference to the void of the Thing in the midst of the symbolic structure, the subject is able to 'bend' the symbolic space she inhabits, and thus to define his/her desire in its idiosyncrasy."[37] To justify his belief in the possibility of a transformative act that would open up a new order not limited to the alternative of either the pure lack of desire or else the pure positivity of drives, Žižek thus raises the question of the originary act that brings order out of disorder and breaks with the constraints of the always already existing state of affairs.

At the constant risk of falling into the trap of mythic-theosophical obscurantism, Žižek's main point of reference for this step back to the beginning is Schelling's act of originary decision or separation: "Schelling's 'materialist' contribution is best epitomized by his fundamental thesis according to which, to put it bluntly, *the true beginning is not at the beginning*: there is something that precedes the Beginning

---

37    Ibid., 107–8, 146.

itself—a rotary motion whose vicious cycle is broken in a gesture analogous to the cutting of the Gordian knot, by the Beginning proper, that is, the primordial act of decision."[38] In a logical rather than a purely chronological order, this act must be presupposed prior to any concrete act or activity of transformation and self-determination—hence presumably prior to what Marx, for example, calls the collective act of self-activation or self-activity, in his early definition of communism in the *Manuscripts of 1844*, but also prior to and more radical than all of Žižek's own concepts of the act since *The Sublime Object of Ideology*, whether as symbolic inscription, as ideological fidelity to principles, or even as the making possible of the impossible.

This fourth intonation, in other words, draws our attention to the presence of an "act before the act" by which the subject becomes who he or she is in the first place. "The real act thus *precedes* the (particular-factual) activity; it consists in the previous restructuring of our symbolic universe into which our (factual, particular) act will be inscribed," writes Žižek: "The 'act before the act' by means of which the subject posits the very presuppositions of his activity is of a strictly formal nature; it is a purely formal 'conversion' transforming reality into something perceived, assumed as a result of our activity."[39] Like the choice of Good or Evil, this decision must be conceived of as "an atemporal, a priori, transcendental

---

38   Ibid., 13.
39   Žižek, *The Sublime Object of Ideology*, 216, 218.

act: as an act which *never took place* in temporal reality but none the less constitutes the very frame of the subject's development, of his practical activity."[40] Dominating Žižek's writings from the mid-to-late 1990s, such as *The Indivisible Remainder*, yet already present as early as in such passages as the ones just quoted from *The Sublime Object of Ideology*, this understanding of the act also continues to cast its shadow over every subsequent invocation of the term, imbuing it with aspects of a quasi-mythic primordiality and negativity that will serve as guarantees of radicalism over and against the alleged naïvety—or worse, the sheer non-thought— which in comparison would beset, for instance, Badiou's understanding of the event.

In effect, the first conclusion to be drawn is that we are now dealing not just with different intonations or with differ- ent moments but also with different levels of application for one and the same concept of the act. There is the cosmic act of God's self-sundering that contracts and expands order out of disorder, but there is also the act of genesis of specifi- cally human subjectivity. The latter, in turn, must be split according to whether we are dealing with the ontogenetic or with the phylogenetic level, that is, the entry of an indi- vidual subject into the symbolic order or the coming into being of the symbolic order as such for the entire human species, as in the founding myths deployed in Freud's *Totem and Taboo* and *Moses and Monotheism* about the killing of

---

40   Ibid., 166–7, 219–20.

the primordial father. Furthermore, we should ask whether the act does not also concern the contingent interventions by which an individual or collective subject sometimes—rarely or intermittently—manages to change the very coordinates of its existing symbolic structure. Finally, in addition to clearly distinguishing these different levels at which the act is operative, we should also ask what kind of relationship should be posited between them. Žižek's answer to this question seems fundamentally to involve a principle of repetition. The act by which a subject at the ontogenetic level is born or thrown into the symbolic order, for example, would repeat the self-sundering experience of God's primordial contraction and expansion at the cosmic level. Similarly, every contingent act of an already constituted subject could be said to repeat elements of the phylogenetic origin of the human species, of consciousness, and of morality, say, to use the Freudian terms, out of the guilt over the crime of killing the primordial father.

What is most important in this discussion, however, is the effect of the logic of the origin and the repetition of the origin, that is, the always-present possibility of turning the prior act against any and all subsequent repetitions or reduplications. No matter how profoundly they may well claim to transform the existing state of things, to the point of miraculously making the impossible possible, all such repetitions cannot but appear as partial disavowals of the arch-radical nature of that *Ur*-act dreamed of by Schelling and allegedly repeated by Lacan's plunging into the death drive, into the pure self-relating negativity that is the abyssal ground of freedom of the subject. At this point, in effect, we are typically treated once again to all the dangerously obscurantist "false poetry" about the "night of the world," the "immortal" substance of zombies and the undead, finitude as the "vertiginous" condition of (im)possibility of human freedom, "madness" and "senselessness" as the origin of "sense," and so on. The radical negativity of the originary arch-act, then, will serve as crucial leverage in the debunking of other notions of the act, of agency, or of the event that cannot but pale in comparison.

For instance, repeating an earlier criticism of Althusser's notion of ideological interpellation as formulated in *The Sublime Object of Ideology* and *Metastases of Enjoyment*, Žižek argues that there is likewise something in Badiou's philosophy of the event that remains necessarily unthought, or worse, something that is disavowed behind a crude non-thought: "When Badiou adamantly opposes the 'morbid obsession with death,' when he opposes the Truth-Event to the death drive, and so on, he is at his weakest, succumbing to the *temptation of the non-thought*."[41] What is more, insofar as "this theoretical gesture involves a 'regression' to 'non-thought,' to a naïve traditional (pre-critical, pre-Kantian) opposition of

---

41   Žižek, *The Ticklish Subject*, 145. On the typical ambivalence of the category of non-thought (both reactive and affirmative, sickly and salvific) within so-called antiphilosophy (which is how we might categorize Žižek's work), see Alain Badiou, *Wittgenstein's Antiphilosophy*, trans. Bruno Bosteels (London: Verso, 2011).

two orders (the finitude of positive Being; the immortality of the Truth-Event) that remains blind to how the very space for the specific 'immortality' in which human beings can participate in the Truth-Event is opened up by man's unique relationship to his finitude and the possibility of death," Badiou's fundamental weakness can be overcome only by radically acknowledging the role of the death drive as a missing third term between being and event: "The Lacanian death drive (a category Badiou adamantly opposes) is thus again a kind of 'vanishing mediator' between Being and Event: there is a 'negative' gesture constitutive of the subject which is then obfuscated in 'Being' (the established ontological order) and in fidelity to the Event."[42] Using Lacan's discourse as an instrument of subversion, much in the same way that Lacan himself used Sade to give us the tormented "truth" of Kant, Žižek thus can claim boldly to lay bare that which cannot but remain obfuscated in Badiou's philosophy: "The 'death drive' is thus the constitutive obverse of every emphatic assertion of Truth irreducible to the positive order of Being."[43]

Ultimately, the philosopher's foolish illusion consists in loving the force of truth, whereas in the analyst's discourse

---

42   Žižek, *The Ticklish Subject*, 163, 160; see also 169 n. 25.

43   Ibid., 159. See Lacan's well-known "Kant with Sade," in his *Écrits*, trans. Bruce Fink (New York: W. W. Norton, 2006), 645–68. I use Lacan's paper as a framing device in order to unravel the logic behind Žižek's criticisms of Badiou, in my "Badiou Without Žižek," *Polygraph: An International Journal of Culture and Politics* 17 (2005): 223–46.

we could say that the real is stronger than the true. Thus, if Lacan began his international career, most notably in his 1953 discourse in Rome, by promising that psychoanalysis would bring not only truth but also wisdom, starting in the 1970s he increasingly moves toward a general antiphilosophical destitution of the category of truth in favor of a peculiar kind of knowledge in the real. For example, in 1970, in a speech to the École freudienne de Paris, he claims: "The truth may not convince, knowledge passes in the act [*La vérité peut ne pas convaincre, le savoir passe en acte*]."[44] Or again, in 1975, in a talk at Columbia University, Lacan suggests that sometimes "the real is stronger than the true [*le réel est plus fort que le vrai*]."[45] Glossing statements such as these, we can say that there is no knowledge of the real without an act. The act happens precisely when something of the real passes into a form of knowledge capable of transmission and as a result of which something must drop out of the existing arrangements of knowledge, including above all their guarantee in the subject who is supposed to know. As Badiou comments: "For Lacan, there is no truth of the real, there is no knowledge of the real, but a function of the real in knowledge. There is also no knowledge of truth, but at best the truth of a knowledge in the real that functions."[46] In sum, *le réel passe en*

---

44   Lacan, "Allocution sur l'enseignement," *Autres écrits*, 305.

45   Jacques Lacan, "Columbia University, Auditorium School of International Affairs—1er décembre 1975," *Scilicet* 6/7 (1976): 45.

46   Alain Badiou, *L'antiphilosophie lacanienne* (seminar of 1994–95 at the École normale supérieure in rue d'Ulm), session of March 15, 1995.

*savoir*, meaning not only "the real passes into knowledge" but also "the real not without knowing," as in the homonymous *le réel pas sans savoir*. And while for the later Lacan this form of knowledge in the real is best transmitted through the impasses of mathematical formalization, we could argue that in the writings of Žižek this role has been taken over by popular culture and jokes. There is thus something archiscientific about the psychoanalytical act in Lacan, whereas for Žižek the genuine act oscillates between an archiaesthetic and an archipolitical dimension. In both cases, however, the crucial point not to be missed is the extent to which the transmission of this knowledge in the real now finds an impediment, rather than an aid, in the category of truth. "The analysis can only have as its goal the advent of a true speech and the realization by the subject of his or her history in its relation to a future," Lacan had written in one of his earlier *Écrits*, but this promise of truth through a kind of full speech later comes to be dismissed as a lure better left to the care of other discourses, such as the university discourse or the master's discourse: "There are four discourses. Each one of them takes itself for the truth. Only the analytical discourse makes an exception."[47] For the later Lacan, therefore, the crucial dividing line is the one that separates truth from a new type of knowledge that involves the relations between fantasy and enjoyment or *jouissance*. Žižek could not be clearer

---

47   Lacan, "The Function and Field of Speech and Language in Psychoanalysis," *Écrits*, 249; and "Transfert à Saint Denis?," *Ornicar?* 17/18 (1979): 278.

in this regard: "So, while the 'classic', structuralist Lacan invites me to *dare the truth*, subjectively to assume the truth of my desire inscribed into the big Other, the later Lacan comes much closer to something like *truth or dare*: (the symbolic) truth is for those who *do not dare*—what? To confront the fantasmatic core of (the Real of) their *jouissance*. At the level of *jouissance*, truth is simply *inoperative*, something which ultimately doesn't matter."[48]

Following the change of position between the earlier and the later Lacan, Žižek's answer to Badiou, then, does not simply oppose truth and knowledge but rather adds another dimension, for which the real of enjoyment constitutes the mediating third term:

In philosophical terms, Lacan introduces here a distinction, absent in Badiou, between symbolic truth and knowledge in the Real: Badiou clings to the difference between objective-neutral Knowledge which concerns the order of Being, and the subjectively engaged Truth (one of the standard topoi of modern thought from Kierkegaard onwards), while Lacan renders thematic another, unheard-of level; that of the unbearable fantasmatic kernel. Although—or, rather, precisely because—this kernel forms the very

---

48  Žižek, "Foreword to the Second Edition: Enjoyment Within the Limits of Reason Alone," *For They Know Not What They Do*, lxvii.

heart of subjective identity, it cannot ever be subjectivized, subjectively assumed: it can only be retroactively
reconstructed in a desubjectivized knowledge.[49]

We thus come to understand how Žižek through his
notion of the act can claim to outstrip the radicalism of
Badiou's notion of the event. Typically, this involves positing the act as a negative gesture that always necessarily
*precedes* the masterly inscription of the event into a new set
of parameters. As we read in *The Ticklish Subject*: "That is
the difference between Lacan and Badiou: Lacan insists on
the primacy of the (negative) *act* over the (positive) establishment of a 'new harmony' via the intervention of some
new Master-Signifier; while for Badiou, the different facets
of negativity (ethical catastrophes) are reduced to so many
versions of the 'betrayal' of (or infidelity to, or denial of) the
positive Truth-Event."[50] The same operation of seeking to
occupy the place prior to that of any given symbolic meaning

---

49    Ibid., cv. The same argument is repeated in Slavoj Žižek, "From
Purification to Subtraction: Badiou and the Real," in *Think Again*,
ed. Peter Hallward (London: Continuum, 2004), 256 n.18. Much
of this polemic in Žižek's article for the volume *Think Again* and
his "Foreword to the Second Edition" of *For They Know Not What
They Do* consists of a reply to my earlier critique of Žižek's reading
of Badiou, in Bosteels, "Alain Badiou's Theory of the Subject: The
Re-commencement of Dialectical Materialism," published in two
parts in *PLI: The Warwick Journal of Philosophy* 12 (2001): 200–29,
and 13 (2002): 173–208.
50    Žižek, *The Ticklish Subject*, 159.

or truth also applies to Žižek's use of the notion of the subject as opposed to the subsequent process of subjectivization, which by contrast he sees as central to both Badiou and fellow ex-Althusserians such as Rancière, Balibar, and Laclau:

> Lacan introduces the distinction between the subject and the gesture of subjectivization: what Badiou and Laclau describe is the process of subjectivization—the emphatic engagement, the assumption of fidelity to the Event (or, in Laclau, the emphatic gesture of identifying empty universality with some particular content that hegemonizes it), while the subject is the negative gesture of breaking out of the constraints of Being that opens up the space of possible subjectivization.[51]

What is pivotal here is the fact that the subject must come before subjectivization, with the latter in a sense already suturing the gap or empty place of which the former is the strict correlate. It is precisely this logical priority that gives the analyst's discourse its leverage in the radical interrogation of any philosophical or political master discourse: "In Lacanese, the subject prior to subjectivization is the pure negativity of the death drive prior to its reversal into the identification with some new Master-Signifier."[52] Indeed, from the point of view of the preceding void, or the prior empty

---

51    Ibid., 159–60.
52    Ibid., 160.

place of the subject, every consequent inscription of a new mark must seem utterly naïve: at best, it is the age-old lure of truth as a symbolic fiction and, at worst, the banality of sheer non-thought. This literally makes it impossible to have faith in the category of truth in the wake of Lacan's return to Freud: "Lacan parts company with St Paul and Badiou: God not only is but always-already was dead—that is to say, after Freud, one cannot directly have faith in a Truth-Event; every such Event ultimately remains a semblance obfuscating a preceding Void whose Freudian name is *death drive*."[53] Thus, Žižek's typical haste to expropriate and often preemptively to vitiate the thought of some of our most provocative philosophers and political theorists today can and perhaps should be seen as part of a larger trend that for purely structural reasons pushes the hysteric, in the name of the analyst's discourse, always to undermine the master's discourse, now shown to be foolishly ignorant with reference to a prior, more originary, or more radically disavowed act: "Whatever you say, that's not it!"

In good Žižekian fashion, then, perhaps I may be allowed to use a joke to illustrate the logic of anticipated certitude and retroactive self-criticism that runs through much of his work. The joke in question puts two madmen together in an insane asylum as they get caught up in a heated shouting match. The first yells: "You're crazy!" The second: "No, *you're* crazy!" "No, *you* are!" "*No, you!*" and so on and so

53   Ibid., 154.

forth, until the first person finally shouts out triumphantly: "Tomorrow, I'll wake up at 5 a.m. and write on your door that you're crazy!"; to which the second person answers with a conceited smile: "And I'll wake up at 4 a.m. and wipe it off!" At its most radical, this is exactly what the act can do for Žižek with regard to the pretense to truth of the event in Badiou. Before any inscription of a new truth or a new political cause even has a chance to take off, the death drive, possibly blocking this process in advance by virtue of a structural necessity, has always already had to come first to wipe the slate clean. In order to undermine the claims of philosophy, a psychoanalytically inspired discourse can always pit the subject against subjectivization, the void against semblance, the real against symbolic fictions, and in the most general terms, the death drive against fidelity to the cause of truth. Thus, before they would join hands in the common cause of communism, in the necessarily lopsided debate between Badiou and Žižek, I cannot help but think that it is the latter's irrefutable and endearing wager—his ever more radically abyssal act—that he will always wake up earlier than the philosopher!

## In Praise of the Non-Act

Finally, as if the withdrawal into the cosmic arch-act supposedly repeated in every genuine act of human history were not radical enough, Žižek in several texts just prior to the renewal of his communist vows also pleads for a radicalism of inactivity, or for what we might call an ethics of the non-act that alone prepares the ground for genuinely transformative political activity. The aim of this new approach, in which Žižek may seem to flirt with the impolitical treatment of inaction and inoperativity, is to avoid the blackmail that calls for action and not just words, practice and not just theory—only to ensure that in the end nothing changes at all. As Žižek writes in *Iraq: The Borrowed Kettle*: "Against such a stance, one should have the courage to affirm that, in a situation like today's, the only way really to remain open to a revolutionary opportunity is to renounce facile calls to direct action, which necessarily involve us in an activity where things change so that the totality remains the same." Instead, it might be better not to act: "The only way to lay the foundations for a true, radical change is to withdraw from the compulsion to act, to 'do nothing'—thus opening up the space for a different kind of activity."[54] And yet, barely two pages further down, we also

---

54  Žižek, *Iraq*, 72. Aside from a controversial reading of Nietzsche as an impolitical philosopher of inaction, which I discussed above in Chapter 2, Roberto Esposito also comments on Karl Barth's *The Epistle to the Romans* in terms of the logic of inaction, or what Barth calls "the inaction in all action [*das Nicht-Tun in allem Tun*] by means of which any action defines its origin [*Ursprung*]," quoted and glossed in an impolitical, inoperative, and non-subjective key in Esposito, "Opera," in his *Nove pensieri sulla politica* (Bologna: Il Mulino,1993), 151–2. In Žižek's case, the more relevant point of reference no doubt is the psychoanalyst's attitude of non-intervention or non-acting, *non-agir*, during analysis. See, for example, Lacan, "The Function and Field of Speech and Language in Psychoanalysis," 255.

receive another definition of the authentic political act that seems once more in line with earlier claims for doing the impossible: "*That* would be a political *act* today—to break the spell of automatically endorsing the existing political framework, to break out of the debilitating alternative 'either we just directly endorse free-market globalization, or we make impossible promises along the lines of magic formulae about how to have one's cake and eat it, about how to combine globalization with social solidarity.'"[55]

Now, if there is one thing that allows Žižek not just to have his cake and eat it, but also to eat all the cakes at the party before anyone else can get to them, it is his continued reliance on all intonations of the act, including the praise of inactivity, at the same time. For instance, if we take one of his recent books, *First as Tragedy, Then as Farce*, we almost immediately find a repetition of the entreaty not to act but to think: "Perhaps it is time to step back, think and *say* the right thing. True, we often talk about something instead of doing it; but sometimes we also do things in order to avoid talking and thinking about them."[56] Soon thereafter, the act is defined in accordance with the miraculous view of making the impossible possible: "This is how the impossible becomes possible: what was hitherto considered unthinkable within the horizon of the established standards of decent working conditions

---

55   Žižek, *Iraq*, 74.
56   Žižek, *First as Tragedy, Then as Farce*, 11.

now becomes acceptable."[57] Yet, in the end, albeit with an added note of violent interruption borrowed from Walter Benjamin, we come back to the earliest modulations of the notion of the act as the assumption of the inconsistency or nonexistence of the big Other: "This is what a proper political act would be today: not so much to unleash a new movement, as to *interrupt* the present predominant movement. An act of 'divine violence' would then mean pulling the emergency cord on the train of Historical Progress. In other words, one has to learn fully to accept that there is no big Other."[58]

The political consequences of this oscillatory movement between the different notions of the act are by no means straightforward. Žižek, on the one hand, certainly ends his ruminations on the ex-Soviet Union in *For They Know Not What They Do*, for example, with an appeal to a leftist-Lacanian political project that would at least keep alive the memory of past revolutionary causes, even if they have been thwarted by the turn to Western-style capitalism

---

57   Ibid., 21. Žižek is here talking about the government bail-out of General Motors after the 2008 crisis, just as elsewhere he mentions the growing tolerance toward using torture against prisoners suspected of terrorist activity. This goes to show that the act of making the impossible possible, or rendering the unthinkable acceptable, is by no means limited to progressive, leftist, or revolutionary politics. In fact, here as elsewhere, the ideological valence of the different intonations of the act is constitutively left open.

58   Ibid., 149.

and neo-racism: "Today more than ever, in the midst of the scoundrel time we live in, the duty of the Left is to keep alive the memory of all lost causes, of all shattered and perverted dreams and hopes attached to leftist projects."[59] Likewise, when in *The Indivisible Remainder* he seeks to illustrate the real genesis of the symbolic order—the process of how someone becomes who he or she is by way of what Lacan calls a precipitate identification—he uses the example of Soviet Communism and Socialism: "When I recognize myself as a 'Socialist,' I thereby posit the very 'objective' frame of reference which allows for my 'subjective' identification. Or—to put it in a slightly different way: I am what (I think that others think that) I am . . ."[60] Lacanian psychoanalysis thus would provide us with many of the tools necessary to establish and understand the identification with a leftist, socialist or communist political cause.

On the other hand, the ultimate paradox might well

---

59  Žižek, *For They Know Not What They Do*, 271.
60  Žižek, *The Indivisible Remainder*, 143. Lacan discusses the notion of precipitate identification in his paper "Logical Time and the Assertion of Anticipated Certainty," *Écrits*, 161–75. Žižek adds: "The significant detail usually passed over in silence is that Lacan quotes as the exemplary political case of such collective identification the Stalinist Communist's affirmation of orthodoxy: I hasten to promulgate my true Communist credentials out of fear that others will expel me as a revisionist traitor . . ." (*The Indivisible Remainder*, 135). Alain Badiou already devoted a lengthy analysis to Lacan's *écrit* in his *Theory of the Subject*, trans. Bruno Bosteels (London: Continuum, 2009), 248–58.

reside in the incompatibility between this hopeful prospect and some of the very same teachings from the Lacanian school that so deeply inspire Žižek. Indeed, as he writes in *The Ticklish Subject*: "For Lacan, negativity, a negative gesture of withdrawal, precedes any positive gesture of enthusiastic identification with a Cause: negativity functions as the condition of (im)possibility of the enthusiastic identification—that is to say, it lays the ground, opens up space for it, but is simultaneously obfuscated by it and undermines it."[61] It would thus seem that any principled recognition of the real of enjoyment and drive strictly speaking undermines in advance the possibility of identifying with a leftist cause—other than a lost one. Indeed, what causes are there to be kept alive from a psychoanalytical perspective, if for the latter the most radical act consists in the subject's defining gesture of pure negativity that precedes and undermines every possible candidate? Or, in a last turn of the screw, perhaps the precipitate identification with a political cause is now something reserved for the Third World: "It appears, in fact, as if the split between First World and the Third runs more and more along the lines of the opposition between leading a long satisfying life, full of material and cultural wealth, and dedicating one's life to some transcendent Cause."[62]

---

61  Žižek, *The Ticklish Subject*, 154.
62  Žižek, "Foreword to the Second Edition: Enjoyment Within the Limits of Reason Alone," *For They Know Not What They Do*, lxxiv.

Žižek himself, in fact, frequently calls for a double act of renunciation, or a twofold *Versagung*. Not only should we give up our innermost idiotic substance and sacrifice everything particular to a cause greater than ourselves, but the modern subject at its most radical is also supposed to sacrifice this cause itself:

> In other words, the modern subject is strictly correlative with the dimension "beyond the second death": the first death is the sacrifice of our particular, "pathological" substance for the universal Cause; the second death is the sacrifice, the "betrayal," of this Cause itself, so that all that remains is the void which is $, the "barred" subject—the subject emerges only via this double, self-relating sacrifice of the very Cause for which he was ready to sacrifice everything.[63]

Seen in this light, there would seem to be little hope of the subject identifying with any cause whatsoever.

---

63   Žižek, *The Indivisible Remainder*, 121. Throughout his work Žižek illustrates this redoubled renunciation and self-sacrifice with a limited set of examples: from Medea to Lacan himself, via Keyser Soeze in *The Usual Suspects* and Sethe in Toni Morrison's *Beloved*. See, for example, *The Fragile Absolute*, 149–55. The call to move from Antigone (sacrificing everything to the Cause) to Medea (sacrificing the Cause itself) is repeated, among other places, in Slavoj Žižek, *The Parallax View* (Cambridge: MIT Press, 2006), 397 n.30.

Perhaps, though, Žižek was right after all. Perhaps this withdrawal into radical negativity and inaction was necessary in order to wipe the slate clean before he could come back to propose the idea of communism and, with it, the return to the political act of instituting a new social order—even a new State. As he puts it in *First as Tragedy, Then as Farce*, in an open polemic with the anti-statist position shared by nearly everyone else at the 2009 London conference "On the Idea of Communism": "If you have no clear idea of what you want to replace the state with, you have no right to subtract/withdraw from the state. Instead of taking a distance from the state, the true task should be to make the state itself work in a non-statal mode," in the strict Leninist sense. "Here, one should shamelessly repeat the lesson of Lenin's *State and Revolution*: the goal of revolutionary violence is not to take over state power, but to transform it, radically changing its functioning, its relationship to its base, and so on."[64] Bolivia is certainly one place where such a takeover of state power in a non-statal manner supposedly is being attempted and where communism, whether old or new, might thus be on the horizon again. Aware of the need not to let home-bred conditions in Western Europe and the United States be surrounded by chauvinistic superstition—as was feared by Marx and Engels as early as *The German Ideology*—I therefore propose in my

---

64    Žižek, *First as Tragedy, Then as Farce*, 130–1.

next and final chapter to foster the spirit of internationalism by turning to the case of Bolivia, its promises and its shortcomings, as seen through the lens of the theoretical work of Álvaro García Linera.

# 5

## *The Actuality of Communism*

What emerges is a Left that operates without either a deep and radical critique of the status quo or a compelling alternative to the existing order of things. But perhaps even more troubling, it is a Left that has become more attached to its impossibility than to its potential fruitfulness, a Left that is most at home dwelling not in hopefulness but in its own marginality and failure, a Left that is thus caught in a structure of melancholic attachment to a certain strain of its own dead past, whose spirit is ghostly, whose structure of desire is backward looking and punishing.

— Wendy Brown, "Resisting Left Melancholia"

### The Communist Horizon

To overcome its melancholic attachment to marginality and failure, should not the Left once again take up the task of the radical critique of the status quo in the name of a communist alternative—including an alternative to the melancholy Left? To what extent can we say that communism today is an actuality and not just a specter; a real movement and not just a ghostly spirit from the dead past, or one whose only

forward-looking move is to postulate the need for a spec-
ulative-philosophical Idea, whether Kantian or Platonic?
Furthermore, can communism offer a way out of the moralization of politics that follows from the endless self-flagella-
tions of the Left? Or is the hopeful invocation of the communist hypothesis, especially when it is no longer tied to any
real movement to abolish the current state of affairs, part and
parcel of the same-old self-sacrificing genealogy of morals?

Álvaro García Linera, Evo Morales's successful running
mate in the 2005 elections and the current vice president of
Bolivia, may help us begin answering some of these questions. Far from denying or disavowing any attachment to
his communist past as either inexistent or else dead and
overcome, which is the response one might expect from an
elected official under the remote but ever-watchful eye of
the United States, García Linera in fact calmly vindicates
this legacy as if it were the most natural thing in the world.
"The general horizon of the era is communist," he states in an
interview with Pablo Stefanoni in which he reflects upon past
expectations and the future tasks ahead for his party MAS
(Movement to Socialism) now that they have democratically
taken over the power of the State. More specifically:

> The general horizon of the era is communist. And this
> communism will have to be constructed on the basis of
> society's self-organizing capacities, of processes for the
> generation and distribution of communitarian, self-
> managing wealth. But at this moment it is clear that

this is not an immediate horizon, which centers on the conquest of equality, the redistribution of wealth, the broadening of rights. Equality is fundamental because it breaks a chain of five centuries of structural inequality; that is the aim at the time, as far as social forces allow us to go—not because we prescribe it to be thus but because that is what we see. Rather, we enter the movement with our expecting and desiring eyes set upon the communist horizon. But we were serious and objective, in the social sense of the term, by signaling the limits of the movement. And that is where the fight came with various *compañeros* about what it was possible to do.[1]

It would be easy to condemn this analysis—and the fight with various *compañeros* no doubt involved precisely such a condemnation—on the grounds that it reverts back to the old stageism in which the generation and distribution of wealth, what García Linera sometimes notoriously refers to as "Andean capitalism," would be the necessary prior condition for the construction of socialism and only afterward can there be talk of a communist future. However, spurred on by Jodi Dean, who has drawn my attention to the untapped richness

---

1   Álvaro García Linera, "El 'descubrimiento' del Estado," in Pablo Stefanoni, Franklin Ramírez and Maristella Svampa, *Las vías de la emancipación: Conversaciones con Álvaro García Linera* (Mexico City: Ocean Sur, 2008), 75.

of this notion of the communist horizon, I would like to read into it the exact opposite of the orthodox if not vulgar picture of the transition from capitalism to socialism to communism. In fact, even for García Linera, the notion resonates not with the banal image of the horizon as an ever-receding line in the distance, so much as with Jean-Paul Sartre's allegedly obsolete definition of Marxism as the untranscendable horizon of our time. This and nothing else is what the invocation of the communist horizon is meant to produce or render actual once again: a complete shift in perspective, or a radical ideological turnabout, as a result of which capitalism no longer appears as the only game in town and we no longer have to be ashamed to set our expecting and desiring eyes here and now on a different organization of social relationships. "'Horizon,' then, tags not a lost future but a dimension of experience we can never lose, even if, lost in a fog or focused on our feet, we fail to see it. The horizon is Real not just in the sense of *impossible*—we can never reach it—but also in the sense of the *actual* format, condition, and shape of our setting (and I take both these senses of Real to be Lacanian)," Jodi Dean explains in her own riff on the notion of the communist horizon that she also borrows from García Linera. "We can lose our bearings, but the horizon is a necessary condition or shaping of our actuality. Whether the effect of a singularity or the meeting of earth and sky, the horizon is the fundamental division establishing where we are."[2]

---

2  Jodi Dean, "The Communist Horizon" (author's manuscript).

## Power to the Plebes?

García Linera is the author not only of important books on Marx and Marxism that he signed as Qhananchiri, including *De demonios escondidos y momentos de revolución* (*Of Hidden Demons and Moments of Revolution*) and *Forma valor y forma comunidad* (*Value Form and Community Form*), this last one written while locked up in the maximum security prison of Chonchocoro in La Paz between 1992 and 1997 on charges of subversive activity and armed uprising, but also of a fundamental collection of political and sociological writings, recently published under the title *La potencia plebeya* (*The Plebeian Potential*). Far from signaling a direct commitment to the communist horizon, however, the title of this collection in the first place seems to suggest a profound indebtedness to leftism. Besides, in several of these writings García Linera also throws some well-aimed punches at those whom he describes as sectarian, catastrophic, or mystical "pseudoleftists," *pseudoizquierdistas*, which would confirm his own implicit self-identification as a presumably "genuine" leftist, rather than as a communist. Moreover, García Linera's ex-*compañera* and fellow guerrilla fighter in the Tupac Katari Guerrilla Army (EGTK), Mexican-born Raquel Gutiérrez Aguilar, writing under the pen name of Qhantat Wara Wara, also formulates a critique of "bourgeois leftism," which once again suggests a commitment to a true leftism, while conversely, from a self-described orthodox Marxist position, both García Linera and Raquel Gutiérrez themselves have come under attack for being "leftist-revisionist."[3]

The multiple references to the "plebes" (*la plebe armada*, *la plebe facciosa*, *las plebes insurrectas*, and so on) in García Linera's recent collection of writings, on the one hand, entail a sustained attempt to bypass the classical figure of the proletariat modeled on the large factory worker, in favor of a wider and much more flexible composition of the revolutionary subject. García Linera calls this composition "motley," or *abigarrada* in Spanish, supposedly borrowing a term from the famous Bolivian sociologist René Zavaleta Mercado. In actual fact, though, this concept and its name already appear in the Spanish translation of Lenin's well-known pamphlet on left-wing communism:

> Capitalism would not be capitalism if the "pure" proletariat were not surrounded by a large number of exceedingly motley types intermediate between the proletarian and the semi-proletarian (who earns his

---

3  Qhantat Wara Wara, *Los q'aras izquierdizantes: una crítica al izquierdismo burgués*, with a presentation by Qhananchiri (La Paz: Ofensiva Roja, 1988); Qhantat Wara Wara, *Contra el reformismo: Crítica al "estatismo" y al "populismo" pequeño burgués*, with a presentation by Qhananchiri (La Paz: Ofensiva Roja, 1989); Carlos M. Volodia, *Contribución a la crítica del revisionismo: Crítica de las posiciones ideológicas de Raquel Gutiérrez* (La Paz: Bandera Roja, 1999); and Fernando Molina, *Crítica de las ideas políticas de la nueva izquierda boliviana* (La Paz: Eureka, 2003).

livelihood in part by the sale of his labour-power), between the semi-proletarian and the small peasant (and petty artisan, handicraft worker and small master in general), between the small peasant and the middle peasant, and so on, and if the proletariat itself were not divided into more developed and less developed strata, if it were not divided according to territorial origin, trade, sometimes according to religion, and so on. And from all this follows the necessity, the absolute necessity, for the vanguard of the proletariat, its class-conscious section, the Communist Party, to resort to manoeuvres, agreements and compromises with the various groups of proletarians, with the various parties of the workers and small masters. It is entirely a case of *knowing how* to apply these tactics in order to *raise*, and not lower, the *general* level of proletarian class-consciousness, revolutionary spirit, and ability to fight and win.[4]

---

4   V. I. Lenin, "'Left-wing' Communism, an Infantile Disorder," *Selected Works* (Moscow: Foreign Languages Publishing House, 1961), vol. 3, 421. For the Spanish translation I have consulted *La enfermedad infantil del "izquierdismo" en el comunismo* (Moscow: Progreso, n.d.). On the notion of "formación social abigarrada," see René Zavaleta Mercado, *Las masas en noviembre* (La Paz: Juventud,1983) and *Lo nacional-popular en Bolivia* (Mexico City: Siglo XXI, 1986; La Paz: Plural, 2008); the massive overview of Zavaleta's thought by Luis Tapia, *La producción del conocimiento local* (La Paz: Muela del Diablo, 2002); and the collection of essays *René Zavaleta Mercado: Ensayos, testimonios y re-visiones*, ed. Maya

This is also how García Linera, drawing on his militant sociological investigations into the phenomena of repro-letarianization and the so-called extinction of the working class, describes the new class composition of that motley social formation of the "plebes" in which socio-economical and cultural-symbolical aspects must constantly be thought together.

More generally speaking, the plebeian reference is consistent with a leftist and populist appeal to various names for the formless or as yet unformed masses: from Hegel's "rabble" to Deleuze's "hordes" and "packs" to Laclau's retrieval of Marx's "lumpen." As Jacques and Danielle Rancière explain in their article on the trajectory of leftism in 1970s France, what many of these names but especially that of the plebes promise are ways of sidestepping the issue of representation as the principal obstacle against which all emancipatory politics run aground. Thus, referring to the use of the notion on the part of New Philosophers such as André Glucksmann, if not already on the part of Michel Foucault, Jacques and Danielle Rancière describe how "the figure of a *plebs* appears whom the intellectual represents just as yesterday he represented the proletariat, but in a way that precisely denies representation, the plebs means both and at the same time all the

Aguiluz Ibargüen and Norma de los Ríos (Mexico City: FLACSO, 2006). This concept is also discussed in Toni Negri, Michael Hardt, Giuseppe Cocco, and Judith Revel's seminar discussion with García Linera and Luis Tapia, *Imperio, multitud y sociedad abigarrada* (La Paz: CLACSO/Muela del Diablo/Comuna, 2008).

positivity of suffering and popular laughter and the part of refusal, of negativity, that each carries with them, realizing the immediate unity of the intellectual and the people."[5] Used in this sense, the plebeian reference is an integral part of the leftist tradition in which political antagonism is purified into a stark dualism that immediately and undialectically pits

---

5    Jacques Rancière (with Danielle Rancière), "La légende des philosophes. Les intellectuels et la traversée du gauchisme," *Les Scènes du peuple (Les Révoltes logiques, 1975/1985)* (Lyon: Horlieu, 2003), 307–8. See also my discussion above in Chapter 3. I should add that this insight into the role of the figure of the plebes did not keep Rancière himself from presenting the work of Gabriel Gauny as that of a "plebeian philosopher," or from delving into the history of "plebeian" appropriations of "heretical" workers' knowledge. Rancière's justification of this earlier use is helpful here: "I use the adjective 'plebeian' rather than 'proletarian' in order to avoid equivocations. Some people, indeed, stubbornly insist on wanting 'proletarian' to designate the worker of a certain type of modern industry. By contrast, it should be clear that 'plebeian' designates a symbolical relation and not a type of work. Plebeian is the being who is excluded from history-making speech." See Rancière, "Savoirs hérétiques et émancipations du pauvre," *Les Scènes du peuple*, 38. For a recent return to Foucault's notion of the plebes, which he began using in 1972 in the debate with the Maoists on the subject of popular justice, see also Tiqqun, *Tout a failli, vive le communisme!* (Paris: La Fabrique, 2009), 39–41. Fredric Jameson also repeatedly speaks of "plebeianization" in *The Hegel Variations* (London: Verso, 2010). In the case of García Linera, another important reference is E. P. Thompson, "The Patricians and the Plebs," *Customs in Common: Studies in Traditional Popular Culture* (New York: New Press, 1993), 16–96; this is a revised and expanded version of the famous article "Patrician Society, Plebeian Culture," *Journal of Social History* 7 (1974): 382–405.

the formless masses against the repressive machinery of the State.

In *La potencia plebeya*, I might add, the unmediated unity of the intellectual and the people that is sought after through the plebeian reference paradoxically also seeks to forego all figures of that mediating third who in Latin America usually comes in the guise of the white *letrado* (literally "lettered" but also more broadly "educated"), or *ladino* (etymologically from "he who knows Latin" but also more broadly meaning "white" or *criollo*). Ironically, though, not only was *un hombre que sabe*, or "a man who knows," a slogan used for posters in García Linera's 2005 electoral campaign, but, what is more, Qhananchiri, the Aymara name with which he used to sign many of his prison writings and pamphlets for the Tupac Katari Guerrilla Army, also means "he who clarifies things" or "he who enlightens," so that many of the stabs in *La potencia plebeya* against the representational figure of the intellectual can be read as prescient self-criticisms. No author writes more ardently and eloquently than García Linera himself against the risks that beset those "committed intellectuals" who claim to speak "for" or "to" the subaltern-indigenous masses, all the while having their eyes fixed high on the benefits, both moral and material, that derive from a privileged position near or inside the Hydra-headed apparatus of the State. Nothing would be easier than to turn these criticisms against their author—and, nowadays, no enterprise is indeed more common on behalf of critics from the Left no less than from the Right.

On the other hand, leading back to a tradition of immanence as the source for a second figure of contemporary leftism, the search for an overcoming of representation is further developed through the element of *potencia* in García Linera's title. The Spanish term *potencia* is certainly as difficult to translate into English as Negri's *potenza*: "potentiality" sounds like an amputated Aristotelianism without actuality à la Whitehead or Agamben; "potency" is overly sexual and anxiously virile; and "power" creates disastrous confusions with the customary translation of the Spanish *poder* or Italian *potere*; so here I will opt for "potential" instead. Still, the English-speaking reader does well to keep in mind that in Spanish a bonus feature of *potencia* is the ease with which this noun turns into a verb, *potenciar*, "to empower," or literally, "to potentialize," meaning both and at the same time to actualize that which otherwise remains as yet merely potential and to retrieve the potential that is actually latent within an existing state of affairs.

Among the most astonishing passages in *La potencia plebeya* are those that refer to the contemporary relevance of *The Communist Manifesto* in which García Linera, also following Marx's *Grundrisse* and Negri's seminal rereading thereof, uncovers the immanent counterfinality of capitalism as the place that at the same time contains the still abstract potential for communism to become actual. "Marx's attitude in the *Manifesto* toward this globalization of capital consists simply in understanding the emancipatory potentials [*potencias*] which are hidden therein but which until now appear

deformed and distorted by the dominant capitalist rationality," García Linera writes, so that a "critical analysis must
bring to light the counterfinalities, the emancipatory counter-
tendencies of labor against capital that are nested materially
in its midst and that Marxists must understand and empower
[*potenciar*] by all the means at their disposal."[6] This also means
that the potential of the plebes, while currently still dormant
and abstract, already lies within the power of capital, instead
of opposing the latter from some utopian or imaginary outside
with the dream of pure nonpower. Communism as the real or
actual movement that abolishes the present state of affairs, in
other words, is not some speculative idealist dream but it is
linked in a properly materialist, critical if not dialectical way
to the tendencies and counterfinalities inherent in capitalism.

---

6   Álvaro García Linera, "El *Manifiesto comunista* y nuestro
tiempo," in *El fantasma insomne: Pensando el presente desde el*
Manifiesto Comunista (La Paz: Muela del Diablo, 1999), reprinted
in Álvaro García Linera, *La potencia plebeya: Acción colectiva e*
*identidades indígenas, obreras y populares en Bolivia*, ed. Pablo
Stefanoni (Buenos Aires: Prometeo Libros/CLACSO, 2008), 59–60.
García Linera's work unfortunately is not yet extensively available
in English. See "State Crisis and Popular Power," *New Left Review*
37 (2006): 73–85; "The 'Multitude,'" in Oscar Olivera with Tom
Lewis, *¡Cochabamba! Water War in Bolivia* (Cambridge: South End
Press, 2004), 65–86; and "The State in Transition: Power Bloc and
Point of Bifurcation," *Latin American Perspectives* 37 (2010): 34–47.
A video of "Marxismo e indianismo" ("Marxism and Indianism"),
García Linera's important 2007 inaugural speech at the "Marx and
Marxisms in Latin America" conference at Cornell University, is
also available in English translation at www.cornell.edu/video.

And yet, the power of the plebes does not emerge spontaneously from the crisis and impotence of capitalism, since capital only produces ever more capital—even in, or especially in, global crises such as the current one. As Marx used to say: "Social reforms are never achieved because of the weakness of the strong but are always the result of the power of the weak."[7] This empowering of the weak depends on a massive and often violent act of torsion or forcing, an act that García Linera—formerly a mathematician by training—also names the curvature of communist self-determination. "In other words, capital unfolds the potentials of social labor only as abstraction, as forces that are constantly subordinated and castrated by the rationality of value of the commodity. The fact that these tendencies may come to the surface is no longer an issue of capital, which while it exists will never allow that they flourish for themselves; it is an issue of labor over and against capital, on the basis of what capital thus far has done," García Linera concludes. He adds: "To break this determination, to *curve* in another direction the domain of classes, otherwise to define labor on the basis of labor itself, is a question of the construction of workers for themselves, of the determination of labor for itself in the face of capital's determination for itself: it is the historical-material problem of self-determination."[8]

---

7    Marx, quoted in García Linera, *La potencia plebeya*, 65.
8    Ibid., 79 and 114. For Linera, such curvature of determination corresponds precisely to Marx's definition of the political party:

## The Current Situation and Our Tasks

From these all too brief remarks about García Linera's recent work as a theorist, I derive two general tasks with regard to the actuality of communism in its never-ending dialectical struggle with leftism, that is, two tasks of theoretical self-clarification that in the end may bring about a common front in which arguments for the subtraction from party and State hopefully no longer need exclude our taking seriously— while neither idealizing nor prejudging—experiments such as the one unfolding today in Bolivia.

The first task requires that we actively continue to historicize the communist hypothesis. We need to carry on beyond the confines of Western Europe and the ex-Soviet Union with what is at once the beauty and disarming simplicity of the idea, or the second-degree idea about the idea, which remains a constant in Badiou's work from *Of Ideology* until most recently *The Communist Hypothesis*, according to which communism is defined, on the one hand, by a series

---

"The party is then the large movement of historical constitution of the proletarian mass into a subject in charge of its destiny through the elaboration of multiple and massive practical forms capable of producing a reality different from the one established by capital. The *party*, in this sense, *is a material fact of the masses*, not of sects or vanguards; it is a movement of practical actions not just theoretical acquisitions; it is the class struggle carried out by the working class itself, not a program or 'an *ideal* to which reality will have to adjust itself'" (ibid., 122).

of axiomatic invariants that can be found whenever a mass mobilization directly confronts the privileges of property, hierarchy, and authority, and, on the other, by the specific political actors who historically and with varying degrees of success or failure implement those same communist invariants. In other words, this first task amounts to writing, as it were, a history of communist eternity, in a counterfactually Borgesian sense. The key concept in this regard is not the orthodox one of stages and transitions in a linear dialectical periodization but rather that of the different aleatory sequences of the communist hypothesis in a strictly immanent determination, with all that this entails in terms of the assessment of failures, including an assessment of the very nature of what is called a failure, and of the legacy of unsolved problems handed down from one sequence to another.

Second, unless the communist hypothesis is to be left to shine for eternity with all the untimely brilliance of a Platonic or Kantian Idea, communism must not only be rehistoricized outside all suppositions of historical necessity and stageism, it must also be actualized and organized as the real movement that abolishes the present state of things. In other words, communism must again find inscription in a concrete body, the collective flesh and thought of an internationalist political subjectivity—even if it may no longer be necessary for such an act of subjectivization to pass through the traditional form of the party for its embodiment. After the historicization of eternity, this would be the second task for the renewal of communism in our current situation. As

Badiou writes in *Of an Obscure Disaster*: "The point where an instance of thought subtracts itself from the State, inscribing this subtraction into being, constitutes the real of a politics. And a political organization has no other goal than to 'hold onto the gained step,' that is, to provide a *body* for that thought which, collectively re-membered, has been able to find the public gesture of the insubordination that founds it."[9] But then, of course, the way in which communism may be organized and embodied is also precisely where all the major doubts and disagreements are to be found.

## Party and State

On several occasions in *La potencia plebeya*, García Linera interestingly enough draws attention to a letter from Marx to Ferdinand Freiligrath, dated February 29, 1860, in which Marx writes that after the dissolution, at his behest, of the League of Communists in November 1852, he himself "*never* belonged to any society again, whether *secret* or *public*; that the *party*, therefore, in this wholly ephemeral sense, ceased to exist for me 8 years ago," but that this does not exhaust the meaning of the term: "By party, I meant the party in the

---

9  Alain Badiou, *D'un désastre obscur: Sur la fin de la vérité d'État* (La Tour d'Aigues: De l'Aube, 1998), 57. *Tenir le pas gagné* is an allusion to Arthur Rimbaud's *A Season in Hell*, just as the book's main title, *D'un désastre obscur*, like that of Badiou's last novel *Calme bloc, ici-bas*, is an allusion to Mallarmé's *The Tomb of Edgar Allan Poe*.

broad historical sense."[10] Based on this letter, García Linera
goes on to call for a retrieval and proper reevaluation of the
dialectic between these two senses of the party, the ephemeral and the grand-historical, in ways that may well dovetail
with some of Badiou's lesser-known pronouncements on the
same subject, even as late as in his *Metapolitics*, a collection
that otherwise pleads for a militant form of politics without
a party and at a distance from the State. García Linera interprets Marx's letter as follows:

> *Historical sense and ephemeral sense of the party* form
> an historical dialectic of the party in Marx, which we
> must vindicate today in the face of a tragic experience
> of the party-state that prevails in the organized experi-
> ences of a large part of the Left worldwide. The party-
> state, in all cases, has been the miniature replica of
> hierarchical state despotism, which has alienated the
> militant will in the omnipotent powers of bosses and
> party functionaries; and no sooner do revolutionary
> social transformations appear than these apparatuses
> show an extraordinary facility to amalgamate them-
> selves with the state machinery so as to reconstruct
> them in their exclusive function of expropriating the

10   Marx to Ferdinand Freiligrath in London, in Karl Marx
and Friedrich Engels, *Collected Works*, vol. 41 (New York:
International Publishers, 1985), quoted in García Linera, *La
potencia plebeya*, 82.

general will, which at the same time reinforces the rationality of capitalist reproduction from which it emerged.[11]

Can we not articulate this idea of retrieving the party in the grand historical sense with a rather surprising defense of the party-form of politics on the part of Badiou in *Metapolitics*? "It is crucial to emphasise that for Marx or Lenin, who are both in agreement on this point, the real characteristic of the party is not its firmness, but rather its porosity to the event, its dispersive flexibility in the face of unforeseeable circumstances," Badiou writes with direct references to *The Communist Manifesto* and *What is to be Done?*

Thus, rather than referring to a dense, bound fraction of the working class—what Stalin will call a 'detachment'—the party refers to an unfixable omnipresence, whose proper function is less to represent class than to de-limit it by ensuring it is equal to everything that history presents as improbable and excessive in respect of the rigidity of interests, whether material or national. Thus, the communists embody the unbound multiplicity of consciousness, its anticipatory aspect, and therefore the precariousness of the bond, rather than its firmness. It is not for nothing that the maxim

11    García Linera, *La potencia plebeya*, 130.

of the proletarian is to have nothing to lose but his chains, and to have a world to win.[12]

The party, in other words, would no longer be the incarnation of the iron laws of historical necessity running things behind our backs while we applaud in unison with the apparatchiks. Instead, it would simply name the flexible organization of a fidelity to events in the midst of unforeseeable circumstances.

With regard to the State, finally, García Linera obviously shares the idea already fully expressed by Marx and Engels after the experience of the Paris Commune and endlessly repeated today by Badiou and Negri, namely: "The modern State, in whatever form it takes, is essentially a capitalist machinery, it is the State of capitalists, the ideal collective capitalist."[13]

---

12   Alain Badiou, *Metapolitics*, trans. Jason Barker (London: Verso, 2005), 74. See Karl Marx and Friedrich Engels, *The Communist Manifesto* (London: Penguin, 1967), 95.

13   Friedrich Engels, "From Utopian Socialism to Scientific Socialism," quoted in García Linera, *La potencia plebeya*, 101 n. 157. Marx's own point of view famously shifted in this regard after and as a result of the Paris Commune. For a commentary on this "rectification" of *The Communist Manifesto* with regard to the State, García Linera refers to the study by Étienne Balibar, "La 'rectification' du *Manifeste communiste*," *Cinq études du matérialisme historique* (Paris: François Maspero, 1974), 65–101. Elsewhere, in his polemic with José Aricó's famous argument about the missed encounter between Marx and Latin America, García Linera draws the conclusion: "There is thus no social revolutionization possible nor therefore any national construction from within the old State. This task can only come into

This is why, in an earlier text written in prison under the pen name Qhananchiri, García Linera repeats the orthodox-leftist viewpoint that communism has nothing to do with apparatuses such as the parliament, except smash them: "Destroy it! Burn it! Make it disappear together with the government and the whole state apparatus! Propose instead the workers, tired of being used as servants by the bosses."[14] And yet, just as he argues against the potential for corruption inherent in the state-form as such, years later the soon-to-become Vice President of Bolivia also warns against what he calls "a kind of non-statehood dreamed of by primitive anarchism":

> The naïvety of a society outside of the State would be no more than an innocent speculation, if it were not

---

being as society's movement of self-organization, as creative and vital impulse of civil society to organize itself as nation," and yet, he adds: "This does not take away the possible role of the State in this task, as Marx signals in the case of absolute monarchism in Europe, or of the creole elites themselves, as in Mexico, but always as condensations, as orienting syntheses of the impulses of society." See Qhananchiri, *De demonios escondidos y momentos de revolución: Marx y la revolución social en las extremidades del cuerpo capitalista, Parte 1* (La Paz: Ofensiva Roja, 1991), 255–6; this section is also included in García Linera, *La potencia plebeya*, 50. For a more detailed discussion of the missed encounter between Marx and Latin America and the debate between Aricó and García Linera on this topic, see the Preface to my *Marx and Freud in Latin America: Politics, Religion, and Psychoanalysis in the Age of Terror* (London: Verso, 2011).

14   Qhananchiri, *Crítica de la nación y la nación crítica naciente* (La Paz: Ofensiva Roja, 1990), 34.

for the fact that it is thus "forgotten" or hidden how the state "lives off" the resources of the whole society, hierarchically assigning these goods in function of the strength of the totality of social fractions and consecrating the access to these powers by means of the coercion that it exerts and the legitimacy that it obtains from the totality of society's members. The state is thus a total social relation, not only the ambition of the "capable" or of the "power-thirsty"; the state in a certain way traverses all of us, which is where its public meaning stems from.[15]

The State, in other words, is ultimately built on and lives off nothing else than the plebeian potential, which can always manifest itself by expropriating the expropriators so as to take back what for the past five centuries has been the defining theft of modern power and sovereignty in Latin America.

---

15   García Linera, "Autonomía indígena y Estado multinacional" (2004), reprinted in *La potencia plebeya*, 231–2 n. 277. The most succinct overview of the ongoing debate over the possible role of the State in popular, indigenous, proletarian and peasant uprisings in Bolivia's recent history can be traced in the articles by Jaime Iturri Salmón and Raquel Gutiérrez Aguilar, in the collection *Las armas de la utopía. Marxismo: Provocaciones heréticas* (La Paz: CIDES/ UMSA, 1996), followed by García Linera's letters in response to the criticisms of his two *compañeros*, 66–76; and García Linera, "La lucha por el poder en Bolivia," in *Horizontes y límites del estado y el poder* (La Paz: Muela del Diablo, 2005), partially reprinted in *La potencia plebeya*, 350–73.

Even in *Crítica de la nación y la nación crítica naciente*, perhaps his most radical text written under the pen name of Qhananchiri, García Linera already invokes not just a "nascent critical nation" but also the possibility of an alternative, "non-capitalist" State. On the one hand: "The current struggle of Aymara and Quechua vindications remits us, therefore, to the problem of a non-capitalist national constitution"; on the other, the possibility for such a non-capitalist state formation will depend on the strength of collective action at the grassroots level:

> Whether in this communal association there is place or not for the formation of a state of Aymara workers, a state of Quechua workers, a state of Bolivian workers, etc., in any case, will be the outcome of the collective decision and will imposed by the vitality of the natural-cultural-historical dimension in the context of the insurgency and of the communitarian links established in all this time between the worker of the city and the country in order to close the scars of distrust borne from the capitalist national oppression.[16]

Finally, in his interview with Stefanoni, García Linera goes so far as to suggest the possibility that the State, provided that it is subjected to a new constituent power, might be one of the

16   Qhananchiri, *Crítica de la nación y la nación crítica naciente*, 18–19 and 28–9.

embodiments that "potentialize" or "empower" the communist horizon from within. Nobody for sure would have expected to hear anything less from a sitting vice president who has gradually come to jettison his more doctrinaire autonomist allegiances to the work of Toni Negri in favor of a well-nigh classical, Hegelian or Weberian view. Even so, García Linera's words as usual are both eloquent and provocative:

> When I enter into the government, what I do is to vali-
> date and begin to operate at the level of the State in func-
> tion of this reading of the current moment. So then, what
> about communism? What can be done from the State
> in function of this communist horizon? To support as
> much as possible the unfolding of society's autonomous
> organizational capacities. This is as far as it is possible to
> go in terms of what a leftist State, a revolutionary State,
> can do. To broaden the workers' base and the autonomy
> of the workers' world, to potentialize [*potenciar*] forms
> of communitarian economy wherever there are more
> communitarian networks, articulations, and projects.[17]

In response to this well-nigh complete turnaround in the interpretation of the relation between communism and the State, which in any case should be no more scandalizing than the turnabouts we can find in the work of other communist

---

17   García Linera, "El 'descubrimiento' del Estado," in *Las vías de la emancipación*, 75.

thinkers with regard to the question of the party—not to mention the apostasies of the repentant that by contrast always meet with the utmost sympathy and compassion on the part of mainstream media—I would argue that we need to avoid two extreme and equally nefarious answers: on the one hand, the wholesale condemnation of all such articulations of the communist hypothesis and the State in the name of a limited historicization focused on Western Europe and on the debacles of both Soviet communism and Eurocommunism; and, on the other, the relativist conclusion that what may be bad for Paris or Bologna may be good for Kathmandu or Cochabamba, or vice-versa.

We have use for neither blind and arrogant universalism nor abject and ultimately patronizing culturalism. Instead, what is needed is a comprehensive and collective rethinking, without epic or apostasy, of the links between communism, the history and theory of the State, and the history and theory of modes of political organization—with the latter including not only the party but also the legacy of insurrectionary mass action and armed struggle, which in the context of Latin America, Asia, and Africa is certainly at least as important as, if not more so than, the old questions of party and State.

## The Future of Communism and Pre-Capitalist Forms of Community

García Linera's most original contribution to the history and theory of socialism and communism, however, concerns the difficult relation of Marx and Marxism to the questions of nation, ethnicity, and community. Not only does he discuss the reasons behind the "missed encounter" or *desencuentro* between Marxism and indigenism, or between Marxism and what in Bolivia is more commonly referred to as *indianismo*. In a painstaking return to Marx's writings on the national and agrarian questions, including the often-ignored ethnological notebooks and the drafts and letter to the Russian activist Vera Zasulich, he also addresses these questions by interrogating the link between communism and community in its pre-capitalist, so-called archaic, ancestral and peasant-agrarian forms. Such is the ambitious task taken up by García Linera in a long process of autodidactic study in the 1990s, before and during his time in prison, and partially reflected in the volumes *De demonios escondidos y momentos de revolución* and *Forma valor y forma comunidad*, both published with prefaces by Raquel Gutiérrez. This debate cannot be dismissed as easily as someone like Žižek seems to think when he rejects offhand Evo Morales's references to nature in the civilizational clash between capitalism and anticapitalism. Far from representing reactive or obscurantist ideological illusions of an original balance and harmony disturbed by modern science and technology, such references can be read as symptoms of the tensions inherent in class-based definitions of socialism and communism with their difficulty in accounting for issues of race, nation, ethnicity, and community.

As he explains in the "Preliminaries" to *Demonios escondidos y momentos de revolución*, the original overarching aim of García Linera's project of self-study was nothing less than to offer "a Marxist explanation of the problem of the ongoing forms of national self-organization and of the meaning of the struggles of the peasant working masses of the last years in what we call Bolivia," that is to say, "a critique of the Bolivian bourgeois nation-State in light of the movement of national Quechua-Aymara and Bolivian popular-proletarian self-determination."[18] In reality, prior to this and in a decision that would forever keep the larger project from reaching completion in published form, García Linera considers a detour necessary in order to develop his own conceptual tools at a distance from the self-proclaimed orthodoxy of existing Marxism: "This is why we have preferred to track this movement of understanding and participation in the 'problematics of the national and the peasant-communitarian' in Marx and subsequently in Marxism in order for us subsequently to tackle their local and actual significance—no longer armed with lifeless and meaningless recipes but with the very movement of comprehension of the national and the agrarian."[19]

---

18   Qhananchiri, "Palabras preliminares," *De demonios escondidos y momentos de revolución*, xii.

19   Ibid. García Linera envisaged four parts in this overarching study: "The first would study the contributions of Marx and Engels to this domain and their treatment would subsequently be used in the remainder of the book as critical arms; the second part would treat the contributions from the time of the Second International and the rise of the Soviets until the contemporary authors; the third

Already the mere timing of these studies makes them quite unique documents. In the 1990s, that is, after the collapse of the Soviet Union, after the electoral defeat of the Sandinista government in Nicaragua, and in the midst of the world-wide imposition of neoliberal policies under the so-called Washington Consensus, there is something at once refreshing and baffling in assertions such as the one that appears in Raquel Gutiérrez's Prologue to *De demonios escondidos y momentos de revolución*: "We are Marxists, that is the initial partisan decision"; or again, in García Linera's own opening words: "Socialism is dead? Idiots! As if the unsatisfied

---

would study the findings of local authors from the founding of the Republic until 1952; in order finally in the fourth part to study the development of the formation of the Bolivian nation-State since 1825 until the emergence of the conditions and possibilities for national Aymara and Quechua self-organization in the last years" (ibid.). Of this overambitious plan, only one third of the first part, namely, the study of the writings of Marx and Engels on the topics of nation, community and the State up to the *Grundrisse*, was published, as the book *De demonios escondidos y momentos de revolución*. However, much of *Capital* as well as Marx's later writings, in particular his famous drafts and letter to Vera Zasulich on the Russian agrarian commune and its possible link to communism, as well as the history of the *ayllu* and pre-capitalist social formations in the Andes, are the topic of García Linera's reflections from prison in Qhananchiri, *Forma valor y forma comunidad: Aproximación teórica-abstracta a los fundamentos civilizatorios que preceden al Ayllu Universal* (La Paz: Chonchocoro, 1995). For the biographical context, see García Linera's introduction to the recent re-edition of *Forma valor y forma comunidad* (La Paz: Muela del Diablo/CLACSO, 2009), 7–12. In what follows, I will quote from the original edition.

needs of three quarters of humanity would have disappeared. Socialism is not the ideal to which destiny will have to be adjusted by force; it is above all the practical movement of the common struggles of living labor in communitarian form to recuperate its expropriated capacities."[20] Theoretically, too, these writings seem to go against the grain of their time. We are after all at a crucial juncture when most leftists are declaring themselves proud post-Marxists if not repentant anti-Marxists; when postcolonial theory is still busy following the example of Edward Said's *Orientalism* into rushed disqualifications of Marx's so-called Eurocentrism; and when the likes of Aijaz Ahmad, Gayatri Spivak or Kevin Anderson have yet

---

20    Qhantat Wara Wara, "Prólogo," in Qhananchiri *De demonios escondidos y momentos de revolución*, no page number; and Qhananchiri, "Palabras preliminares," ibid., vii. This untimely assertion of socialism or communism, combined with Marxism as the untranscendable horizon of our time in the Sartrean sense, obviously does not exclude the need for rectifications. "Thus, it is a matter of advancing 'paradigmatic rectifications,' precisions such as the ones Marx proposed in 1871 on the occasion of the Paris Commune, that is, the moment of the maximum conquest and defeat of the international proletariat's self-determining act in the nineteenth century. At that time, the rectification concerned the role of living labor vis-à-vis the apparatus of the State; subsequently, with the Chinese peasants, this rectification was expanded to include the sphere of the productive forces and, with the European and Chinese workers of the early 1970s, the terrain of the organization of work and, in part, culture." See María Raquel Gutiérrez Aguilar and Álvaro García Linera, "A manera de introducción," in Qhananchiri, *Forma valor y forma comunidad*, xv.

to demand a more thorough reassessment of Marx's views on India and on the margins of capitalism in general.[21] Even in this broad international context, García Linera has precious little company in his attempt in the early 1990s to continue the dialogue with work in Marxist theory from the 1970s and 1980s such as Lawrence Krader's presentation of *The Asiatic Mode of Production* or Teodor Shanin's *Late Marx and the Russian Road: Marx and "the Peripheries of Capitalism,"* with the latter including the correspondence between Marx and Zasulich and the former Marx's so-called Kovalevsky note-

---

21   Edward W. Said's all-too-brief indictment of Marx's colonialist prejudices can be found in his classic *Orientalism* (New York: Vintage, 1979), 153–7. Aijaz Ahmad corrects Said's cavalier approach in "Marx on India: A Clarification," in his collection *In Theory: Classes, Nations, Literatures* (London: Verso, 1992), 221–42; and Gayatri Chakravorty Spivak offers a symptomatic rereading of the role of the Asiatic mode of production in Marx's writing, in *A Critique of Postcolonial Reason: Toward a History of the Vanishing Present* (Cambridge: Harvard University Press, 1999), 67–111. More recently, see also Kevin B. Anderson, *Marx at the Margins: On Nationalism, Ethnicity, and Non-Western Societies* (Chicago: University of Chicago Press, 2010). Even so, Said's dismissal of Marx's Eurocentric prejudices continues to be a tempting approach in postcolonial studies. Witness a recent study such as Olivier Le Cour Grandmaison, "F. Engels et K. Marx: le colonialisme au service de 'l'Histoire universelle,'" *ContreTemps* 8 (2003): 174–84; and the succinct rebuttal from Sebastian Budgen, "Notes critiques sur l'article d'Olivier Le Cour Grandmaison," ibid., 185–9. For a careful overview of the question, see Kolja Lindner, "L'eurocentrisme de Marx," *Actuel Marx* 48 (2010): 106–28.

book for which García Linera previously had prepared a Spanish edition in Bolivia.[22]

What then are some of the conclusions to be drawn from García Linera's investigations of the national, communal, and agrarian questions from the point of view of the Andean periphery? A first insight to be culled from these investigations concerns precisely the much-debated issue of Marx's Eurocentrism. Referencing case studies about Prussia, Ireland, India, Poland, Turkey, Spain, Russia, and Latin America, among others, García Linera shows how in Marx and Engels's writings, despite the persistence of

---

22　See Lawrence Krader, ed., *The Ethnological Notebooks of Karl Marx (Studies of Morgan, Phear, Maine, Lubbock)* (Assen: Van Gorcum, 1974); Lawrence Krader, ed., *The Asiatic Mode of Production: Sources, Development and Critique in the Writings of Karl Marx* (Assen: Van Gorcum, 1975); Teodor Shanin, ed., *Late Marx and the Russian Road: Marx and "the Peripheries of Capitalism"* (New York: Monthly Review Press, 1983). For the Bolivian edition of the Kovalevsky notebook, with a preface by García Linera, see Marx, *Cuaderno Kovalevsky* (La Paz: Ofensiva Roja, 1989). Earlier, García Linera also prepared a Bolivian edition of Marx's *Ethnological Notebooks*; see his "Introducción a los estudios etnológicos de Karl Marx," in *Cuadernos etnológicos de Marx* (La Paz: Ofensiva Roja, 1988). In *Forma valor y forma comunidad*, García Linera expands upon these materials from the late Marx with abundant references to Spanish and American, mestizo and indigenous chroniclers, from Pedro de Cieza de León to Guamán Poma de Ayala to Tupac Katari, as well as to contemporary ethnographic and sociological studies of Aymara and Quechua communities from Claude Meillassoux to Silvia Rivera Cusicanqui.

prejudices about the allegedly innate revolutionary or counterrevolutionary nature of certain nations and about the so-called backwardness of peasant communities and peripheral countries in general, the measure for evaluating a given situation is always this situation's potential for radical emancipation from an internationalist perspective. Even more importantly, he shows how gradually the study of those cases leads Marx ever more clearly to confirm a principle he first formulated in *The Class Struggles in France*: "Violent outbreaks naturally erupt sooner at the extremities of the bourgeois body than in its heart, because in the latter the possibilities of accommodation are greater than in the former."[23] Instead of having to yield to the inexorable laws of historical progress whereby so-called primitive or pre-capitalist modes of communal production would have to wither away or in any case be allowed to become extinct, the task is to foster change at the international level starting precisely from those extremities of the capitalist body. "It is not a question of waiting for the fall of the most powerful capitalist country but of impelling its fall from within the revolution in the least powerful ones," writes García Linera. "The point is not to limit the social revolution to a single country, which in the long run will only lead to its partiality and eventually its defeat, but immediately to extend it to other countries until reaching the most powerful one; not

---

23   Marx, quoted in Qhananchiri, *De demonios escondidos y momentos de revolución*, 153.

to wait and see but to act with the available materials in the global perspective."[24]

A methodological corollary of this critique of the alleged Eurocentrism in Marx and Engels's writings about dependent nations concerns what is supposed to be the Marxist treatment of history. Here, the aim is to avoid the twin extremes of either turning Marx's account into "a historico-philosophical theory whose supreme virtue consists in being supra-historical" or else lapsing into "a historicism of basically disconnected singularities."[25] Especially after 1870, Marx himself insists on the need for a site-specific, circumstantial, and multilinear view of history that—far from being limited to the study of peripheral and dependent countries or to what nowadays might be called alternative modernities—would also apply to Western Europe. García Linera comments:

> In fact, in a famous letter Marx emphatically rejects any attempt to convert his historical outline about the development of capitalism in Western Europe, expounded in *Capital*, into "a historico-philosophical theory of the general course, fatally imposed upon all peoples, regardless of the historical circumstances

---

24   Ibid., 153–4.
25   Ibid., 204, 171. Michael Löwy offers similar insights in his reading of Rosa Luxemburg's work on Marx's *Ethnological Notebooks*, in Löwy, "Rosa Luxemburg et le communisme," *Actuel Marx* 48 (2010): 22–32.

in which they find themselves placed." Against this scornful use of his thought, which seeks to make it into "the master key of a general theory of the philosophy of history," Marx calls for the separate study of "each historical process" so as to find the material forces and possibilities that point toward its transformation into a new social regime.[26]

This principle is particularly important to take into account today insofar as García Linera's current view of the indigenous and peasant communities in Bolivia, now that he is vice president, has come under attack for adopting precisely the kind of linear-developmentalist philosophy of history that he is at pains to debunk throughout *De demonios escondidos* and *Forma valor y forma comunidad*. Then again, few of García Linera's recent critics show the same degree of seriousness in actually studying his views in the way he does for Marx and Engels in his writings from the 1990s about the emancipatory potential coming from the extremities of the capitalist body.

By far the most important insight in these writings, especially in the last chapter of *Forma valor y forma comunidad*, stems from García Linera's careful return to Marx's

26  Qhananchiri, *De demonios escondidos y momentos de revolución*, 204–5. The reference is to Karl Marx, "A Letter to the Editorial Board of *Otechestvennye Zapiski*," in Teodor Shanin, ed., *Late Marx and the Russian Road*, 136.

correspondence from February–March 1881 with Vera Zasulich about the communist potential of the agrarian commune in Russia. Expanding upon the idea of a unique, non-linear, and contingent course of history, this correspondence highlights the possibility for a transformed revival of elements of the pre-capitalist community in superior—communist-universal—conditions: "In the words of Marx, referring to the possible future of the Russian agrarian commune, what is needed to 'salvage' for our actuality the communal form in those places where it has been preserved on a national scale is to 'develop' it by transforming it into 'the direct *starting point*' for the construction of a new system of social organization based on communitarian-universal production and appropriation."[27] This is neither a nostalgic return to pastoral dreams from the past nor a developmentalist illusion of inevitable progress. Instead, it is only from within the contemporaneity of international exchange and the universalization of capitalism that simultaneously the possibility arises for a rearticulation of communism and community as envisioned in Marx's correspondence with Zasulich:

This monumental work of reconstructing the ancestral community into a "superior form" of "an archaic social

---

27   Qhananchiri, *Forma valor y forma comunidad*, 335. The internal quotations are drawn from "Marx-Zasulich Correspondence: Letters and Drafts," in Shanin, ed., *Late Marx and the Russian Road*, 121.

type" nowadays is made possible thanks to the counter-finalities that are made to erupt by the same regime that seeks to annihilate all communal forms: capitalism as world system, since the latter's contemporaneity with communal forms permits these to "appropriate all its positive achievements without undergoing its frightful vicissitudes," in particular by recuperating under a new social form the worldwide intercommunication and interdependence of producers, certain qualities of the scientific-technological form of development, the search for the overcoming of labor time as the measure of social wealth, etc. But all this, in order to realize itself as society's authentic reappropriation of its own creative forces, has as its prerequisite and its guiding thread the subjective and material self-unification of the community that allows it to liberate itself from the frustration and local isolation in which communities find themselves with regard to one another and with the rest of contemporary society's laboring forces. Nothing else is social emancipation.[28]

García Linera is well aware of the risks of localism and dispersion that beset the emancipatory actions of autonomous communities. In fact, in several passages from *Forma*

---

28  Qhananchiri, *Forma valor y forma comunidad*, 335. The quotations are from "Marx-Zasulich Correspondence: Letters and Drafts," 106–7.

*valor y forma comunidad* he seems to repudiate in advance the kind of defense of cultural autonomy and difference that nowadays he is accused of subordinating to a new hegemonic politics centralized in the State. The irony is that such accusations frequently take the form of a surprised discovery of Marx's drafts and letter to Zasulich, which are then turned back against the Bolivian Vice President as though the latter had not devoted hundreds of pages to the continued relevance of this correspondence! "Contrary to what Marx argued, for whom the Russian commune can be the platform for the construction of a new world of communism, for García Linera this 'traditional' world is an obstacle for change," Raúl Zibechi claims in an argument quickly seconded by José Rabasa: "The will to suppress this millennial common sense at the root of the *ayllus*' ethos, politics, and cognitive structures, and their power to mobilize the masses, would in turn reenact the violence of conquest and colonization—be it in the mode of the Spanish conquest, neoliberal colonization, or 'state capitalism.'"[29] For García Linera, however, it is not the effort at executive empowerment but the cultural defense of otherness that risks being silently complicit with the legacy of colonial dominance:

> By contrast, those who advocate the adoration of the disintegrating martyrdom of communities, behind their suspect "tolerance" of "others," of cultures, and of "differences," harbor a silence that is complicit with the frightful colonial mutilation, abuse, and pillaging that the

---

29  Raúl Zibechi, *Dispersar el poder: los movimientos como poderes antiestatales* (La Paz: Textos Rebeldes; Buenos Aires: Tinta Limón, 2006), 195–6; and José Rabasa, *Without History: Subaltern Studies, the Zapatista Insurgency, and the Specter of History* (Pittsburgh: University of Pittsburgh Press, 2010), 280. In these criticisms there is not the slightest sign of awareness of García Linera's extensive work on the Marx–Zasulich correspondence in light of the traditional *ayllu*. Finally, it should be noted that García Linera himself lays out the possible options and outcomes of an "indigenous" State for Bolivia, for example, in "Autonomía indígena y Estado multinacional," 240–2; and in "Indianismo y marxismo. El desencuentro de dos razones revolucionarias" (originally from 2005), reprinted in *La potencia plebeya*, 373–92. He soberly concludes: "What remains to be seen about this varied unfolding of indianist thought is if it will be a worldview that takes the form of a dominant conception of the State or if, as seems to be insinuated by the organizational weaknesses, political mistakes, and internal fractures of the collectivities that vindicate it, it will be an ideology of a few political actors who merely regulate the excesses of state sovereignty exerted by the same political subjects and social classes who habitually have been in power" (*La potencia plebeya*, 391).

regime of capital imposes against the communities via an infinity of capillaries, from commerce to racial-political exclusion, from cultural disdain to barefaced exploitation of the communal working capacity, vitality, and objective and subjective force. Hypocritical "tolerance" is the archaeological curiosity for the vanquished, it is the radical negation of their communitarian self-determination, their right to subvert the politics, culture, and sociality of those who implacably destroy theirs, those who deny them the effective right to exist and realize themselves politically, economically, and culturally as they are: in short, against those who deny them their humanity. This contemplativeness, in sum, is a renewed attempt to convert the historical endeavor of the universalized community into an inoffensive folkloric curiosity.[30]

As Marx also repeatedly says, there is never an option of purely turning back in time. Without presupposing the slightest historical inevitability, the available conditions are in fact those of global capital and it is only from within these conditions that we can raise the question of the communist revival of the archaic community. "The ancient nations cannot exist or reproduce themselves independently because they already find themselves incorporated into the potential space of existence of the bourgeois nation. Either they succumb to it after the abuse of pillaging and savage exploitation or they strengthen and

---

30    Qhananchiri, *Forma valor y forma comunidad*, 333–4.

raise themselves up against it to defend their forms of sociality. Indifference amounts to the subjugation and destruction of these non-capitalist forms," adds García Linera. "The ancestral aspect of use value as the direct component of the social form of the product of labor remains tied to the novelty of the universal character of use value, which leads to a superior synthesis that overcomes all that exists: the social-universal community, or what we must call the Universalized Ayllu."[31]

## Society Against the State?

Even so, today there is certainly no shortage of critics of the idea of empowering the plebeian potential of communism both from the supposed grassroots level of the community and at the same time from within the heavily centralized apparatuses of the modern State. Interestingly enough, one of the most forceful and eloquent among these critics is Raquel Gutiérrez, García Linera's one-time partner-in-arms and co-author of numerous texts on revolutionary and communal politics that by several years pre-date his seeming turnabout with regard to the relation of communism to the State. Both personal and political, the split between these two figures is in many ways symptomatic of the core issue confronting the history and theory of communism today. Thus, while García Linera abandoned his more rabid anti-State rhetoric to join the electoral campaign of Evo Morales

---

31  Ibid., 195–6.

for MAS that would eventually bring him to his country's vice presidency, Gutiérrez left Bolivia for her home country of Mexico, where she is now a political activist and a journalist for the newspaper *La Jornada*, after having studied in Puebla with John Holloway, the author best known for the anti-statist politics summed up in his book *Change the World Without Taking Power: The Meaning of Revolution Today*.

In the concluding observations to her own major book, *Los ritmos de Pachakuti: Movilización y levantamiento indígena-popular en Bolivia (2000–2005)*, Gutiérrez distinguishes two main trends among the array of movements and insurrections in Bolivia's recent history, one communitarian and anti-statist and the other national-popular and always aimed at taking over the power of the State. According to her, the second of these trends has, fatally—by means of the idea of a necessary delegation—seemed to channel, absorb, and silence the first. For Gutiérrez, this is what happened starting in 2005 with the uprisings and mobilizations from the beginning of the twenty-first century in Bolivia:

> Thus, the expansive actions of confrontation and struggle unfolding on the part of multiple social forces in 2005 practically throughout the entire Bolivian

territory, while certainly similar in their external—
apparent—form to the struggles of 2001, 2002 and
2003, did not have the same inner quality: little by
little they anchored themselves in a national-popular
horizon in which the reverberations of the popular-
communitarian perspective ended up as internal noise,
as past echoes, manifested in discomfort and silence,
undergirding the weight of ignorance and isolation,
speaking with difficulty through the voice of those
absent from the hegemonic project of MAS and its still
contradictory national-popular limits.[32]

As a matter of fact if not also in principle, then, there would
be no transitivity between the communist-communitarian

32   Raquel Gutiérrez Aguilar, "Cuatro reflexiones finales," *Los
ritmos de Pachakuti: Movilización y levantamiento indígena-popular en Bolivia (2000–2005)* (La Paz: Ediciones Yachaywasi/Textos
Rebeldes, 2008), 305. Raúl J. Cerdeiras has written an important
rejoinder to Gutiérrez's book: "La transmisión de la política al
Estado," *Acontecimiento: Revista para pensar la política* 38–39
(2010): 27–79. For a similarly critical assessment of the Bolivian
situation, see Forrest Hylton and Sinclair Thomson, *Revolutionary
Horizons: Past and Present in Bolivian Politics* (London: Verso,
2007), 127–43. James Petras and Henry Veltmeyer are even more
critical of MAS and the Morales/García Linera electoral formula,
in *Social Movements and State Power: Argentina, Brazil, Bolivia,
Ecuador* (London: Pluto, 2005), 175–219. For an all-round evaluation, see the two special issues of *Latin American Perspectives*
37.3–4 (May and July 2010); and, most recently, Jeffery R. Webber,
*From Revolution to Reform in Bolivia: Class Struggle, Indigenous
Liberation, and the Politics of Evo Morales* (Chicago: Haymarket
Books, 2011).

horizon and the national-popular ambitions of the State. With Morales and García Linera, in other words, we would still remain locked within the traditional hermeneutics of the Left, which sees in the State the only possible agent of change and the sole transmission belt between social movements and politics.

Raquel Gutiérrez finds this aporetic tension between society and the State, between movement and apparatus, or between the subjective and the objective, reproduced in the work and even in the very person of her partner of fifteen years. "In the work of García Linera in general there are always two strains that confront each other: one has a certain family resemblance to an almost positivistic objectivity, whereas the other, by contrast, is situated in the depths of the emancipatory will of Bolivia's social struggle," she writes in a rare personal aside. "These two tendencies coexist in García Linera's work, perhaps due to his own difficult and discontinuous vital trajectory: from guerrilla fighter to maximum security political prisoner to academic to commentator on the public opinion linked to the social movements to Vice-President in the government of Evo Morales."[33] In the end, though, I would propose that we revisit the theoretical strategies that accompany the different moments along this discontinuous trajectory. Not only would we then find that García Linera in many of his early writings provided us

---

33   Raquel Gutiérrez Aguilar and Luis A. Gómez, "Los múltiples significados del libro de Zibechi," in Zibechi, *Dispersar el poder*, 22.

with the conceptual tools necessary for assessing his own achievements or shortcomings under President Morales. But Raquel Gutiérrez herself, in some of those same early texts co-authored with García Linera, also seems to have envisioned a more dialectical and less aporetic understanding of the links between emancipatory mass movements and the political power of the State.

Gutiérrez and García Linera on the one hand warn against the risks inherent in the traditional idea of taking over the power of the State: "We must abandon once and for all the vulgar idea of the 'conquest of power' that has translated itself into the occupation of alien power, after alien property and alien organization, by an enlightened elite subsequently turned administrator of the same power, property, and organization that are still alien to society."[34] On the other hand, however, all such warnings are only meant to situate the source of power firmly within the immanence of society: "The point is for society to construct its power so as to emancipate itself from the dominant private power, to install the power of society as the sole form of power in society. If the whole society does not construct its power (from the most capillary levels to the global and fundamental centers), emancipation is a supplanting hoax."[35]

Time and time again, this is also how García Linera

34 Gutiérrez Aguilar and García Linera, "A manera de introducción," in Qhananchiri, *Forma valor y forma comunidad*, xvi–xvii.
35 Ibid.

himself, later on in *De demonios escondidos y momentos de revolución*, proposes to articulate society and the State—the whole question being, of course, whether the Morales/García Linera formula has been able to overcome the legacy of a century-old impossibility in this regard:

> The State in over a century has not been able to produce society as an organic whole, much less to revolutionize it. To the contrary, the culminating moments in the reform and organization of society as nation have been linked to great movements of mass insurrection, of the self-organization of society against the State, of the unfolding of the organizational and revolutionary vitality of society confronting the State. Outside of these movements, and in spite of efforts from above, the construction of the nation and social reform has been nothing more than a seignorial, oligarchical and large-landowning fiction.[36]

Positively speaking, what this assessment presupposes is nothing less than a notion of communism as the act of all-round collective self-emancipation by which a people—as community, civil society, nation, or international organization—takes hold of its own destiny.

---

36  Qhananchiri, *De demonios escondidos y momentos de revolución*, 255.

# *Conclusion*

> Even if communism *were* dead, it is still possible to
> *refuse* to "mourn," *refuse* to "work it through," even
> *refuse* to work at all. It would still be possible and
> desirable to continue to "act out" communism's best
> features, especially if there are no better alternatives.
> — Geoff Waite, *Nietzsche's Corps/e*

From the preceding theoretical investigations, I should now
like to derive the following set of conclusions about the horizon for leftism and communism in the present age. Five
conclusions, to be precise, having to do respectively with
the relation between politics and philosophy; the relation
between history and the ahistorical; the increasing moralization of politics; the ambivalent status of speculative leftism
in a generically understood communism; and the relation of
communism to internationalism.

First, precisely insofar as the preceding analyses are
meant to be theoretical, rather than philosophical in the
strict sense, I also intend them to be read as interventions
in the ongoing polemic over the delimitation of politics and
philosophy. Thus, the question with which I approached
the works under analysis concerns the extent to which they

open up (or not) a passageway from present-day philosophy to the actuality of communism. This means neither to fall back on old schemes for the derivation of politics from some higher or first philosophy, nor to replace these metaphysical schemes with the Marxist or perhaps more properly Leninist definition of the rapport between theory and practice, with its underlying pedagogical hierarchy. Philosophy, like art or literature, certainly is capable of anticipating the future in a fictive extension, or a generic supplementation, of the status quo that is neither dogmatic nor utopian. We might even say that, insofar as it breaks with the given assignation of tasks and aptitudes supposedly inscribed in our very own bodily frames, all emancipatory politics relies on a degree of fiction, namely, on the fictive gap between a given task and the aptitude that alone is supposed to make a subject or group of subjects fit for it.

What we witness in the wake of some of the most sophisticated exercises in the critique of metaphysics, however, is exactly the opposite of such a revalorization of the power of fiction that we can find in different versions in the work of Rancière or Badiou. After, in lieu of, or by way of compensation for yesterday's common references to Hegel or Marx, today's references to Kant or Heidegger thus often lead to a redrawing of the boundaries of what can and cannot legitimately be thought or presented as falling under the purview of a concept or Idea. Unfortunately, such a critical or deconstructive delimitation also often leads to the dismissal of all emancipatory or revolutionary politics as being based on a transcendental or metaphysical illusion, rather than on an enabling fiction for the abolition and overcoming of the present state of things. "Revolutionary politics," as Lyotard writes with exemplary clarity in his *Enthusiasm: The Kantian Critique of History*, "is based on a transcendental illusion in the political domain: it confuses what can be presented as an object for a cognitive phrase with what can be presented as an object for a speculative and/or ethical phrase; that is to say, it confuses schemata or examples with *analoga*."[1] What is more, the careful policing of boundaries of the thinkable or presentable in the name of the deconstruction of metaphysics or the critique of the speculative language game not only frequently seems to involve a philosophical ratification of what is already said to have been the verdict of history anyhow, it also oftentimes preemptively cancels and represses—without future sublation—any and all possible political alternatives. In "Community and Violence," a recent talk summarizing his work from the last few years, Esposito for example adopts a skeptical-conservative tone that we can also find in contemporary reflections on politics inspired by Freud or Lacan. Referring to the culmination of biopolitics in our present epoch of globalization, he unhesitatingly asserts that "current immunitary attempts to neutralize global dynamics are doomed to failure in the first

---

1    Jean-François Lyotard, *Enthusiasm: The Kantian Critique of History*, trans. Georges Van Den Abbeele (Minneapolis: University of Minnesota Press, 2009), 22.

place because these attempts are impossible to mount and in the second because, even if they were possible, they are counter-productive. They are destined to empower disproportionately the conflict that they want to suppress."[2] Should we not read this condemnation or prohibition of what is in any case supposed to be impossible as the very textbook definition of repression?

Whether tacit or explicit, two presuppositions are at work behind this self-confident reliance on the wisdom of philosophy or on the worthiness of thinking for the deconstruction of politics. On the one hand, the assumption is that all hitherto existing modes of politics, whether fascist or communist, liberal or reactionary, have been essentially misconceived. Marx's fundamental mistake, and the reason for the failure of really existing socialism, for example, would on this account have consisted in a metaphysical, humanist, or essentialist dependence on the transparent self-production of the subject. Now, in the wake of the ontological turn in political philosophy, we should have come to learn our lesson that all such notions of productivity, transparency, actuality, fullness, and immanence are, for the self-professed leftist, nothing but ill-conceived liabilities in need of a thorough and most likely interminable deconstruction. Summing up

---

2    Roberto Esposito, "Community and Violence," talk at the international conference "Commonalities: Theorizing the Common in Contemporary Italian Thought," organized by Timothy Campbell under the auspices of *diacritics: review of contemporary criticism*, at Cornell University (September 24–25, 2010).

this first presupposition, which can also be found in different guises in the work of post-Heideggerian philosophers such as Derrida, Nancy, or Lacoue-Labarthe, Esposito even goes so far as to suggest that the failure of the Marxian-inspired idea of human emancipation, as opposed to merely political emancipation, would be due to an insufficient understanding of the ontological difference. "Naturally, the 'community' that Marx looks at as the place of the maximal potentialization of liberated humanity is not the one in which the individual always already finds himself 'thrown': rather, the complete negation of the latter is possible only through a politics that 'sublates' itself into philosophy while at the same time philosophy 'realizes' itself in politics," Esposito writes in an entry on "Myth" from his *Nove pensieri sulla politica*. "With Hegel (and against Kant) evil lies in the obstinacy of the finite to remain as such, the refusal on the part of the individual to disappear into the whole, the obstacle to the 'putting into work' of the negativity of the dialectic. Leading the problem of evil back to that of alienation, historically determined by particular conditions that can be overcome, Marxist human-ism leads to the most explicit negation of all 'ontological difference.'"[3] On the other hand, philosophy derives much of its prominence in the recent return of the political from the presupposition that these failures of the Left can be remedied only by addressing, if not also correcting, the metaphysical

---

3   Roberto Esposito, "Mito," in *Nove pensieri sulla politica* (Bologna: Il Mulino, 1993), 120.

illusions that undergird all previously existing emancipatory practices and that assimilate them with totalitarian practices. Whence the pathos—but also, it must be said, the stylistic sublimity—with which these philosophers announce the possible coming into being of a new understanding of the political as a task urgently assigned to philosophy, or, to use the mandatory jargon, as the only task worthy of thought, if we want to avoid what is then often alluded to simply and menacingly as the worst.

In the face of such grandiose claims for the salvific dignity of philosophy or of postmetaphysical thinking, my plea for the work of theory is not meant as a mere substitute or envious competitor in the after all quite petty turf-battle among disciplines, methods, or fields of investigation. Rather, my goal is to instill a degree of modesty and realism in the reflection concerning politics and philosophy. Really existing socialism and communism, if in fact they are now bankrupt beyond salvage, did not fail but were defeated; their defeat and bankruptcy—or, alternatively, perhaps, their continuing actuality—are primarily not philosophical but political and ideological issues. Of course, this does not mean that we have no use for militant investigations into the theoretical limits and promises of the philosophy of praxis. But, again, such investigations should not mistake themselves for politics in the way critical (post-Kantian) or ontological (post-Heideggerian) inquiries into the essence of the political frequently present themselves as already being political—and, furthermore, as being more radically political because less metaphysically deluded than all hitherto existing politics. As Lyotard, for example, asserts: "Philosophy of the political, that is, 'free' reflections or critique concerning the political, shows itself to be political by discriminating between the heterogeneous phrase families that present the political universe and by following the 'passages' (the 'guiding thread,' writes Kant) that are indicated between them (for example, is the 'enthusiasm' of 1968 like what Kant analyzes for that of 1789?)."[4]

A second conclusion, closely linked to the question about the status of theory or philosophy, concerns the relation between politics and history. In fact, in the recent revival of the communist hypothesis, we can easily observe that the dominant tendency is for a push away from history and toward the affirmation of the eternity or, at the very least, the trans-historical availability of communism qua invariant Idea. As Badiou writes already in *Of an Obscure Disaster*: "From Spartacus to Mao (not the Mao of the State, who also exists, but the rebellious extreme, complicated Mao), from the Greek democratic insurrections to the worldwide decade 1966–1976, it is and has been, in this sense, a question of communism. It will always be a question of communism, even if the word, soiled, is replaced by some other designation of the concept that it covers, the philosophical and thus eternal concept of rebellious subjectivity."[5] In *The*

---

4    Lyotard, *Enthusiasm*, xviii.
5    Alain Badiou, *D'un désastre obscur: Sur la fin de la vérité d'État* (La Tour d'Aigues: De l'Aube, 1998), 14.

*Communist Hypothesis*, following up on a brief suggestion from *Logics of Worlds* to the effect that "a passion for history" with its "cult of genealogies and narratives" is "the authentic historical materialism" complicit with "democratic materialism" and that, therefore, "it is crucial to disjoin the materialist dialectic, the philosophy of emancipation through truths, from historical materialism, the philosophy of alienation by languages," Badiou even goes so far as to affirm that all history belongs only to the State: "History as such, made up of historical facts, is in no way subtracted from the power of the State. History is neither subjective nor glorious. History should instead be said to be the history of the State."[6] Žižek, similarly, argues for his radical act as the repetition of some nonhistorical kernel without which no true historicity, as opposed to mere historicism, would be possible in the first place. Against Judith Butler's claim that the Lacanian psychoanalytical framework for thinking of politics and ideology is insufficiently historicized insofar as it relies on a point of the real as an insuperable limit or stumbling block, Žižek argues that what is needed today is not a greater awareness of historical contingency so much as a recognition of the ahistorical ground of history: "My ultimate point is thus that Kantian formalism and radical historicism are not really opposites, but two sides of the same coin: every version of historicism

---

6  Alain Badiou, *Logics of Worlds*, trans. Alberto Toscano (London: Continuum, 2009), 509; and *The Communist Hypothesis* (London: Verso, 2010), 245.

relies on a minimal 'ahistorical' formal framework defining the terrain within which the open and endless game of
contingent inclusions/exclusions, substitutions, renegotia-
tions, displacements, and so on, takes place."[7]

In the present circumstances, this recourse to the eternal, the invariant, or the ahistorical can certainly be justified. Given the depoliticizing effects of the call constantly to
historicize, not to mention the even more damning effects of
the invocation of some figure or other of the world-historical tribunal, it can indeed be argued that history in and of
itself no longer possesses the emancipatory power it once
had in the nineteenth century, say for Marx in his critique
of classical political economy with its presupposition of the
eternal—because natural—evidence of the capitalist mode
of production. Today, the drive to historicize everything is
rather part and parcel of late capitalist ideology as such, as
is the emphasis on difference, flux, and multiplicity. "This
also explains why the fetishism of history is accompanied by
an unrelenting discourse on novelty, perpetual change and
the imperative of modernization," adds Badiou in *Logics of
Worlds*. "Everything changes at every instant, which is why
one is left to contemplate the majestic historical horizon of
what does not change."[8]

---

7   Slavoj Žižek, "Class Struggle or Postmodernism?" in Judith
Butler, Ernesto Laclau, and Slavoj Žižek, *Contingency, Hegemony,
Universality: Contemporary Dialogues on the Left* (London: Verso,
2000), 111.
8   Badiou, *Logics of Worlds*, 509–10.

For all these reasons, the renewed insistence on the eternal, invariant, and untimely nature of communism no doubt has an important tactical and even strategic efficacy today. And yet, given the equally pressing need to avoid lapsing into an ultra-leftist purification of communism outside of any given time and place, I would also want to argue for a dialectical articulation of the nonhistorical with concrete analyses of the historicity of leftist, socialist, and communist politics. This would mean giving more attention than hitherto has been the case to the first half of Žižek's proposal for such a dialectic: "The truly radical assertion of historical contingency has to include the dialectical tension between the domain of historical change itself and its traumatic 'ahistorical' kernel qua its condition of (im)possibility."[9] Only the recognition of an eternal or ahistorical kernel would open up the possibility of changing the very terrain upon which history plays itself out. But then should we not also assume the task of investigating the concrete historical changes that this structural recognition would enable?

Taking up the dialectic between concrete historicity and the ahistorical kernel of emancipatory politics, in my view, also ought to mean writing the history of the people, not from the point of view of the State but from below, by delving into the archives of popular insurrection and plebeian revolt without sinking them even deeper into the dustbins of history where they risk being crushed under the heavy paperweight of philosophical reflections whose perverse

---

9   Žižek, "Class Struggle or Postmodernism?" 111–12.

effect consists in obliterating a second time in theory what has already been defeated in practice. After all, we should not let the Cold War or the "war on terror" make us forget that, even in the United States, communism has been the name for an impressive range of struggles for justice, equality, solidarity, and an end to exploitation. To refuse participation in the politics of oblivion that is often disguised under the name of the politics of memory, though, also requires that we first come to grips with the effects of anti-communism on the historiography of communism in relation to the Left: "The logic of the Cold War is with us today, as much as it was two decades ago, even though the content to which that logic most directly applies is no longer exclusively substantiated by reference to Communist parties or governments."[10]

Now part of the anti-communist history of the Left in the latter half of the twentieth century—this will be my third conclusion—involves the effects of a growing moralization of politics. Particularly starting in the years of global reaction with the imposition of neoliberal policies in the 1980s and countering the street-fighting years of the 1960s and 1970s, this process has tended to rephrase questions of power and strategy in the melodramatic vocabulary of Good and Evil— most often nihilistically reducing the Good to being nothing

---

10  Michael E. Brown, *The Historiography of Communism* (Philadelphia: Temple University Press, 2009), 26. With thanks to Randy Martin for bringing this important collection of essays to my attention.

more than the avoidance of Evil. As Wendy Brown suggests, we should read this renewed moralism in politics as the symptom of the lost dream of another political, social, and economic world. "Previously I argued that certain contemporary moral claims in politics issue from a combination of attachments—both to Truth (as opposed to power) in a postfoundational era and to identity as injury in a political domain of competing survivor stories," Brown writes in *Politics Out of History*, summarizing her previous argument in *States of Injury*. "Here, I reconsider moralizing politics as marking a crisis in political teleology. I propose to read such politics not only as a sign of stubborn clinging to a certain equation of truth with powerlessness, or as the acting out of an injured will, but as a symptom of a broken historical narrative to which we have not yet forged alternatives."[11] We are thus in part remitted back to the aforementioned task in the continuing historiography of the Left after the Cold War.

Crucial in this regard has been the history and theory of "totalitarianism" in the back-to-back dismissal of both Nazism and Stalinism, with the Gulag but above all the Holocaust, particularly after the Arab-Israeli war of 1967, becoming key references in the accusation—and frequently the remorseful self-accusation and apostasy—of leftist politics as somehow

---

11    Wendy Brown, "Moralism as Anti-Politics," in *Politics Out of History* (Princeton: Princeton University Press, 2001), 22–3. See also Brown, *States of Injury: Power and Freedom in Late Modernity* (Princeton: Princeton University Press, 1995).

being intrinsically anti-Semitic. On the conceptual level, this major shift in the history of the Left—most of which remains to be written—has involved a displacement from categories such as the worker or the militant to those of the victim and the survivor. Sometimes dressed in the Levinasian language of an ethics of respect for the Other and other times in a post-Heideggerian critique of history as the history of metaphysical violence exemplified in the camps, this displacement wittingly or unwittingly also has had the effect of obliterating, if not of canceling out in advance, any and all figures of subjective militancy or activism. In their stead, and as an admonishing reminder of the evil nature that is said to lurk behind such figures, we are confronted with a generalized state of victimhood in which everyone, already from the sheer fact of being born, is the traumatic victim of one's sameness or of another's originary violence. "Today, evil, with its innocent and guilty parties, has been turned into the trauma which knows of neither ignorance nor guilt, which lies in a zone of indistinction between guilt and innocence, between psychic disturbance and social unrest," writes Rancière. "Childhood trauma has become the trauma of being born, the simple misfortune that befalls every human being for being an animal born too early. This misfortune, from which nobody can escape, dismisses the very notion that injustice could be dealt with by enforcing justice."[12]

---

12  Jacques Rancière, "The Ethical Turn of Aesthetics and Politics," in *Dissensus: On Politics and Aesthetics*, ed. and trans. Steve Corcoran (London: Continuum, 2010), 186–7.

This antipolitical effect of the ethical turn or of the shift toward moralism in politics was perhaps nowhere more evident than in the perverse rewriting of the paradoxical logic of emancipatory universalization, when the once-mobilizing slogan from May 1968, "We are all undesirables" or "We are all German Jews" (in reference to the then student leader Daniel Cohn-Bendit's singular status as an unwanted and illegal alien in the eyes of the French government), immediately after the 9/11 attacks became transmogrified into the false sharing of particularistic victimhood and trauma under the slogan "We are all Americans now" (as the headlines read in a number of European newspapers at the time).

To escape from the reign of depoliticization, or from the pseudopolitical rhetoric of moral outrage and indignation, though, the answer cannot consist in seeking to wipe the slate clean in the name of a return to pure politics outside of morality, history, economics, or the social. The Gnosticism or Manichaeism of this desire for a tabula rasa is what I have diagnosed repeatedly as speculative leftism, following also in this regard the work of Rancière and Badiou—even to the point of finding certain elements thereof in texts by these same authors such as *Disagreement* or *The Communist Hypothesis*. The conclusion—my fourth—to be drawn from this, however, is not to adopt the attitude of the Marxist-Leninist-Maoist thought police by merely denouncing speculative leftism as an infantile disorder or childhood disease to be cured and overcome by a fully matured communism. But neither should we be content to settle for Daniel and Gabriel Cohn-Bendit's clever inversion of Lenin's famous diagnostic of left-wing communism, when in 1968 they proposed leftism as a remedy for the senile disorder of communism. Rather, I believe there is room for what I have called a communism of communisms in which speculative leftism is not just the symptom of a maddening desire for purity but also serves as a constant source of revitalization for communism.

After all, something of this kind—a proposal for the actuality of communism in which there is room for movements and hypotheses no less than for tactics and strategies—is also in my view part of the dream bequeathed to us by Daniel Bensaïd:

Communism is neither a pure idea nor a doctrinaire model of society. It is not the name of a state regime, nor of a new mode of production. It is the name of the movement that permanently overcomes/abolishes the established order. But it is also the goal that, borne from this movement, orients it and, as different from politics without principles, actions without consequences, or day-to-day improvisations, enables it to determine what comes close to the goal and what strays from it. In this regard, it is not a scientific knowledge of the goal and the path to obtain it, but a regulative strategic hypothesis. It names, indissociably, the irreducible dream of another world of justice, equality, and solidarity; the permanent movement that seeks to overturn the existing order in the age of capitalism; and the hypothesis that orients this movement toward a radical transformation of the relations of property and power, at a far remove from the accommodations to a lesser evil that would be the shortest path toward the worst.[13]

Finally, communism cannot and will not be actual without also being international. Or, not to make too fine a point of this last conclusion: "Any socialist claiming that socialism, when it is arrested in one country or region, *is* communism is an idiot or a criminal," as Geoff Waite writes. "This is certainly not an argument against socialist-inspired revolution, nor a deprecation of the struggles to build communism by means of socialism under horrific internal and external pressures. Rather it is to say that communism is in principle dynamic and international—still the only major international ideology that might combat and destroy capitalism's patented brand of internationalism."[14] Thus, when Marx and Engels, in a passage from the end of *The Communist Manifesto* to which I already had a chance

---

13   Daniel Bensaïd, "Puissances du communisme," *ContreTemps: Revue de critique communiste* 4 (2009): 16.

14   Geoff Waite, *Nietzsche's Corps/e: Aesthetics, Politics, Prophecy, or, the Spectacular Technoculture of Everyday Life* (Durham: Duke University Press, 1995), 5.

to allude in my reading of García Linera's work, define what sets communists apart from the various kinds of feudal, critical-utopian, scientific, or "true" socialists surrounding them at the time in the movements against the existing social and political order of things, the only two distinctive features they offer are the following: "In all these movements they bring to the front, as the leading question in each, the property question, no matter what its degree of development at the time"; and "they labour everywhere for the union and agreement of the democratic parties of all countries."[15]

---

15  Karl Marx and Friedrich Engels, *The Communist Manifesto* (London: Penguin, 1967), 120. In the same way, earlier, we can read: "The Communists do not form a separate party opposed to other working-class parties"; "The Communists are distinguished from the other working-class parties by this only: 1. In the national struggle of the proletarians of the different countries, they point out and bring to the front the common interests of the entire proletariat, independently of all nationality. 2. In the various stages of the development which the struggle of the working class against the bourgeoisie has to pass through, they always and everywhere represent the interests of the movement as a whole" (95). Raquel Gutiérrez also invokes this passage to define generically and in the broadest possible terms what she labels a "leftist political organization," in "Leer el *Manifiesto* 150 años después," in Álvaro García Linera et al., *El fantasma insomne: Pensando el presente desde el* Manifiesto Comunista (La Paz: Muela del Diablo/ Comuna, 1999), 9–34; and again in "México 2006: el incierto tránsito desde la impotencia civil hacia la soberanía social," in Raúl Zibechi et al., *Los movimientos sociales y el poder: La*

Perhaps we have not yet come to grips with the profoundly aporetic tension that runs between these two features and the two corresponding targets, private property and chauvinistic nationality, with which communists are supposed to concern themselves equally. "What seems to me to be lacking today in order for us to be able to continue thinking of communism in these terms," as Balibar writes, "is the possibility of considering the critique of property and that of the nation as being automatically convergent, and *a fortiori* of rooting one in the other by way of an ontology, albeit a 'negative' one."[16] Finally, perhaps we have not yet come to grips with the fact that the critique of political economy with its focus on the question of property and commodity fetishism, which thus far has been the dominant if not the exclusive concern of communism as well as the favorite measuring stick with which orthodox communists denounce the excesses of ultraleftism, cannot in fact be performed without at the same time adopting an internationalist point of view. This means that we cannot let the Western European history lessons, regardless of whether their master-teachers are despondent or enthusiastic or both at once in a manic-depressive oscillation, determine the agenda for the rest of the world. It also suggests, as I have minimally tried to do

*otra campaña y la coyuntura política mexicana* (Guadalajara: Brigada Callejera, 2007), 281–312.

16    Etienne Balibar, "Remarques de circonstance sur le communisme," *Actuel Marx* 48 (2010): 39.

in the last chapter of the present book and as I hope others will do for other regions, that we look elsewhere for models or counter-models to put to the test the hypothesis of the actuality of communism.

# Acknowledgments

Chapter 1 is a revised version of my "Afterword: Thinking, Being, Acting; or, On the Uses and Disadvantages of Ontology for Politics," in Carsten Strathausen, ed., *A Leftist Ontology: Beyond Relativism and Identity Politics* (Minneapolis: University of Minnesota Press, 2009), 235–51.

Chapter 2 is a revised version of my essay "Politics, Infrapolitics, and the Impolitical: Notes on the Thought of Roberto Esposito and Alberto Moreiras," *CR: The New Centennial Review* 10: 2 (2010): 205–38. The second section also reworks materials from my contribution "Archipolitics, Metapolitics, Parapolitics," in Jean-Philippe Deranty, ed., *Jacques Rancière: Key Concepts* (Durham, UK: Acumen, 2010), 80–92.

Chapter 3 is a revised version of "Rancière's Leftism, or, Politics and Its Discontents," in Gabriel Rockhill and Philip Watts, eds., *Jacques Rancière: History, Politics, Aesthetics* (Durham, NC: Duke University Press, 2009), 158–75; originally published in French as "La Leçon de Rancière," in Laurence Cornu and Patrice Vermeren, eds., *La Philosophie déplacée: Autour de Jacques Rancière* (Lyon: Horlieu Editions, 2006), 49–70.

Chapter 4 was read in an earlier version at the Seventh Annual Conference of the Association for Psychoanalysis and Cultural Studies on the topic of "Psychoanalysis and Social Change," Rutgers University, November 9–11, 2001.

Chapter 5 reworks the final section of my contribution to the London conference "On the Idea of Communism," published as "The Leftist Hypothesis: Communism in the Age of Terror," in Costas Douzinas and Slavoj Žižek, eds., *The Idea of Communism* (London: Verso, 2010), 33–66.

Special thanks to my friend Sebastian Budgen for believing in this project early on, for pestering me about the missed deadlines along the way, and eventually for making the book a reality with Verso; to Tim Clark for his editing skills; and to my father, Raf Bosteels, for painstakingly combing over the page proofs in the final stretches.

Like everything else I do, this book is dedicated to Simone Pinet and to our kids, Lucas and Manu.

# Index